THE JEWISH
PRESENCE

About the Author

A NATIVE NEW YORKER, Lucy S. Dawidowicz was educated at Hunter College and Columbia University. She teaches modern Jewish history at Yeshiva University. She is the author of *The Golden Tradition: Jewish Life and Thought in Eastern Europe* (Holt, Rinehart and Winston/Beacon), *The War Against the Jews 1933–1945* (Holt, Rinehart and Winston/Bantam), *A Holocaust Reader* (Behrman House), and has written for many journals. A recipient of a Guggenheim fellowship, Mrs. Dawidowicz is presently at work on a history of the Jews in the United States.

Lucy S. Dawidowicz

THE JEWISH PRESENCE

Essays on Identity and History

HBJ

A Harvest/HBJ Book
Harcourt Brace Jovanovich
New York and London

FOR SZYMON

Harvest/HBJ edition published by arrangement with Holt, Rinehart and Winston.

Library of Congress Cataloging in Publication Data
Dawidowicz, Lucy S
The Jewish presence.
(A Harvest/HBJ book)
Reprint of the ed. published by Holt, Rinehart and Winston, New York.
Includes bibliographical references and index.
1. Jews—Identity—Addresses, essays, lectures. 2. Jews in the United States—Addresses, essays, lectures. 3. Judaism—United States—Addresses, essays, lectures. 4. Yiddish language—United States—Addresses, essays, lectures. 5. Holocaust, Jewish (1939-1945)—Addresses, essays, lectures. 6. United States—Social conditions—Addresses, essays, lectures. I. Title.
[DS143.D36 1978] 909'.04'924 78-6236
ISBN 0-15-646221-4

First Harvest/HBJ edition 1978

A B C D E F G H I J

Contents

Contents

Preface

THESE ESSAYS, most of them published during the last fifteen years, now revised and some enlarged, sketch out the odyssey of American Jews in search of themselves, their Jewish heritage and identity. Some of these essays are personal, some are commentaries on books, but all are written with the perspective of Jewish history and all are permeated by a Jewish presence. By "Jewish presence" I mean the preoccupation of Jews with themselves and with the nature of their Jewishness. By "Jewish presence" I also mean the space that Jews occupy in the minds of non-Jews and the ambience that Jews have created in the non-Jewish world. In my lifetime the Jewish presence in its several senses has been especially visible in the world. Indeed, many times Jews desperately wished to be less visible, to be offstage and unstarred in the drama of human events. But Jews have always, for better and worse, lived in the vortex of history. The Jewish presence is the outcome of that turbulence.

The essays in Part I, "Full Life: Being Jewish," explore what it means to be a Jew in the modern world, taking stock of the accommodations and rapprochements that Jews have made between past and present, between tradition and modernity. The story of the American metamorphoses of Judaism and Jewish life is told in Part II, "Transformations: The American Catalyst." Here, in describing American Judaism as seen in its variant forms of Orthodoxy, Conservatism, and Reform, the essays try to illuminate the continuities and discontinuities between Old World and New World Judaism, to probe the modern Jew's struggle between faith and secularism, and to appraise the mutations of American Jewish religious and cultural life.

As offspring of East European Jewish immigrants, American Jews are the heirs of the culture of Yiddish which long ago they had scorned and disowned. Today, aware that to be whole the present needs its past, recognizing that tradition and continuity are integral to culture, many American Jews want to learn about the culture which they or their parents once repudiated and whose living community in Eastern Europe the Germans destroyed in World War II. Part III, "Heritage: The World of Yiddish," imparts something of the history of that culture and its language.

The specter of the Holocaust continues to haunt Jews everywhere and to define their priorities. The imperative is Jewish survival, above all, the security of Israel. Anti-Semitism has not ceased to cast its shadows, especially in an atmosphere of brightness. Part IV, "Torment: Anti-Semitism and the Holocaust," examines some aspects of the subject which I did not discuss in *The War Against the Jews 1933–1945.*

I wish to express my thanks to Norman Podhoretz, editor of *Commentary,* and to Neal Kozodoy, its executive editor, for their continuing interest in my work and for having published twelve of these essays.

For assistance in tracking down elusive facts I thank Dina Abramowicz, librarian of the YIVO Institute for Jewish Research; Harry J. Alderman, former director of the Blaustein Library of the American Jewish Committee, and his successor, Cyma Horowitz; and Lotte Zajac, head of the Committee's clippings service. I am, as always, indebted to Rose Grundstein for her assistance. The Memorial Foundation for Jewish Culture provided a small grant for research on the subject of Jewish identity.

Finally, I would like to express my gratitude to Thomas C. Wallace, editor-in-chief of Holt's General Book Division, for his support and encouragement. He is an editor every writer hopes for.

New York, December 1976   Lucy S. Dawidowicz

To be a Jew in the twentieth century
Is to be offered a gift.   If you refuse,
Wishing to be invisible, you choose
Death of the spirit, the stone insanity.
Accepting, take full life, full agonies:
Your evening deep in labyrinthine blood
Of those who resist, fail and resist; and God
Reduced to a hostage among hostages.

The gift is torment.   Not alone the still
Torture, isolation; or torture of the flesh.
That may come also.   But the accepting wish,
The whole and fertile spirit as guarantee
For every human freedom, suffering to be free,
Daring to live for the impossible.

—*Muriel Rukeyser*

I

Full Life: Being Jewish

1

JEWISH IDENTITY: A Matter of Fate, a Matter of Choice

IN THE VILNA GHETTO in 1942 the subject of what or who was a Jew preoccupied some intellectuals who had never given the matter much thought before the German occupation. Now they were confined in a ghetto together with all sorts of people called Jews, with whom they appeared to have little in common. Their confinement appeared to be punishment for a crime they had committed—the crime of being a Jew.

At the same time, in the same Vilna, in a ghetto school, a child from a home where not much attention had been paid to being Jewish was learning the story of Jacob and Esau. It was her first encounter with the Jewish tradition. "Teacher," she called out in the classroom, "aren't we really the descendants of Jacob? Aren't *They* the descendants of Esau? Isn't that so? I like it that way. Because I want to belong to Jacob and not to Esau."*

* "Pondering Jewish Fate: From Zelig Kalmanovich's Diary," in *A Holocaust Reader*, ed. Lucy S. Dawidowicz (New York: Behrman House, 1976), pp. 231–232.

In the prison house of the Vilna ghetto, where the only freedom that Jews could enjoy was the exercise of imagination and the pursuit of ideas in the mind's privacy, that child chose to be a Jew. Even there, to be a Jew was not just a matter of birth and fate. It was also a matter of choice, of wanting to be a Jew.

Unambiguous criteria in the *Halakhah,* Jewish law, which govern lineage and conversion, define who is a Jew, but no such clarity prevails as to what is a Jew in the modern world. You may be a Jew only in the sense that you were born to Jewish parents. You may be a Jew because you were raised as one, in a family informed by Jewish tradition and molded by Jewish history. You may be a Jew if you were educated to be one, parents and teachers having transmitted to you a body of Jewish knowledge and a system of Jewish beliefs. You may be a Jew because your family reared you to observe Jewish law and because the milieu in which you choose to live observes that law and enforces its conduct. You may be a Jew by speaking Yiddish, by proclaiming you love Yiddish, even by denying you know Yiddish. You may be a Jew just by not being a Christian or a pagan. Or you may be a Jew only by living among Jews. You may be a Jew just by being marginal, poised between two cultures, never quite at home in either. Or your Jewishness may be evident only in a stamp of restlessness, a cast of skepticism, an affinity for irony. Or by the contempt you inflict on yourself and the destructiveness you discharge on others. You may be a Jew in your own eyes, in the eyes of other Jews, or only in the eyes of non-Jews. You may curse the day you were born a Jew or celebrate your being one.

What makes one a Jew? Identity, as Erik H. Erikson has told us, has its locus "in the core of the individual and yet also in the core of his communal culture." Each person's individuality is determined by his unique psyche developing in mutual interaction with his social milieu, his culture. That culture, in turn, is shaped by history. The intersection of individuality, culture, and history becomes the crucible where selfhood is forged.

With mother's milk the child imbibes the values and traditions of his group and culture. Nearly every Yiddish lullaby that East European Jewish mothers sang to their babies embodied that culture's ideal: the little Jewish boy would grow up to study Torah, he would become a pious Jew; the little Jewish girl would grow up to marry the Jewish boy who studied Torah. Modern Jewish mothers no longer sing Yiddish lullabies, but like mothers in all cultures, classes, and societies, they rear their babies into awareness that the world is divided in two camps: We and They. The Italian mother draws the perimeter of We around the family, excluding the rest of the world. The Greek mother extends the community of We to include the village. The Jewish mother enlarges the We to embrace all Jews, those living now and those of the past, those living here, there, and everywhere. The Jewish child is taught stories and myths about the Jewish past that are intended to build and reinforce his commitment to the Jewish group* (though not necessarily nowadays to study Torah).

Before long, Jewish children growing into adolescence learn other lessons too. Living in the modern world, often in an open society, they come to see that the terms and conditions of their Jewish world are at variance with the terms

* An excellent exposition on the formation of Jewish identity is Mortimer Ostow, "The Psychologic Determinants of Jewish Identity," paper delivered at a conference on Jewish identity, Graduate Center of the City University of New York, May 26, 1976. For penetrating studies on the function of group myths in the formation of identity, see Jacob A. Arlow, "Ego Psychology and the Study of Mythology," *Journal of the American Psychoanalytic Association* 9 (1961):371–393; also Arlow's "Some Uses of Mythology in Politics," unpublished address delivered on the occasion of the founding of the St. Louis Psychoanalytic Institute, October 25, 1974.

and conditions of the non-Jewish world, a world they believe to be neutral with regard to Jew and Christian. That is the world of the street, the public school, the ball park—a world that beckons with expansiveness, tantalizing with its possibilities of unknown joys, untried exploits, forbidden fruits. It is a world that distracts them from their Jewish connections, a world where the action is—where the Yankees and Dodgers triumph or fail, where the flag is raised at Iwo Jima, where men walk on the moon.

That lesson—to be a Jew in the neutral world—counterbalances another lesson which all young Jews eventually learn: growing up Jewish in a gentile world, confronting the fears and anxieties of belonging to a pariah people, of enduring contempt and humiliation. Some learn it firsthand, others through the glass of the past. Young people whose psychological health is rooted in self-esteem and in ties of mutual regard binding them to family and community emerge strengthened and fortified from this encounter with anti-Semitism, their definition of self clarified, their group loyalties invigorated by their personal struggle with historic hostility. "For nothing can be sole or whole," wrote W. B. Yeats, "that has not been rent." William James declared that need and struggle are what excite and inspire us: "It is only by risking our persons from one hour to another that we live at all." Max Nordau dramatized this inner struggle in confrontation with anti-Semitism: "It has had the effect of a sharp trial which the weak cannot stand, but from which the strong emerge stronger and more confident in themselves."

The unhealthy responses to anti-Semitism are familiar and stereotypic: at one extreme, the aggressive super-Jew; at the other, the pathological self-hater. The super-Jew veers between states of jingoistic euphoria (Jewish is joyous) and indiscriminate paranoia. He regards every phenomenon in the universe from an exclusively Jewish perspective (the elephant and the Jewish question; is fluoridation good for the Jews?). He is the Jewish chauvinist, the thousand percent Jew. He turns his back on the non-Jewish world, persuaded that every gentile is an unadulterated anti-Semite. Still, the Jewish superpatriot, being animated by an excess of self-love and pride, is more tolerable than the self-hater. For the self-hater, in contrast, is warped by the misery of his enforced identity with Jews, obsessed by a desperate wish to be someone else, somewhere else. He is in limbo between his own rejection of his Jewishness and his being rejected by Them because of his Jewishness. Wanting to shed his Jewishness, to be a non-Jew, the self-hater does not know what Ludwig Lewisohn learned: that which one chooses to be must also be able and willing to be chosen. "Choice," Lewisohn wrote, "requires for its completeness a complete harmony between the chooser and the thing chosen." Every minority spins off self-haters, persons who fashion for themselves a negative identity distilled from precisely those values of the majority culture which denigrate their own. The Jews, for so long persecuted and humiliated, have had more than their share of self-haters—the self-deniers, universalists who elevate every interest over that of the Jews (revolution, proletariat, blacks, Arabs), rebels, mutineers, apostates, renegades, runaways, heretics, dissidents, and secessionists.* Sartre called them the "non-authentic Jews."

Commitment to people, country, or faith is, for most

---

* An anecdote: A German Social Democrat fled Germany in 1933 and came to England. The Fabians expressed sympathy for his situation as a Jew. "I'm sorry," he said, "I'm not a Jew," explaining that while it was true he was Jewish from the "racial" point of view—his parents were Jews—he himself, back in 1924, had sent in his formal resignation from the Jewish community of Berlin. "Oh, I see," said one of the Fabians, "the Jews are a club."

people at most times, slack and habitual, undemanding, subordinated to the claims of personal affections. But when communal crisis erupts, when national disaster threatens, when the very existence of one's people is imperiled, the individual summons up his psychic vigor to stake his life, to put his selfhood on the line for his group. Crisis thus provides the occasion for self-discovery and self-avowal, dredging up dormant or repressed feelings, transforming them into affirmations of self.

Situated, as they have been in their turbulent history, at the center of social upheaval, at the crossroads of intellectual ferment, in the midst of violence and terror, objects of envy and hate, the Jews have had a profusion of opportunities for testing themselves and their communal identity. From the French Revolution to the Bolshevik Revolution, the question of Jewish identity and the individual Jew's relationship to the Jewish collectivity continued to confront the Jews. Wherever the Enlightenment penetrated, whether in its West European rationalist guise or its East European Hebrew form, Jews began to search for answers to the question of what is a Jew. Every pogrom, from the "Hep! Hep!" attacks in Germany in 1819 to the bloody massacres in the Ukraine in 1919 to 1921, became a catalyst of Jewish identity. In our time, the aftereffect of the Holocaust, in which 6 million Jews were destroyed, has been the mobilization of Jewish energies toward Jewish goals. The rise of nationalist movements everywhere provoked both Jews and non-Jews to consider the nature of Jewish identity and its constituent elements. Above all, Israel—whose very right to exist still remains at stake—has galvanized Jews everywhere for the ordeal of survival.

History has supplied the Jews generously with occasions to test their selfhood, to forge their personal and communal identity. But the modern world has been niggardly in providing viable forms or formulas for that identity. Since the Enlightenment, the question of Jewish identity, of what is a Jew, of how one lives as a Jew, has continued to perplex and confound.

The Enlightenment, invading the traditional world of European Jewry in the late eighteenth century with its promise of Progress, with its intellectual allurements, launched the relentless erosion of faith. That, in turn, undermined rabbinic authority among Jews, thus hastening the collapse of the rule of *Halakhah* in the Jewish community. Enlightenment bred secularism, humanism elevated man to godlike status. Always in the forefront of modern movements, Jews began to join the ranks of the humanists, the secularists. Some ceased to believe in the God of Abraham, Isaac, and Jacob. Some no longer observed the commandments of *Halakhah*. Some no longer submitted to the discipline of the Jewish community. They were still Jews, yet the nature of their Jewish commitment remained elusive.

The rise of the nation-state, in the wake of the Enlightenment, exacerbated the question of Jewish identity. Whereas the Enlightenment had attacked the validity of the individual Jew's faith and his system of beliefs, the nation-state —as it was becoming and as it eventually became—directly assaulted the concept of the Jew as a people, the corporate Jewish identity. Traditionally, a Jew was not just someone who believed in the Jewish God and observed His commandments: a Jew was also someone who belonged to the Jewish people, whose Covenant with God bestowed nationhood upon them, even though that nationhood in modern times had no political sovereignty, no fixed territorial abode. But the emergent nation-state held a different view of nationhood and nationality. As the ideologues of the French Revolution formulated it, citizenship in the nation was premised on belonging to the nation. To be part of the nation it was not enough to reside on the nation's territory. The would-be national had to adopt the language and the culture of the nation. Culture, then even more than now, meant common law, customs, traditions, history, and not least of all religion.

Those West European Jews already committed to secularism and Enlightenment, identifying themselves as Frenchmen or Germans, appealed to the state to recognize them as such. They asked to be emancipated, to be granted citizenship and civic equality. The French Revolutionary National Assembly argued, however, that the Jews were alien, different; besides, they were "a nation within a nation." But Count Clermont-Tonnerre's famous formula provided a solution to the problem: "To the Jews as a nation—nothing; to them as individuals—everything." The westernized Jews accepted the principle, contending that the Jews were not any more a nation but only adherents of a particular faith.

In asserting that the Jews of Europe shared with each other only their common faith in Judaism, and that the primary loyalties of Jews in each country were solely and uniquely to the country in which they lived, the French Jews (later the German Jews) split the atom of Jewish identity, in which for millennia faith and peoplehood had been—so it had seemed—indissolubly united. The irony was that precisely those Jews who protested most fervently that the Jews were nothing more than believers in Judaism did not believe very much in it or observe its law.

How then could they reconcile themselves to being Jewish? What was the nature of their Jewishness? Would it be, like the color of one's eyes, merely another inherited characteristic, a feature without significance? For some, then as now, that nominal acceptance of being Jewish was indeed no more than a formal acknowledgment of, a passive assent to, the fact of birth. Other Jews, however, needed more self-definition, moved perhaps by a desire for personal wholeness, perhaps by an indefinable sense of solidarity with other Jews, perhaps by the need for intellectual integrity. They began to search for ideas or ideology, for an intellectual framework, even for a communal institution that could clarify, justify, underpin, or give substance and satisfaction to what it meant to be a Jew in the modern world.

Not the French Jews during the French Revolution, but the German Jews before and thereafter provide us with the models, the prototypes for all the versions of Jewish identity that we know today. All modern Jews, Milton Himmelfarb observed, walk in the footsteps of German-speaking Jewry, the pioneers of Jewish modernity.* Since the old mold of being Jewish no longer fit the new times, the German Jews began to innovate, invent, experiment with new modes of being Jewish, to modulate and mutate the old and familiar ones, to refashion traditional and prescriptive ways, to challenge the conventional and time-honored forms. The path-breaker was Moses Mendelssohn. With calculated deliberateness, he organized his life to be an exemplar, to demonstrate that it was not only theoretically possible but indeed fully realizable that a man could be at the same time a faithfully observant Jew and also a philosopher, a rationalist, both product and producer of Enlightenment.

In his youthful maturity Mendelssohn nearly plunged into the abyss of disbelief.† In one of his early works, *On the Sentiments*, whose autobiographical character is gen-

* See his book *The Jews of Modernity* (New York: Basic Books, 1973), for its erudite, penetrating, and witty essays on the modern Jewish condition.

† For the life and work of Mendelssohn, see Alexander Altmann, *Moses Mendelssohn: A Biographical Study* (University, Ala.: University of Alabama Press, 1973), a magnificent magisterial study.

erally acknowledged, Mendelssohn's protagonist confesses how near he once came to "complete ruin," his feet slipping "from the happy path of virtue," tortured by "doubts even in the existence of God and in the worthwhileness of virtue." His "faithful guides"—Locke, Leibniz, and Christian von Wolff—returned him to the firm path of true philosophy, to knowledge of himself and of his origin. Was that really so? Did rationalist philosophy enable Mendelssohn to come to terms with himself as a Jew, to remain steadfastly observant of Jewish law, and to interpret Judaism as a natural religion? Or was it that he, fundamentally a cautious, conservative man, was inhibited by the fear of becoming a figure of controversy, perhaps even an outcast of the Jewish community? Mendelssohn was fascinated by Spinoza, with whom he identified, yet he was haunted by Spinoza's fate. Was that why he remained committed to Jewish law and tradition?

Mendelssohn was an ambitious man, despite his timidity. Did he perhaps harbor the impudent idea that he could, by his own accomplishments, prove to the gentile world, to the men of Enlightenment, that those despised Jews whom they regarded as backward and superstitious were capable of the highest intellectual activity, the mastery of philosophy? Did he hope that by his exemplary life as a good Jew and a good philosopher he could wrest from the gentile world approval and recognition which would eventually redound to the benefit of the Jews—at least to those educated and enlightened Jews who deserved civic equality as well as respect?

Mendelssohn's life and ideas raise these questions, but they do not supply clear answers. Mendelssohn lived a compartmentalized, dichotomized life. He spent half his days in business (he became manager of a silk factory) among businessmen, the other half in the study of philosophy and in the company of Europe's most distinguished intellectuals.

His life as an observant Jew was private; his life as a philosopher was public. By the time he reached forty, in his intellectual prime and at the height of his renown, Mendelssohn appeared to have proved the viability of his way of life. He was a Jew at home, a philosopher abroad. In the Age of Enlightenment, for the first time in Christian Europe it would seem, Jews and Christians, regardless of their private religious commitments, could share common interests in the ostensibly neutral areas of philosophy, science, and literature.

The eruption of the Lavater Affair in 1769 shattered the fragile structure of Mendelssohn's dichotomous life. Johann Kaspar Lavater, a Christian theologian in the grip of millennial visions, publicly challenged Mendelssohn— Europe's most eminent Jew—to refute, if he could, arguments offered as incontrovertible proof of Christianity's superiority. Wishing to avoid headlong and dangerous controversy, Mendelssohn pleaded for religious toleration. Convinced of the truth of his own religion, he asked for the right to adhere to his own faith without being answerable to the world for his private beliefs. Besides, since the Jews were "an oppressed people that had to implore the ruling nation for patronage and protection," Mendelssohn indicated the delicacy of the situation in which he, as a member of that oppressed people, might find himself, were he to undertake an attack on Christianity.

The Lavater-Mendelssohn debate soon became the center of religious and philosophic argumentation, a subject for gossips and bigots. It dragged on until January 1771, when Mendelssohn wrote his last letter to Lavater. Some weeks later, after a restless night, Mendelssohn awoke to an attack of paralysis, accompanied by palpitations and burning sensations. For the next six years such attacks recurred and subsided, with decreasing severity and reduced frequency.

Mendelssohn's doctors held that the illness was caused by mental strain. Besides prescribing medication and treatment, they advised against reading, writing, and thinking. When, after six years, Mendelssohn resumed normal intellectual activity, philosophy no longer occupied a central place in his work. Thenceforth, till the end of his life, Mendelssohn committed himself to the enlightenment of the Jews and the improvement of their political status.

Were those paralytic attacks psychosomatic? Mendelssohn's friend Friedrich Nicolai thought so, if only because Mendelssohn, a "peace-loving man," had been forced into an unwanted battle. That strange illness must surely have been induced by the emotional aftereffects of the Lavater Affair. For the controversy had shown that even in the Age of Enlightenment a Jew who was a philosopher still had to justify himself to the world because he was a Jew. The Lavater Affair had frustrated Mendelssohn's ambition to be accepted as a philosopher who happened to be a Jew. In his last years he became something else—a Jewish philosopher. One hundred years later, the goal that Mendelssohn had striven for as a model for Jewish identity was attained when Hermann Cohen, a believing Jew and founder of neo-Kantianism, was appointed to teach philosophy at the University of Marburg.

Although Mendelssohn dutifully observed Jewish law, his Jewish endeavors were directed toward reforming— that is, "naturalizing" and modernizing—Judaism, a purpose that becomes even more evident when viewed from a later perspective. (Heine, born a decade after Mendelssohn died, labeled him "the reformer of the German Israelites.") Mendelssohn's disciples, less timorous than he about the communal criticism they might provoke and less respectful than he of Jewish tradition, held that reform of Jewish worship was a matter of urgency both for Jews and for the future of Judaism. To win emancipation and equality, the Jews, according to the Reformers, had to prove their worthiness, to give evidence that they were not a nation within a nation but merely a confession. Furthermore, that confession would have to be a system of beliefs and a form of worship that were consistent with rationalism, natural religion, and Enlightenment. Thus, Reform would be the precursor of emancipation. Besides, since Reform would transform Judaism into something of a Jewish variant of enlightened Protestantism, it would succeed also in emancipating the Jews from the stigma of inferiority which—so the Reformers believed—justly attached to them because of their "outmoded," supernatural, particularistic religion.

The Reformers wanted Reform also as an end in itself, not merely as a means to hasten emancipation. The early decades of the nineteenth century in Germany were lean years for Judaism and the synagogue. Young people in large numbers were abandoning Judaism, converting to Christianity. Judaism's very existence was threatened by apostasy and apathy. The Reformers—who abbreviated the synagogue service and removed the particularistic prayers, who translated the Hebrew liturgy into German and introduced organ music into the Sabbath worship, who patterned Jewish education upon the Protestant catechism—were genuinely and honestly concerned about the survival of Judaism. Better to have Reformed Jews, they argued, than to have no Jews at all. Their advocacy of Reform had something of medieval gallantry in it, for many rejected conversion as dishonorable, even though the baptismal certificate was, in Heine's lapidary phrase, the admission ticket to European culture.

For all their ambivalence to Jewish tradition, for all their Protestantization of Judaism, these Reformers were trying to fashion a mode of Jewish identity and a form of Jewish observance that enabled them and other Jews like them to feel pride rather than humiliation in being Jewish, to feel that they rightfully belonged in German society and German culture, while retaining their basic Jewish commitment. Reform—enlightened Judaism based on ethical imperatives—became a viable option for German Jews. In its early decades it nearly swept traditional Judaism from its moorings in Germany. For later generations, in Germany and especially in America, Reform succeeded as a mode of staying Jewish without the fervor of feeling Jewish. Located on the outer marches of Judaism, as it were, Reform became a kind of border station of Jewish belonging—the last stop on the way out, the first stop on the way back. Its weakness has been its strength: still committed to a universalist rather than a particularist doctrine, Reform asks less of its constituency than any other branch of Judaism. For the *baal-teshuvah*, the returner to Judaism, the penitent rejoining his people, a person whose commitments may still be hesitant and tentative, Reform offers identity and security without demanding much in return, without asking for a down payment. The sense of identity that Reform generates is passive rather than active, perhaps because Reform is still burdened by its rationalist heritage of the Age of Enlightenment.

In 1836, Heinrich Graetz, then only nineteen, read and was overwhelmed by a new book just published in Germany, *Nineteen Letters on Judaism*. Written by Samson Raphael Hirsch, a young rabbi in Altona, it was an impassioned poetic defense of Orthodox Judaism. "With avidity I devoured every word," Graetz noted in his diary. "Disloyal though I had been to the Talmud, this book reconciled me with it."* Written in impeccable German, its argument

* Quoted in Noah H. Rosenbloom, *Tradition in an Age of Reform: The Religious Philosophy of Samson Raphael Hirsch* (Philadelphia: Jewish Publication Society of America, 1976), p. 71.

presented in a then fashionable style combining philosophic rationalism and poetic allegory, the book had a stunning impact. Hirsch managed to demonstrate that a person could be, at one and the same time, a strictly observant Orthodox Jew, a loyal German, and an educated man.

Himself reared by parents whom he once characterized as *erleuchtet religiös* (enlightenedly religious), Hirsch undertook to bring Enlightenment and Orthodoxy together, to reconcile those two elements which had been thought until then to have been irreconcilable. Whereas Mendelssohn felt an affinity for Spinoza, Hirsch's ideal was Maimonides, the rationalist philosopher who, reinterpreting traditional Judaism in contemporary terms, demonstrated its immutable validity. Hirsch enunciated his accommodation of Torah to the Enlightenment in the celebrated formula: *Torah im derekh eretz* (Torah together with secular knowledge). His second formula was *Jisroel-Mensch*, a prescription for integrating those two elements that Mendelssohn had tried to keep apart: the Jew and the *Mensch*, the essential human being, in this instance the man of culture, the man of pride.

As much a product of the Age of Enlightenment as the Reformers against whom he later waged war, Hirsch superimposed a rationalist mode on Judaism, thus enabling traditionalist Jews to accommodate to the changing world around them, to shore up their universe, to hold fast to *Halakhah*. Gershom Scholem is probably right in his charge that *Torah im derekh eretz* represented a capitulation to the forces of modernity—Progress and Enlightenment.* Frankfurt Orthodoxy, the corporate product of Hirsch's teachings and politics, which approached Judaism with German discipline and rigor, could scarcely supply Jewish fervor. Still, Hirsch provided a new model of being Jewish in Germany

---

* See his savage critique of Hirsch's grandson, "The Politics of Mysticism: Isaac Breuer's New Kuzari," in *The Messianic Idea in Judaism and Other Essays on Jewish Spirituality* (New York: Schocken, 1971).

that enabled traditional Judaism to survive in Germany until 1933, however dry and formalistic that Frankfurt mold turned out to be. Desiccation is, after all, a form of preservation.

But Frankfurt Orthodoxy could not satisfy the hunger for mystery and mysticism. Later in the nineteenth century, when Romanticism had displaced rationalism, the search for faith, the longing for wholeness and holiness, animated many intellectuals. Jews too were caught up in those currents. Some, in the quest for self-fulfillment, eventually turned to Christianity. Those came, for the most part, from homes without commitment to Judaism, often without spirituality. Reared in ignorance of even the fundamentals of Judaism, unaware of its possibilities for sacredness and transcendence, even for ecstasy, they chose Christianity to heal their inner division, to restore inner harmony. Some have eminent names: Henri Bergson (a Catholic *in voto* when he died), Eugen Rosenstock-Huessy, Edith Stein, Simone Weil, Boris Pasternak. But others found their way back, reverting to Judaism and to the Jewish community.

Repentance, a central concept in Judaism, applies to the believer who sins and to the unbeliever who returns. Sometimes it seems that the tradition extends a greater measure of divine grace to the *baal-teshuvah*. The Midrash says that God goes halfway to meet those who return. The paradigm of the repentant returner is, of course, Franz Rosenzweig, but there are other known names: Nathan Birnbaum, Edmond Fleg, Jiri Langer, Ludwig Lewisohn. The obscure men and women who returned have been a multitude.

Franz Rosenzweig had studied modern history under Friedrich Meinecke and earned a doctorate in philosophy with a dissertation on Hegel. One evening in July 1913, when he was in his twenty-sixth year, Rosenzweig had a decisive conversation with his friend Eugen Rosenstock, a

Jew who had converted to Christianity.* "Disarmed,"
Rosenzweig wrote later, by his friend's "simple confession
of faith," he began to rethink his own views of Christianity.
In that reconstructed world, he confessed, "there seemed to
me to be no room for Judaism."

Having decided to become a Christian that night,
Rosenzweig set about his task with high purposefulness. He
would come to Christianity through Judaism, not "through
the intermediate stage of paganism." That fall he attended
Rosh ha-Shanah services with his parents in the Liberal
synagogue in Cassel. Upon their return home, Rosenzweig
told his mother, in a rush of fervor, that the New Testament
was everything, the truth. "There is only one way," he said,
"Jesus." They quarreled. To his declaration that he would
attend the synagogue on Yom Kippur, his mother replied,
"In our synagogue there is no room for an apostate."
Rosenzweig went to Berlin, where, by chance it would appear, he attended Yom Kippur services in a small Orthodox
synagogue. There he encountered a Judaism he had never
known, a faith that transformed him. Some days later he
wrote to his mother that he seemed to have found his way
back. To his friend he wrote: "I will remain a Jew." Thenceforth he immersed himself in the study of Judaism and its
basic sources. He became a wholly committed, fully observant Jew and, in a few years, one of the seminal Jewish
thinkers of our time, an achievement particularly astonishing
in view of the seven-year progressive paralysis that afflicted him and which he bore with surpassing fortitude.
His intellectual creativity continued undiminished until
his untimely death on December 10, 1929, at the age of
forty-three.

* The indispensable source on Rosenzweig is Nahum N. Glatzer, *Franz
Rosenzweig: His Life and Thought*, 2d ed., rev. (New York: Schocken,
1961).

Rosenzweig only once attempted to describe his transfiguring experience. In a letter written in 1920 to his former professor, Friedrich Meinecke, he tried to explain why he could not accept a lectureship at the University of Berlin. Rosenzweig had then just become head of the *Freies Jüdisches Lehrhaus* in Frankfurt, organized on principles which he himself had developed to help reintroduce Judaism to others who, like him, had returned. Judaism, he explained, had become the center of his existence and he felt that he could not serve two masters. He went on:

In 1913 something happened to me for which *collapse* is the only fitting name. I suddenly found myself on a heap of wreckage, or rather I realized that the road I was then pursuing was flanked by unrealities. Yet this was the very road defined for me by my talent, and my talent only! I began to sense how meaningless such a subjection to the rule of one's talent was and what abject servitude of the self it involved. . . . Amidst the shreds of my talents I began to search for my self, amidst the manifold for the One. It was then (one can speak of such matters in metaphors only) that I descended into the vaults of my being, to a place whither talents could not follow me; that I approached the ancient treasure chest whose existence I had never wholly forgotten, for I was in the habit of going down at certain times of the year to examine what lay uppermost in the chest: those moments had all along been the supreme moments of my life. But now this cursory inspection no longer satisfied me; my hands dug in and turned over layer after layer, hoping to reach the bottom of the chest. They never did. They dug out whatever they could and I went away with armfuls of stuff—forgetting, in my excitement, that it was the vaults of myself I was thus plundering! Then I climbed back again to the upper stories and spread out before me what treasures I had found: they did not fade in the sheer light of day. These, indeed, were my own treasures, my most personal possessions, things inherited, not borrowed! By owning them and ruling over them I had gained something entirely new, namely the right to live—and even to have talents; for now it was *I* who had the talents, not they who had me.*

In the half century since his death, Rosenzweig has exercised a continuing fascination and fundamental influence on Jews in search of the security of identity. He speaks for a maximalist Judaism that combines rapturous faith with the discipline of observance and the rigor of religious study. His Judaism addresses itself to sensibility as well as intellect, satisfying the need for privacy as well as collectivity, answering skepticism in the language of modernity, with the power of mystical symbolism.

The potency of traditional Judaism as a viable option of Jewish identity today is seen also in East European Hasidism, which still speaks with persuasiveness to the fallen away. The classic case in the twentieth century was Martin Buber, who at twenty-six rediscovered Judaism while reading the Baal Shem Tov's testament. "It was then," he wrote in a memoir, that "something indigenously Jewish rose in me, blossoming, in the darkness of Exile, to a new conscious expression." Nowadays, competing with varieties of faddish Eastern mysticism, Hasidic sects—notably the Lubavitcher movement—have succeeded in reaching some anguished and soul-sick young Jews and healing them.

The commitment to modernity and secularism precluded many Jews from searching for personal fulfillment in religion. But secularism devised new outlets for the repressed religious sensibility. The compensatory surrogate forms of

* Ibid., pp. 95–96.

collective emotionality that swept the Western secularized world were nationalism and socialism, the prime expressions of secular messianism.* For the secular Jew in search of authentic selfhood, the discovery of national belongingness as a viable form of identity was as transfiguring as the discovery, for religious converts, of God. Moses Hess's declaration of his return to the Jewish people still vibrates with the ring of revelation. In 1862, when he was fifty years old, having spent his life in the cause of socialism, he published a small book, *Rome and Jerusalem*, with a confessional introduction:

> Here I stand once more, after twenty years of estrangement, in the midst of my people; I participate in its sacred days of joy and mourning, its memories and hopes, its spiritual struggles in its own house and with the civilized peoples among whom it lives, but with whom, despite two thousand years of common life and struggle, it cannot attain organic unity.
>
> One thought which I believed I had suppressed forever within my heart is again vividly present with me: the thought of my nationality, inseparable from the heritage of my fathers, the Holy Land and the Eternal City—the birthplace of the belief in the divine unity of life and in the future brotherhood of all men.

When, in his youth, Hess had become involved in the rising socialist movement, he appeared to have abandoned his Jewishness, forgetting, repressing the traditional Jewish upbringing which his observant grandfather had given him from the time he was five until after he became bar mitzvah.† Hess's sense of Jewish identity was stirred briefly

---

* See Zevedei Barbu, *Problems of Historical Psychology* (New York: Grove Press, 1960).

† A regrettably brief (49 pages) but unexcelled exposition of Hess's life and ideas is Isaiah Berlin, *The Life and Opinions of Moses Hess* (Cambridge: Jewish Historical Society of England, 1969).

by the Damascus Affair of 1840, an ugly ritual-murder libel leveled by Syrian Christians and Moslems against the Jews of Damascus. He wrote an essay on the Jewish need for nationhood but, setting it aside, he then forgot it, once more unmindful of the Jews. A few months later he met Karl Marx, who became his idol.

Twenty years later, without forewarning, without displaying any prior preoccupation with Jewish matters, Hess began to write *Rome and Jerusalem*. A moving testament of his return to the Jewish people, the book diagnosed the condition of Jewish pariahism and homelessness which the emancipation had failed to resolve and prescribed a remedy —a program to establish the Jewish nation in its own home in Palestine. "Jewish patriotism," Hess wrote, "is a natural feeling which, in its primordiality and simplicity, needs neither to be demonstrated nor to be demonstrated away." In elaborating his argument on Jewish nationhood, Hess affirmed the nationally binding character of Judaism, adducing the pious Jew as the Jewish patriot and the Reform Jew who denied the existence of the Jewish nation as the traitor to his people.

Nineteenth-century European nationalism, especially the contemporary events of the Italian Risorgimento, prompted the national ideas in *Rome and Jerusalem,* but surely the underlying catalyst was the resurgence of Hess's Jewishness and his sense of its importance. Though Hess never explained what had motivated him, it is likely that the recurrent exposure to anti-Semitism that he suffered—even, he admitted, among his own party comrades—sharpened his self-awareness; to reinforce his self-esteem, it is likely that he drew upon the childhood memories of traditional Judaism which his grandfather had instilled in him. Hess secularized the religious concepts of the Jews as a people and of the return to Zion, transforming them into a modern nationalist program whose accomplishment hinged upon politics and organization instead of the coming of the Messiah. Thus, he was the first to envision the Jews as a modern nation, in contrast to his proto-Zionist contemporaries, Yehuda Alkalay and Zvi Hirsh Kalisher, who just wanted to apply practical means to hasten the messianic redemption.

Did Hess provide a model of Jewish identity for others of his time? We know that within a decade his book penetrated into Eastern Europe and stirred the Jewish imagination. Even in Western Europe there must have been young people who, upon reading *Rome and Jerusalem*, experienced the thrill of recognition, the sense of discovery that Hess spoke for them and to their condition, offering them—as Jews—the possibility of grandeur and the opportunity for a noble experiment.

The crises of Jewish history continued to press on Jewish consciousness, as European Jews endured alternate cycles of liberalism and persecution. The tidal wave of pogroms in 1881 and 1882 in czarist Russia launched a new search for national identity, especially among young Jews who had, only yesterday, preached russification or radicalism as solutions to the Jewish problem. Such a one was Leo Pinsker, a doctor in Odessa, who had been deeply involved in efforts to russify the Jews and thereby hasten their assimilation into Russian society. The Easter pogrom of 1871 in Odessa, the most tolerant of Russian cities, had shocked Pinsker and his organization into paralysis. For the next decade Pinsker concentrated on his medical career, abstaining from Jewish communal activity. It was surely a time of emotional crisis.

Then, in 1881, at the age of sixty, stunned perhaps more by the silence of Russian liberals after the pogroms than by the pogroms themselves, Pinsker underwent a radical change of beliefs. He set his ideas down in a small book, *Auto-Emancipation*. The Jews, he argued, were a people, even though they lacked the normal attributes of nationhood.

The persistence of the Jews as a spiritual nation through the ages, "without unity or organization, without land or other bond of union," generated in the gentile nations a fear of Jews as a ghostly apparition of a people. This fear of Jews, this anti-Semitism, which Pinsker diagnosed as a form of demonopathy, could be overcome only if the Jews had a national home of their own.

Pinsker's *Auto-Emancipation* electrified the Russian Jews, especially those who, like him, had been committed to the ideals of the Enlightenment and imbued with the hopes of fraternity. Moshe Leib Lilienblum, the most influential writer of his time, became Pinsker's disciple. "I was exalted by this lofty thought of return," he wrote. "The oppressive weight rolled from my heart. It was a revelation. I became exalted and transfigured." His language and the experience it described have a mystical cast. The oppressive weight is the burden of humiliation and the purposelessness of life. The revelation is the avowal of self-worth through the redemption of an ancient tradition of moral transcendence. Thus, the fusion of modern nationalism with Jewish tradition continued to fire the Jewish imagination.

More than a decade later, Theodor Herzl, completely unaware of Hess and Pinsker and their books, found out for himself what they had discovered before him. Like them, Herzl early in life had turned his back on Judaism and the Jewish community, making a career as a journalist and playwright in Vienna. For a while, unsettled by the rising political anti-Semitism in Vienna, Herzl toyed with erratic and capricious notions of "solving" the Jewish problem. Then, when Karl Lueger, Christian Socialist and political anti-Semite, was elected mayor of Vienna, and when the drama of the Dreyfus case began to unfold in Paris, Herzl wrote *Der Judenstaat*, an open proclamation of his Jewishness and an affirmation of Jewish national existence.

Shortly after he began working on *Der Judenstaat*, on

July 6, 1895, Herzl recorded in his diary a conversation he had had with his friend Max Nordau. "Nordau and I agreed," Herzl noted, "that only anti-Semitism had made Jews of us." But that was not quite the whole story. The idea of Palestine and of the return to Zion had lain fallow and forgotten in his memory since childhood. Alex Bein, Herzl's biographer, has described the near trauma that the story of the Exodus had upon Herzl as a child in Hebrew school in Budapest. Even more telling is Bein's surmise about the influence of Herzl's paternal grandfather, who lived in Semlin, the home also of Yehuda Alkalay. Surely the elder Herzl, during his prolonged annual visits to his son in Budapest, told stories about the famous rabbi's work for Palestine that was designed to hasten the coming of the Messiah. Those stories must have impressed the young Theodor, burrowing into his subconscious mind, eventually to come to the surface and inspire him to national mission. To be sure, anti-Semitism turned Herzl into a Jew, but only because it inflamed him to seek self-definition. In this search for self, he summoned up from his submerged memories those formative fragments of Jewish tradition that had been inculcated in him in his childhood.

Jewish national consciousness continues to exert a galvanic effect on the formation of Jewish identity. The idea of the Jewish state, once the catalyst for Jewish identity, has now been supplanted by the Jewish state itself, by Israel, which has become both substance and symbol of Jewish being for Jews throughout the world. Its existence threatened since its creation, its very right to live put in question, Israel has mobilized Jewish energies everywhere in its defense. In a way, the Jewish state has become the corporate paradigm for the ideal image of the Jew in the modern world, whose pluck and stamina under beleaguerment evoke admiration, whose daring exercises of self-defense arouse pride. Israel has redeemed those Jews who felt humiliated by Jewish powerlessness in the Dispersion. For those without childhood memories of tales of Jewish heroism and fortitude, for those without a sense of the Jewish past, Israel serves as the positively charged nucleus of Jewish identity, the affirmation of Jewishness in response to the negative force of anti-Semitism and self-hate. How common were those stories about Jewish self-discovery during the Six Day War of 1967, and how commonplace they began to appear when they recurred, with new actors, during the Yom Kippur War of 1973, when even the most committed among Jewish universalists capitulated to the realities of We and They.

The story of how Israel's existence affected the Jews of the Soviet Union is, however, neither common nor commonplace. For the Soviet Jews, Israel became the very pith of their Jewish identity, their ancestral heritage. How this happened remains both mystery and miracle, an unpredicted and unpredictable chapter in modern Jewish history.

A population of 3 million, the Russian Jews had already been subtracted from the statistics of the Jewish people, having for decades been coerced into assimilation, dispossessed of faith, community, language, literature, and custom, and then ravaged by the Holocaust. The Soviet Jews appeared to have come to the end of the line of Jewish history. By the logic and cunning of Communism, they seemed surely destined for extinction as an ethnic and cultural entity. Judaism no longer existed in Russia except for a few encapsulated communities in Asia and a fragile underground in a few Russian cities. Yiddish as a living language was in decline. There were no authorized opportunities to learn Hebrew, to study Jewish history, to read Jewish books (other than Soviet-style). To be a Jew was fraught with peril. Yet in the late 1950s a Jewish under-

ground began to organize clandestine groups to study
Hebrew, to read Zionist literature, and to circulate Jewish
samizdat, crudely duplicated editions of forbidden works.
The earliest *samizdat* consisted of the story of the Warsaw
ghetto uprising in 1943, Ben-Gurion's speeches on the 1956
Sinai campaign, and extracts from Simon Dubnow's *World
History of the Jews*. Then extracts of the historical material
in Leon Uris's *Exodus* began to appear spontaneously in
different cities, even in labor camps. In its several abbreviated versions in Russian translation, *Exodus* became the
Bible of the Jewish *samizdat*, the "greatest Jewish inspiration," according to an underground Zionist activist, read by
tens of thousands of Soviet Jews.[*]

The Six Day War stoked the defiance of the dissident
Jews, kindling their courage, bringing to the public surface
their underground Jewish activities, their muffled Jewish
feelings. Economic reprisals and arrests followed. Then came
trials and the impetuous clamor of ringing declarations: "I
am a Jew!" "I am a Zionist!" By now, more than 100,000
Jews have joined the exodus from the Soviet Union. Those
who remain—and most will—will be charged with Jewish
national consciousness to the end of their days.

Some Jews who no longer believed in Judaism, who
wanted to be part of the larger society, yet for whom
Jewish particularity remained a real, if indefinable, element
of personality, discovered a mode of Jewish identity through
the pursuit of Jewish scholarship. If one could not practice
Judaism, at least one could study it.

The seven young university-trained intellectual Jews
who assembled late in 1819 in Berlin to form an association
were unclear about what made them Jews and bound them

[*] Leonard Schroeter, *The Last Exodus* (New York: Universe Books,
1974), pp. 64–68.

together. Discussing the dilemma of being Jewish without observing Judaism, they concluded that each of them had an inner Jewish consciousness, a sense of Jewish belonging (though not, they stressed, a "national" feeling) whose specific character they could not altogether define. Some referred to the unique culture of Judaism, and consequently these young men formed a society to study that culture—*Verein für Kultur und Wissenschaft der Juden* (Society for the Culture and Scholarship of Jews). That scholarship in later mutations through the nineteenth century became known as *Wissenschaft des Judentums*, traditionally translated "Science of Judaism" (I prefer "Scholarship of Judaism").

Neither the vague sense of Jewish identity, which these young men were hard put to define, nor the profession of Jewish historical study long sustained them as Jews. All but one, in pursuit of career and success, abandoned Judaism for Christianity. Only Leopold Zunz loyally applied himself to *Wissenschaft des Judentums* until the end of his days, but not with any expectation that the study of the Jewish past would improve the Jewish present or ensure the Jewish future. Disbelieving in the possibility of a viable Judaism in the future, Zunz reconciled himself to the task, in Milton Himmelfarb's characterization, of being the necrologist of Judaism and its culture. The story is told that late in life Zunz was introduced to Judah Leib Gordon, the Hebrew poet of the Russian *Haskalah*, and asked him, "And when did you live?"

Moritz Steinschneider, an early disciple of Zunz who became the master builder of Jewish bibliography, devoted his whole long life to *Wissenschaft des Judentums*. When he was very old (he died in 1907, at the age of ninety-one), a young disciple came to him, fired with passion about a Jewish renaissance. Steinschneider discouraged those hopes.

Pointing to his bookshelves (his own publications among them numbered some 1,400 items), he said, "We have only one task left: to give the remains of Judaism a decent burial."*

Only when Jewish scholarship is used as an expressive outlet for Jewish identity rather than as a substitute for it has it avoided antiquarian sterility or nostalgic sentimentality. From Nahman Krochmal through Simon Dubnow to Max Weinreich and Gershom Scholem,† Jewish scholarship has served not primarily as an end in itself for the sake of itself, though its practitioners have, to be sure, been rewarded not only with accomplishment but with a sense of fulfillment. Committed as these men have been to modern critical scholarship, their studies have nonetheless been enlisted in the larger cause of Jewish survival, imbued with the hope that knowledge of the Jewish past—of Jewish languages, literature, traditions, and history—communicated to new generations of Jews, would help ensure Jewish continuity.

What of those Jews who, though asserting their sense of Jewishness, cannot, for one reason or another, commit themselves or their children to the Jewish collectivity of faith or peoplehood? Only fate, the unchosen destiny of being born Jewish, has brought them to the threshold of the Temple. The definition of the anti-Semite alone keeps them within the Jewish pale. "The black mystery of what happened in Europe is to me indivisible from my own identity," writes George Steiner. "To be a Jew," says Alfred Kazin in

---

* Gershom Scholem, "The Science of Judaism—Then and Now," in *Messianic Idea*, p. 307.

† For portraits of some of these Jewish scholars, see Lucy S. Dawidowicz, *The Golden Tradition: Jewish Life and Thought in Eastern Europe* (Holt, Rinehart and Winston, 1967), pp. 225–269.

Walker in the City, "meant that one's very right to existence was always being brought into question." But those definitions of Jewish identity, as they stand, are incomplete, unconsummated. They are the torment without the gift, the infliction without the reward, the enforcement of being Jewish without the choice of being Jewish.

Goethe once said that only he earns his freedom and existence who daily conquers them. The reward of being Jewish lies in defining oneself, not in being defined. The gift is in possessing one's heritage and in affirming one's existence on one's own ground.

but here is — how the rub: to do this

2

ARNOLD SCHOENBERG: A Search for Jewish Identity

IN DECEMBER 1966, more than fifteen years after the composer's death, Arnold Schoenberg's unfinished opera *Moses and Aaron* was given a belated American premiere by the Opera Company of Boston.* The occasion was full of ironies. The performance, which took place in America's historic citadel of high culture, was staged in a shabby one-time movie palace; the impresario was Missouri-born and Arkansas-reared; the work itself, a twelve-tone opera glorifying Jewish monotheism, was written by a Jew who had become a Lutheran but returned to Judaism. As a further affront to Boston's traditions, the opera contained an orgy scene which, in another day, would certainly have been banned.

* Since then, the only other American performance has been a concert version given by the Chicago Symphony under Georg Solti in November 1971.

Producing *Moses and Aaron* demands immense resources. Sarah Caldwell, the artistic director whose previous productions of other seldom-heard works have put Boston on the national operatic map, assembled for *Moses and Aaron* a cast which included two stars—a bass-baritone for the role of Moses (Donald Gramm, one of the Metropolitan Opera's best acting singers) and a tenor to sing Aaron (Richard Lewis, who sang the role in the British production of 1965); twenty singing principals; a chorus of fifty-five sopranos, mezzos, and altos; forty-eight actors and dancers; and members of the Boston Symphony Orchestra under the direction of Osbourne McConathy. What with seventy Elders, twelve Tribal Chieftains, four Naked Virgins (not to speak of the Golden Calf), and who knows how many supernumeraries, it is no surprise the production cost $300,000. (Boston has a tradition of sorts for big musical settings: In 1869, to celebrate the National Peace Jubilee, 10,000 singers, 1,000 musicians, and 100 firemen beating anvils with sledgehammers performed the "Anvil Chorus" from *Il Trovatore*.)

Both the libretto and the music of *Moses and Aaron* are fully Schoenberg's creation.* As to the music, it is a complex contrapuntal composition whose absorbing twelve-tone structure and atonality serve to enhance and amplify the terror and awe of the libretto. The opera opens with God's summons to Moses before the Burning Bush, as told in Exodus 3–4. The Voice from the Burning Bush (sung by six solo voices behind the stage and a six-part speaking chorus) calls Moses to bring the Israelites the message of the One God and to lead them to freedom. Moses pleads that

---

* The complete libretto, in German and in Allen Forte's English translation, appears in Karl H. Wörner, *Schoenberg's "Moses and Aaron,"* trans. Paul Hamburger (London: Faber and Faber, 1963), and also in Columbia's recording, K3L–241.

he is unfit; because he is slow of speech and of a slow tongue, the people will not believe him. God promises that He will perform wondrous things to convince the people of Moses's message. Aaron will be Moses's spokesman to the people.

In the next scene the brothers confront one another (Exod. 4:27–28). Text and music stress the discrepancy between word and image, thought and feeling, idea and myth. Moses speaks earnestly, in inflected, accented speech (*Sprechstimme*), while Aaron sings sensuous floating melodies, florid, with a hint of the cantorial. Aaron fails utterly to understand the new and religiously revolutionary basis of Moses's monotheism—that man's reward lies in his freedom to act righteously. Instead, he translates this idea back to the pagan concepts of reward for obedience to the gods and punishment for disobedience.

In the third scene, against nervous orchestral runs, the Israelites exchange fearsome rumors about the impending arrival of Moses and Aaron. The intricate contrapuntal choral composition gives expression to their fears and superstitions, and to the divisions among them. In the closing scene of Act I, Moses and Aaron bring God's message (Exod. 4:29–31). The Israelites at first mock the new God who cannot be seen or heard. As Moses despairs of his ability to communicate his message, Aaron performs "the signs in the sight of the people." He turns Moses's rod into a serpent, and back into a rod; Moses's hand becomes leprous and then whole again; the Nile waters turn into blood. (In the Boston production, all these actions were pantomimed.) "And the people believed." The act closes with a rapturous hymnal chorus in march tempo as the Israelites go off into the desert wasteland: "We are His chosen folk before all others,/We are the chosen ones,/Him alone to worship,/Him alone to serve."

Between the end of Act I and the choral interlude that

precedes Act II, the Jews have left Egypt, crossed the Red Sea, and journeyed into the desert. Moses has ascended Mount Sinai (Exod. 24:18). The Israelites fear that Moses and his God have abandoned them. The small chorus whispers its anxiety in hushed tones: "Where is Moses? Where is his God?" The musical theme recalls God's promise to Moses, but its repetitive syncopated staccato heightens doubt and insecurity.

Act II opens to show the disarray in the Israelite camp in the forty days since Moses's ascent. Violence and lewdness prevail; the seventy Elders can no longer exercise authority. The people turn on them savagely, demanding their old gods back. The fearful elders turn to Aaron for direction. Unsure of himself, he yields quickly.

The jubilation begins, introduced by great fanfares. The Golden Calf (Exod. 32:3–6) is brought onstage. The stupendous scene of "The Golden Calf and the Altar" is, according to Karl Wörner's analysis, a symphony in five movements for solo voices and choruses. It opens with a ritualistic dance of the slaughterers who prepare the animal sacrifices; then follow worshipful processions of the sick, the poor, and the old. The music has an eerie, abnormal character. Fanfares introduce the tribal leaders who come to pay homage to the Golden Calf. The tempo accelerates. When a youth exhorts the Israelites to remember their religion of freedom and to destroy "the image of temporality," the tribal leaders murder him, to a fury of brass and drums. Then a gentle swaying dance tempo is heard as the people begin to exchange gifts and kindnesses. But coarseness and drunkenness soon overtake them. The priestly ritual begins: the four Naked Virgins give themselves to the embrace of the priests, who then sacrifice them upon the altar to the Golden Calf. Music and action intensify in a frenzy of syncopated tension, ending in a percussive, delirious finale.

As the killing, self-destruction, and sexual debauchery come to an end and the sacrificial fires are extinguished, a voice from afar proclaims that Moses is descending from the mountain. Moses appears and destroys the Golden Calf with these words: "Begone, you image of powerlessness to enclose the boundless in an image finite!" The brothers confront each other. Moses demands an explanation. Aaron justifies himself: he loves his people—"I live just for them and want to sustain them." Moses insists that his love is for the idea of the One God. Aaron answers that the common people can comprehend only part of that idea, the perceivable part, that they need feeling and hope. Moses refuses to "debase" his idea; he will remain faithful to it, as it is set forth in the tablets. Aaron counters that the tablets, too, are images, "just part of the whole idea." At that, Moses smashes the tablets. (In Exod. 32:19–20, Moses smashes the tablets first, then destroys the Golden Calf.) In despair, he asks God to relieve him of his mission as Aaron chides him for faintheartedness. Then the pillar of fire by night and the pillar of cloud by day appear, and the people follow them in religious ecstasy. Aaron explains that "the Infinite thus shows not Himself, but shows the way to Him and the way to the Promised Land." Once again believing in, and reconciled to, their chosenness, the Israelites sing the marchlike hymn with which Act I closed. But Moses sinks to the ground, despairing of the possibility of expressing the idea of the inconceivable God. The violins sustain taut legatos of unbearable poignancy as Moses cries out in defeat, "O word, thou word, that I lack!"

Schoenberg's text for the unfinished third act departs rather drastically from the biblical original. Aaron, a prisoner in chains, is dragged in by soldiers. Moses calls him to account for having betrayed God's word, wrought miracles, believed in the physical reality of a land flowing with milk and honey, and given the people false gods. Now, Moses charges, Aaron has disobeyed God's word by smiting the rock, instead of speaking to it, to make the waters of Meribah flow. (In a letter to Walter Eidlitz in 1933, Schoenberg complained about "incomprehensible contradictions in the Bible" which made it difficult for him to complete the act. He was referring to the variants in Exod. 19:5–6 and Num. 20:7–12.) When the soldiers ask to kill Aaron, Moses orders them to "set him free, and if he can,/he shall live." But Aaron, freed, falls dead.

There is in Schoenberg's *Moses and Aaron* an almost uncanny intuition of the meaning of biblical Judaism and of Moses's historic role as the founder of Israelite monotheism. It is doubtful whether Schoenberg read any serious scholarly literature on the subject; in any case, much of what was then available had been written under the influence of Wellhausen and the higher critics who dated Israel's ethical monotheism from the later period of classical prophecy. Schoenberg's artistic conception, on the other hand, is essentially traditionalist (and quite in accord with recent archaeological findings and modern scholarship), and it is thus interesting to speculate on how he arrived at his position. He was quite obviously not a fundamentalist, of either a Jewish or a Christian variety, and he had been remote from traditional Jewish thought. Is this operatic exaltation of monotheism and condemnation of idolatry to be seen then as a confession of Jewish identity? Or did he perhaps undertake it as a celebration of Jewish morality at a time when European society was poised at the brink of pagan violence and destruction?

Schoenberg completed the first two acts of *Moses and Aaron* in March 1932. While he was still at work on the third act, the Reichstag passed the Enabling Act (March 23,

1933), which gave Hitler and the National Socialists the power to enact any legislation at will. A month later, the Jews were driven by Nazi law from their positions in government and cultural institutions. Dismissed from his post at the Prussian Academy of Arts, Schoenberg left Berlin for America. On July 24, 1933, in a simple ceremony at the Liberal Synagogue of Paris, he was readmitted to the Jewish community. (His two witnesses were David Marianoff, Albert Einstein's son-in-law, and Marc Chagall.) On October 16, 1933, he wrote to Alban Berg: "As you have doubtless realized, my return to the Jewish religion took place long ago and is indeed demonstrated in some of my published work . . . and in *Moses and Aaron*. . . ."*

Schoenberg himself considered his return to Judaism to be a political rather than a religious act. Yet such matters are seldom as simple as one would like to believe; indeed, the complex twists of Schoenberg's own life would indicate that religion and politics cannot in his case be easily separated, and that faith and identity, self-esteem and group pride, all played a part in the formulation of his final intellectual and emotional position.

Arnold Schoenberg was born in Leopoldstadt, Vienna's Jewish quarter, on September 13, 1874. His father, Samuel, a shopkeeper, had come from Pressburg, now Bratislava, the stronghold of Jewish Orthodoxy in Hungary. No doubt Samuel Schoenberg had brought some Jewish traditions and practices with him when he migrated to the big city. Until his death in 1889, when Arnold was fifteen, the family still observed the Jewish holidays, according to Gertrud Schoenberg, the composer's widow, with whom I spoke in

* This and other quotations are from Arnold Schoenberg, *Letters*, ed. Erwin Stein, trans. Eithne Wilkins and Ernst Kaiser (New York: St. Martin's Press, 1965).

California in 1966. It is unlikely that Schoenberg himself had any Jewish education.

At the age of seventeen, Schoenberg began working in a bank, and at the same time continued his self-education in music and composition. Around 1895, as a cellist in an amateur student orchestra in Vienna, he met the conductor Alexander von Zemlinsky, who became interested in his compositions. In 1901, Schoenberg married Zemlinsky's sister Mathilde (she died in 1923).

In 1898, at twenty-four, to his family's deep shock, Schoenberg became a Lutheran. No one knows exactly why he converted. His cousin, Hans Nachod, says that Schoenberg was persuaded to make the move by a singer friend, but Gertrud Schoenberg probably was closer to the truth in maintaining that his conversion was prompted by cultural rather than by religious motives. It was, she said, "quite a usual procedure for educated Jews, as the belief in assimilation at this time flourished."

Schoenberg's parents had come to Vienna during the great Jewish migration from the hinterlands of Galicia, Hungary, and Bohemia after the enactment of the 1867 Constitution, which erased the legal inequities under which Jews had suffered. In thirty years, from 1860 to 1890, the Jewish population of Vienna rose from 1 to 12 percent. Jews flocked to the *gymnasia* and the universities, where they were overwhelmingly concentrated in the faculties of law and medicine. They also went into journalism—en masse, it seemed to the Austrians. Yet although (or because) Jews shaped Vienna's literary and artistic tastes, anti-Semitism continued to prevail in most professional, academic, and government circles, even before Karl Lueger became *Burgermeister* and Christian Socialism a vehicle for political anti-Semitism. At a time when a birth certificate should have sufficed, many positions still required proof of baptism.

Freud, for example, a *privatdozent* for seventeen years, was kept from being appointed at the University of Vienna, according to Ernest Jones, by "the anti-Semitic attitude of official quarters. . . ."

The keys to musical Vienna were similarly held by men who did not like to open doors to Jews. Mahler's baptism, in 1897, constituted his ticket of admission to the directorship of the Vienna Opera. It seems entirely likely that Schoenberg, too, became a Christian in order to have easier access to important musical institutions and influential musicians. Perhaps, like others of his generation and upbringing who stood neither here nor there in their Jewishness, he was attracted to what must have seemed the dazzlingly brilliant cultural life of the non-Jewish and ex-Jewish intellectuals, poets, composers, and artists. (Schoenberg was also a painter, active in the Expressionist movement and a participant in the *Blaue Reiter* exhibition of 1912.) Among themselves, young Jewish cosmopolitans often attributed Vienna's accelerating anti-Semitism to the bearded traditionalist Jews who had migrated from the Galician towns and villages with their baggage of poverty, Orthodoxy, and Yiddish. For many, the baptismal waters represented a means of escaping identification with these Jews.

Religion—Judaism or Evangelical Lutheranism—meant little to Schoenberg in the time following his conversion. One of his biographers has characterized it as a period of "positivistic atheism." Later he developed an interest in Swedenborgian ideas. Schoenberg himself described this process in a letter to the German poet Richard Dehmel on December 13, 1912:

For a long time I have been wanting to write an oratorio on the following subject: modern man, having passed through materialism, socialism, and anarchy, and despite having been an atheist, still having in him some residue of ancient faith (in the form of superstition), wrestles with God (see also Strindberg's "Jacob Wrestling") and finally succeeds in finding God and becoming religious.

Dehmel could not provide the poetic text Schoenberg wanted. Eventually, using Balzac's now quite unknown theosophical novel, *Seraphita*, Schoenberg began composing both text and music for the oratorio, *Die Jakobsleiter.** The work contained suggestions of ideas he was later to use in *Moses and Aaron*: "this Either and this Or," "instincts" versus "commandments," spirit versus matter. But Schoenberg never finished *Die Jakobsleiter*. For one thing he was drafted into Franz Josef's army, where he became a *Kapellmeister*. Later, groping his way back toward Judaism, and more rigorous in his religious thinking, he may have become uneasy with alien and pseudoliterary texts and have decided to turn to more appropriate and authentic ones.

In 1922 a small incident set Schoenberg on an irrevocable course back to Jewishness and Judaism. At a resort in Mattsee near Salzburg, where he had gone to spend the summer, he was told that Jews were not welcome. He came to realize that the Christian promise to accept Jews at the price of assimilation (read: conversion) was a fraud. "For I have at last learnt the lesson that has been forced upon me during this year and I shall never forget it," he wrote to Wassily Kandinsky. "It is that I am not a German, not a European, indeed perhaps scarcely even a human being (at least, the Europeans prefer the worst of their race to me), but I am a Jew."

* Dr. Dika Newlin, who studied with Schoenberg, wrote about *Die Jakobsleiter* in a program booklet on the occasion of its London premiere, November 1965.

In a second letter to Kandinsky on May 4, 1923, in which he referred to "that man Hitler" who would make no exception even for a "good" Jew like himself, Schoenberg prophesied that though the anti-Semites would try to "exterminate" Einstein, Mahler, and himself, they would not succeed with those "much tougher elements thanks to whose endurance Jewry has maintained itself unaided against the whole of mankind for twenty centuries. For these are evidently so constituted that they can accomplish the task that their God has imposed on them: to survive in exile, uncorrupted and unbroken, until the hour of salvation comes!"

Thereafter, Schoenberg's immersion in Jewish themes seemed inevitable. Until his death in 1951, Jewish subject matter continued to attract him. During 1926 and 1927 he worked on a play, *Der biblische Weg*, which he said had been "conceived in 1922 or '23 at the latest"—that is, at the very time his self-esteem rebelled at German anti-Semitism. The drama, never published, was, in his own words, "a very up-to-date treatment of the story of how the Jews became a people." Its protagonist, Max Aruns (Moses and Aaron in one), attempts to unite his people and lead them to the fulfillment of their God-given mission. But dissidents beat him to death, and his leadership falls to another. *Der biblische Weg* foreshadowed the dramatic core and conflict of *Moses and Aaron*. Thus, Asseino (from "Sinai"?), the spokesman of traditional Jewry, speaks to Max Aruns:

> Max Aruns, you want to be Moses and Aaron in one person! Moses, to whom God gave the idea but denied the gift of speech; and Aaron, who could not grasp the idea but could formulate it and move the masses.*

* Quoted in Peter Gradenwitz, "Gustav Mahler and Arnold Schoenberg," in *Year Book V* (New York: Leo Baeck Institute, 1960), p. 275.

Thenceforth, the idea of an opera about Moses and Aaron seized Schoenberg's imagination. On April 10, 1930, he wrote to Alban Berg that after a year of "very strenuous work," he needed a holiday and he was playing tennis instead of working. (Oscar Levant said Schoenberg once told him that if he had not been a composer, he would have liked to have been a champion tennis player.) At the end of the letter, he said he would like best to do an opera: ". . . perhaps I shall do *Moses and Aaron*." By August 1930 he was already at work on it. He completed the second act just as National Socialism stood at Germany's threshold.

Theodor W. Adorno has suggested that the composition of *Moses and Aaron* was Schoenberg's defense against the rise of Hitler. (Hence the fall of the Third Reich eliminated the need to complete the opera.) This must surely have been a major motive. The figure of Moses served to reinforce Schoenberg's Jewish self-esteem, to strengthen his rejection of the world that National Socialism was then fashioning in Europe, a world governed by paganism, violence, and bloodshed. (Something akin to this motive probably animated Freud's interests in Moses as well.) It has also been suggested that Schoenberg saw himself as a revolutionary herald of a new musical system—atonality—and identified his own lack of popular success with Moses's failure to communicate with the people. I myself, however, prefer to think that Schoenberg intended *Moses and Aaron* as a challenge—musically, philosophically, politically, and culturally—to Wagner's *Parsifal*, the only other religious music drama to which it might legitimately be compared.

The two operas are total opposites. Musically, Wagner was the last great Romantic, while Schoenberg, the great adversary of Romanticism, advocated musical cerebralism and classicism. Philosophically, or theologically, *Moses and Aaron* and *Parsifal* appear to represent the antagonism between Judaism and Christianity, between monotheism and trinitarianism. *Parsifal*, Wagner's version of the legend of the Holy Grail, glorifies compassion and repentance through Christ. It is religious drama in that it leads from conflict to a renewal of faith and a restatement of religious values.

Yet notwithstanding its exaltation of Christianity, *Parsifal* remains pseudoreligious; it is not genuinely Christian. Wagner hardly identified himself as a Christian, in part because he could not accept Christianity's Jewish origins: "For us it is sufficient to derive the ruin of the Christian religion from its drawing upon Judaism for the elaboration of its dogma." Rather, he defined the Holy Grail as the spiritual aspect of the Nibelungen hoard, Amfortas with the German kaiser, Parsifal with Siegfried. He wrote once that "the abstract highest God of the Germans, Wotan, did not really need to yield place to the God of the Christians; rather could he be completely identified with him. . . . Christianity has been unable in our day to extirpate the local native gods." Thus, Wagner's Christianity turns out to be Teutonic paganism; as others have pointed out, *Parsifal* is not a religious Christian drama but the fifth opera in the Ring, welding Teutonic paganism, medieval Christianity, and modern German nationalism into one romantic *Gesamt-kunstwerk*, a stage-consecrational-festival play.

It is, I think, plausible that Schoenberg felt the need to define himself in opposition to this kind of German Christianity, which was, at different levels of consciousness, inextricably associated with paganism and idolatry. Perhaps, in *Moses and Aaron*, he wished not only to surpass Wagner as a composer but also to distinguish himself decisively from the Wagner who was a Christian-pagan, German nationalist, and anti-Semite, and from the rising Nazi culture that Wagner would have applauded. Thus, *Moses and*

Aaron, the vehicle through which Schoenberg asserted his Jewishness, comes to symbolize the antithesis of everything that *Parsifal* represents, a reassertion of the intrinsic and superior value of Jewish monotheism—in itself, for Schoenberg, the purest concept of belief.

3

ON BEING A
WOMAN IN SHUL

"It is better to pray at home, for in the synagogue it is impossible to escape envy and the hearing of idle talk." Thus the advice of Elijah ben Solomon, the Gaon of Vilna, in a letter to his wife. "The more so," he added, "on Sabbaths and festivals, when people assemble in order to talk; on such days it would be better not to pray at all." The Vilna Gaon even advised his wife to keep their daughter away from the synagogue, "for there she would see garments of embroidery and similar finery." Consequently, she "would grow envious and speak of it at home, and out of this would come scandal and other ills."

Since the Vilna Gaon wrote this letter about 200 years ago surprisingly little has changed, Reform Judaism notwithstanding. Indeed, people who are nowadays lax in such matters are even more likely to agree with his judgment of the synagogue than those who are themselves strict in Jewish observance. To be sure, the synagogue does not *generate* envy and gossip; it merely happens to be one of the sites, particularly on Sabbaths and festivals, where they are commonly found. *Pirke Avot* counsels, "The more flesh, the more worms," and this is to the point: the more affluence, the more finery; the more finery, the more envy; the more envy, the more gossip.

My shul is better than most, I think, partly because it has only a modest share in the affluence that many American Jews enjoy. It is an Orthodox shul in the middle-middle-class community of Jackson Heights in Queens.* Most of its congregants are native Europeans who fled to the United States from Poland, Hungary, Austria, and Germany, some by way of Auschwitz and displaced-persons camps. Neither rich nor poor, they are small businessmen, retailers, accountants, salesmen, a few professionals.

The women, for the most part, are not prosperous enough to own the embroidered garments that the Vilna Gaon warned against or the mink habiliments that are de rigueur for bar mitzvahs. Their mode of dress and adornment would hardly necessitate any such sumptuary legislation as that enacted by Jewish communal officials in Poznan (for example) in 1629, forbidding tailors, under penalty of a fine, to accept orders "for a garment of satin or damask even from the leading families of the province." Besides, being Orthodox (more or less), the women in my shul are by nature, as it were, decorous in their dress: the vagaries or vulgarities of individual taste are curbed by the insistence of tradition on modesty and propriety.

I like this shul. The male congregants themselves conduct the services, and once you have heard them, no cantor will do. Florid phrases and fluttering quavers are a poor substitute for the spontaneity, inwardness, and genuineness with which

* For more on that community, see "Middle-Class Judaism," pp. 67–91.

these men pray. When I arrive, Saturday mornings, a little late, I can almost feel the ascent of their urgent voices, their exaltation of God.

This shul is, above all, a place where people come to pray. When there is a bar mitzvah ceremony, it does not usurp the service. The boy reads the haftarah; the rabbi acknowledges the occasion in his sermon and bestows upon the celebrant the sisterhood's gift of a *siddur*; then the service goes on as usual. The women, too, come to pray. Whenever they arrive—no matter how late—they recite the Shemoneh Esreh. Then they catch up with the rest of the congregation. Even behind the partition of lattice and scrollwork, the women of this shul can find their place in the prayerbook, without assistance from their menfolk.

To my astonishment—for I consider myself modern—I find I like the partition. Because of it, men are more intent on the liturgy (and, for that matter, women are too) than they might otherwise be. The original reason for separating the sexes, a practice which dates all the way back to the Temple, when women were assigned to the *ezrat nashim*, was, presumably, to discourage amorous thoughts. Later, to ensure the same purpose, rabbinic leaders prescribed special galleries for women in the synagogue so that they "should look down from above and men look from below." (This was not a uniquely Jewish problem. Some English churches in the Middle Ages separated the sexes to discourage philanderers who, as John Gower put it, "in churches and in minstres eke,/That gon the women for to seke." The Duke of Mantua, a notorious operatic seducer second only to Don Giovanni, used to go to church to find girls when things got dull at his court.)

Separation by partition or gallery does, as a matter of fact, help the congregants concentrate on prayer. Separation also ensures that the service remains a men's service, that women do not usurp it. Judaism has always depended on its males to maintain the congregation. That is their prime responsibility. Because women do not share this responsibility, we are told again and again that Judaism regards women as inferior creatures. Every Jewish male, on arising, recites these benedictions:

> Blessed art thou, O Lord our God, King of the universe, who hast not made me a heathen.
> Blessed art thou, O Lord our God, King of the universe, who hast not made me a slave.
> Blessed art thou, O Lord our God, King of the universe, who hast not made me a woman.

Christians who like to argue the relative merits of religions often adduce Paul's annulment of these discriminatory distinctions as evidence of Christianity's greater tolerance for women: "There is neither Greek nor Jew, there is neither bond nor free, there is neither male nor female, for ye are all one in Christ Jesus" (Gal. 3:28). To propagandize his new religion, Paul promised equality both here and in the hereafter to heathens, slaves, and women. But on those women who were already committed to Christianity, he imposed total subservience. *"Mulieres in ecclesiis taceant,"* he wrote: "Let your women keep silence in the churches: for it is not permitted unto them to speak; but they are commanded to be under obedience, as also saith the law" (1 Cor. 14:34). And he commanded them also to dress and act modestly, and to pray in silence and subjection. For their sins, and Eve's original sin, they could be saved only by childbearing and "faith and charity and holiness with sobriety" (1 Tim. 2:9–15). What an easy argument for a Jewish polemicist to rebut: Compare the honor accorded the woman of valor in the Book of Proverbs.

Judaism is a man's religion not only in substance and in practice but also in its symbolic theology. God is male. Israel in relation to God is female: the Bridegroom God and the Virgin Israel. The *Shekhinah*, the Divine Presence, represents the feminine potency within God. The Torah is female, the Sabbath is female. In relation to them, Israel is male. In the books of the Prophets and, of course, in the Song of Songs, marriage and sexual relations symbolize the ties between God and Israel, Israel and the Sabbath, Israel and Torah. The Torah, according to the Talmud, is betrothed to Israel, and therefore forbidden to every other nation. When a Jewish boy comes of age, his assumption of the responsibilities of manhood is solemnized by his being called up to the Torah.

Professor Gershom Scholem has illuminated and explicated the mystic-mythic conceptions of masculine and feminine— begetting and receiving—which the Kabbalists derived and amplified from the traditional sources and in which the symbolism of the sacred marriage between God and Israel occupies a central place.* The ritual of the Sabbath in particular, Scholem tells us, became associated with the myth of the sacred marriage. On the basis of Talmudic passages about a rabbi who, on the eve of the Sabbath, used to put on his best clothes and say, "Come, let us go and meet the Queen Sabbath," and another who cried out, "Come, O bride, come O bride," the Kabbalists personified the Sabbath as a celestial bride with whom Israel entered into a mystical union. The traditional service for the inauguration of the Sabbath has sanctioned this view by incorporating into the liturgy the *Lekhah Dodi* ("Come, my friend, to meet the bride; let us welcome the presence of

---

* See his *On the Kabbalah and Its Symbolism*, trans. Ralph Manheim (New York: Schocken, 1965).

the Sabbath"), a poem written by the sixteenth-century Kabbalist Solomon Alkabetz.

On the festival of Simhat Torah (Rejoicing in the Law), the marriage symbolism is patent and exposed, even in the most exoteric, austere, rationalistic style of worship. At the morning service the men called up to the reading of the last and first portions of the Pentateuch are designated, respectively, as *Hatan Torah* and *Hatan Bereshit*—Bridegroom of the Law and Bridegroom of Genesis. During the service they hold the sacred scrolls in their arms. The ceremony is obviously a representation of the symbolic marriage between Israel and the Torah. The festival begins on the previous evening when the Torah scrolls, dressed in their richly embroidered silk and velvet coverings and adorned with elaborately chased silver crowns and shields, are removed from the Ark and paraded in processions (*hakkafot*) seven times around the reading desk. (At an Orthodox wedding, the bride is led seven times around the groom.) In my shul the *hakkafot* summon forth the congregants' normally inhibited Hasidic heritage. Dancing and singing, shouting and stamping their feet, downy-cheeked yeshiva students and gaunt patriarchs embrace the Torah scrolls. After each *hakkafah* their dancing becomes more frenzied, their faces flushed, their voices more rapturous as they sing *Ve-nosan lonu Toras emes* ("And He has given us the Torah of truth").* Little boys ride upon their father's shoulders, merrily waving Torah flags; the old men raise the Torah scrolls high above their heads in exaltation. The women stand behind the latticed partition, watching, beating out the rhythm, clapping and stamping, singing too—but still only spectators. They are envious—more likely, jealous.

* My shul, like most Orthodox synagogues, retains the Ashkenazic pronunciation in the liturgy.

The Torah has seduced the men, and earthly women are forgotten. The men are dramatizing Israel's marriage to the Torah. This is the only time during the cycle of Sabbaths and festivals of the Jewish year that I suffer a sense of deprivation from being a woman in shul.

On Simhat Torah morning once, I attended services at a Reconstructionist synagogue, where I had been urged to come because the Torah reading was said to be beautiful. It was indeed, but Reconstructionists are much too rationalistic to observe Simhat Torah as it ought to be observed, and Simhat Torah is too transcendental, too supernatural for the Reconstructionists to assimilate. But I did not mind the dry-as-dust service so much as I did the feminist spirit which informed it. Women have equal rights in this synagogue all year round, and Simhat Torah was no exception. Not only were women called up to the Torah for *aliyot* (that is an ordinary Sabbath routine here), but they were also given the privilege of *Hatan Torah*, which, Reconstructionists being strict rationalists, was renamed *Kallat Torah*. Watching these women embrace the Torah, I found myself seized by wicked and perverse thoughts. Wicked: how insensible was this movement to the festival's symbolism, to its music and poetry. Perverse: only here could transvestitism appear as innocent farce.

If ever men abdicate their synagogal responsibilities to women, the synagogue will, I fear, succumb either to Italianization or to Hadassah-ization. Women, when passive, can turn the synagogue into something like a provincial Italian Catholic church. The rabbi assumes all sacerdotal functions: the women become his dutiful parishioners whose religion is part devotion, part ignorance, and part superstition. Religion, then, becomes a womanish thing. Men stay away out of contempt. But even more forbidding—to me at least—is the threat of female power, female usurpation of the synagogue. Women are efficient: they can organize, raise funds, bring order out of chaos. They can turn the shul into a Hadassah chapter. Not that I disapprove of Hadassah, its activities, or its ladies. But I do not like the idea of their taking over the synagogue. To my mind, the assumption by a woman of a rabbinic or priestly function in the synagogue undermines the very essence of Jewish tradition. To say that the "Jewish women's movement" is inherently antitradition-alist and implicitly antinomian is only to speak tautologically.

In Judaism, women are assigned primacy at home, not in shul, and despite the reformers, this traditional religious role of women seems appropriate also biologically and sociolog-ically. Though the women's libbers deny it, everyone knows, and empirical scientific studies have shown,* that differences between the sexes—not just the sexual and, consequently, the biologically determined—are manifested in behavior (in-tellect, perception, affect) that need not be culturally conditioned. The Talmud exempted women from the per-formance of "positive commandments which depend on stated times," and the rabbis said women acquire merit "by sending their children to learn [Torah] in the synagogue, and their husbands to study in the schools of the rabbis, and by waiting for their husbands until they return from the schools of the rabbis."

But women were not exempt from praying: they were expected to recite the Shemoneh Esreh and say the benedic-tion after meals. (The Vilna Gaon, maximalist that he was, ruled that women were also obligated to recite the *Shema*.) Nor were women discouraged from attending services in the synagogue. But women's obligations at home seldom per-

* See, for instance, Eleanor Emmons Maccoby and Carol Nagy Jacklin, *The Psychology of Sex Differences* (Stanford, Calif.: Stanford University Press, 1974).

mitted them the leisure to go to shul for daily morning prayers. (Dr. Isaac Rivkind recounted an anecdote of a pious East European woman who used to come to shul early each morning and recite a prayer of her own: "Good morning, God! I haven't got much time to spend here; I must go home and feed Abraham my son, so he will have strength to study your holy Torah. Good day, God!") For the most part, women have gone to shul on Sabbaths and festivals.

Women know less of the liturgy and the Torah than men do or, if they are modern women, than they ought to. Traditionally, though it was considered improper to teach women the Oral Law, there was no prohibition against a woman's learning to read the Torah. Still, most Jewish women used to be what we would today describe as functional illiterates.

One solution to female liturgical illiteracy was a female prayer-leader, known in Yiddish variously as a *zogerin*, *forzogerin*, *zogerke* (all meaning "reciter"), or *voylkenevdike* (a learned woman). Proficient in Hebrew, with mastery of the liturgy, the *zogerke* would recite and translate the set prayers for the women in the gallery, simplifying, paraphrasing, enlarging, embellishing, and interpreting in a fashion appropriate for her listeners. They, if they could, repeated the Hebrew after her.

In time, the oral tradition of the *zogerke* became formalized in print. The *Korban Minhah* prayerbook, containing a Yiddish translation and commentary on the whole liturgy, first published in 1725, became the standard *siddur* for women and the most widespread in Eastern Europe even until 1939. In my shul several older women still pray from it. Private prayers (*tehinnot*) or prayers for private occasions also became standardized in print. Composed chiefly by women, these *tehinnot* provided for all sorts of personal and ritualistic contingencies which Jewish women might confront. The most famous of the *tehinnot* composers was Sarah, known by her own appellation as *Sore bas tovim*—Sarah, daughter of pious parents—who lived early in the eighteenth century. Her *tehinnot* were so popular that some 150 years after her death, her name continued to appear on devotional compositions which indigent and somewhat cynical rabbinical students wrote on demand for publishers, imitating her touching and sentimental style. The granddaughter of a rabbi, Sarah was probably a *zogerke*, traveling from town to town, from one women's gallery to another. Her self-imposed condition of homelessness, she explained in one of her collections of *tehinnot*, was by way of expiation for the sins of her youth: "I talked in the synagogue while the dear Holy Torah was being read." She cautioned her readers to benefit from her sad experience:

I do recall those times when I used to come to the dear synagogue in costly jewels, sneering and scoffing . . . but God remembers and does not forgive. Therefore, you should come with reverence, knowing before Whom you have come and to Whom you pray.

The hour at which the reading from the Torah scrolls takes place is generally conceded to be the best time for conversation in shul; at least that has been the practice from the days of Sarah *bas tovim* (and surely before) until today. But in the good old days, on the very first occasion the Torah was read before a congregation, there was no talking at all. According to the Bible, when Ezra brought the Law before the congregation, both men and women, "the ears of all the people were attentive unto the book of the Law" (Neh. 8:3). But thereafter, though the *Shulhan Arukh* proscribed conversation during Torah reading, even about Torah, the ruling was honored, as they say, more in the breach.

That there is too much talking in shul is a criticism Jewish universalists are prone to make of Jewish particularists, as if idle conversation during services were unique to Jews or to Jewish women. But the complaint is more universal than the universalists may care to concede, because they are so particularist in their criticism of particularism. Bertold of Regensburg, a thirteenth-century Franciscan preacher, used to grumble at churchgoers who,

> while God is being served with singing or reading . . . laugh and chatter as if they were at a fair. . . . And ye women, ye never give your tongues rest from useless talk! One tells the other how glad the maidservant is to sleep and how loth to work; another tells of her husband; a third complains that her children are troublesome and sickly!

One reason why women gossip in shul is, of course, that they have an innate feminine proclivity for it: "Of ten measures of talk that came down to the world, women took nine." Another reason is that they simply do not understand what is going on. I have discovered that many women in my shul who can recite the prayers more fluently than I seldom know their meaning, although they can locate them immediately in the *siddur*. Least of all do they understand the Torah reading. This, too, was not always the case. When Ezra first read the Torah, everyone knew what was going on: "And they read in the book, in the Law of God, distinctly; and they gave the sense, and caused them to understand the reading" (Neh. 8:8).

The Hasidim of medieval Germany believed that understanding the liturgy was the key to *kavanah*, the mystical meditation on the meaning and words of the prayers, inducing communion with God. The *Sefer Hasidim* (Book of the Devout) counseled God-fearing men who knew no Hebrew and women, "who certainly do not understand Hebrew" but who wanted to pray with *kavanah*, to pray in the language they understood: "For prayer is the heart's pleading. If the heart understands not what the lips utter, what good is such prayer?" Presumably, the Reform movement solved this problem with the Union Prayer Book. Reform women can understand the prayers; but if they don't gossip, or gossip less, in Reform Temple, it may be because the service is too short for social intercourse. The *Shema* and the *Shemoneh Esreh* have been so truncated that there is little left of the original liturgy either to understand or to misunderstand. And since hardly any Torah is read, that problem, too, has been solved by being done away with. I, for one, prefer ignorant piety to literate brevity. Besides, I find decorum more unnerving than talk.

Nevertheless, in my shul the hubbub of conversation during Torah reading often annoys me. But then, too, I can afford to be self-righteous because I have no one to talk to. Though I pay my way, I am an anonymous creature there. Sometimes, when I get lonesome, I daydream about my ideal *ezrat nashim*, about shul-going women I would like to talk to. When I come back to reality, I find I like things pretty much as they are. Still, it would be nice to have a friend with me once in a while so that I, too, could talk and be like other women in shul.

II

Transformations: The American Catalyst

4

EXPLAINING
AMERICAN JEWS

THE UNITED STATES, it has often been noted, was the first
society in history to have been founded consciously as a
nation, its own history, in effect, being the evolution of the
social processes that forged national unity. Moreover, as
these things go, America's history spans but a moment in
time, lacking the centuries-old accretions of traditions and
tensions—social, political, economic, religious, and cultural
—that mark European politics. There is a further distinction.
Brief as American history may be, in its entirety it belongs
to only a part of its citizenry—to the Sons and Daughters of
the American Revolution, to be precise. For America is
preponderantly a nation of immigrants and in the main has
only part-time heirs, so to speak, of its past. At the time of
the Civil War the American population numbered some
31 million, but in the period between 1865, when the war
ended, and 1925, when the restrictive immigration laws went
into effect, America took in more than 32 million immigrants

—which means that close to half of the present-day U.S. population, the descendants of the immigrant masses, have no direct ancestral memories or family traditions that trace back as far as the Civil War.

The children of the immigrants learned about America's past from teachers and from books, and not as part of inherited family traditions. Thus were they assimilated into the American ethos, the process of assimilation itself becoming a factor in American history. The history of America which the immigrants and their children might themselves recount was, in all likelihood, not the history they had learned at school, but that of their own acculturation, of the immigrant struggles and adjustments and accommodations that form the very center of the American historical experience.

This experience as it affects American Jews has been described by Marshall Sklare, American Jewry's most eminent sociologist, in most of his works, and probably most succinctly in *America's Jews* (New York: Random House, 1971). The focus of this work is on Jewish identity—its private and public faces, its normal and pathological aspects, the formal and informal means through which it is transmitted and reinforced. From this central investigation Sklare proceeds to an exploration of American Jews in relation to the two basic forces acting upon them: the influences of world Jewry, past and present; and the countervailing influences of America, Christian, secular, and pluralist. The result is sociological topography of a very high order, comprising an imaginative mapping of the American Jewish experience in all its facets.

The term "Jewish identity" has come to signify the Jew's acceptance of his Jewishness and of his sense of belonging to the Jewish group. In America, Jewishness is a matter of personal choice, in contrast to most prewar European states, where Jews became members at birth of a legally constituted and officially defined Jewish community having governmental status. A Jew could take his leave from such a community only by submitting a formal petition to the municipality; upon approval, the petitioner was then classified as a "nonbeliever." In Poland, where the Ministry of Religion did not recognize "nonbelievers" as a category, the only effective way of withdrawing from the Jewish group was through conversion. But America, as they say, is different. Here group membership is considered strictly a private matter, and nonidentification with the Jewish group involves no communal penalty or public sanction, since it requires no public declaration of disaffiliation (as in Weimar Germany, for instance, where the local Jewish communities, informed by the municipality of Jewish withdrawals, used to publish notices in the newspapers under the heading *Austritte aus dem Judentum*). Nevertheless, as Sklare points out, even though in America the state is neutral on the matter of group identity, the decision to be or not to be a Jew (or a member of any other minority group) is not entirely a matter of individual choice; for the choice must be legitimated not only by the individual's own group but also by the larger society. The discrepancies between self-definition and external legitimation are often at painful variance—witness the case of those black Jews who are full-fledged Jews by all the criteria of rabbinic law yet are rejected as such by most American Jews and regarded simply as blacks by society at large.

Given this situation, where the decision of Jewish affiliation is a personal and voluntary one, the extraordinary thing is that the overwhelming majority of America's Jews do in fact identify themselves as such and, for the most part, try to give shape and substance to that identity. The most common form which this takes is organized religion, though religious observance, as we all know, is not practiced too scrupulously.

Secularization has made greater inroads in Judaism than among other religions in America, and this, as Sklare explains, is due to the special nature of the Jewish sacred system, which, more than any other, encompasses almost the entire round of diurnal activity. But even before the mass immigration to America, secularization, abetted by urbanization and industrialization, had begun to invade traditional Jewish society and to chip away at the traditional patterns of faith. In America the process was hastened by an eagerness to acculturate to American society. Thus, many Jewish observances came to be seen, in Sklare's phrase, as "disharmonious with the environment"; the Judaism practiced in the Old World underwent a series of adjustments to accord with the American situation, where the Jew "is guided by a new personalism rather than by an old prescriptionism." (Sklare is quick to note, however, that the personalism in question is not all that individualistic, but is determined by the prevailing environment.) Speculating on why some observances have been retained and others dropped, Sklare concludes that the highest degree of retention occurs when a ritual "is capable of effective redefinition in modern times," when it "does not demand social isolation or the adoption of a unique life style," when it "accords with the religious culture of the larger community while providing a 'Jewish' alternative when such is felt to be needed," and when it "is centered on the child."

Traditionally, it was the family that was charged with the responsibility of transmitting a sense of Jewish affiliation to the child and of imbuing Jewish values in the young. But most American Jewish parents, lacking even rudimentary knowledge of Judaism or familiarity with the Jewish past, are not able to fulfill their traditional task. Consequently, they have transformed the functions of certain communal institutions—primarily the synagogue and the school—and given them a surrogate parental role. It is not altogether a discouraging development, for, in Sklare's words, "community persists, because identity persists." Once having been brought into existence, the community and its institutions operate out of a dynamic of their own, and while serving the need for identity, they also stimulate and foster it.

To be sure, wherever Jews have lived, the synagogue has been the central Jewish institution. In this respect America is not different, yet in America the synagogue has undergone a profound sea change. In its European habitat, the synagogue was primarily a place of worship and of religious study. In America it vastly expanded its functions to become a communal center as well, thus accommodating the needs and desires of its members to maintain and transmit their Jewish identity.* The behavior of American Jews indicates that their choice of this religious identity does not necessarily affirm a personal commitment to Judaism, but rather to membership in the Jewish people.

The gaping discrepancy between some of the more egregious Jewish practices and the historic Jewish tradition they are meant to represent is an easy target for adolescent rebels and self-righteous literalists. But the form which Jewish identity has taken, whether one likes it or not, is the heritage of the modernism that Jews have been trying to live with ever since the late eighteenth century, when the French Revolutionary National Assembly reluctantly enfranchised the Jews at the price of membership in their own corporate communities. It is a heritage fraught with paradox.

---

* But not only in America. In the Soviet Union young Jews—totally secularized and totally ignorant of Judaism—congregate outside local synagogues on the festival of Simhat Torah to demonstrate their Jewish affiliation. Their behavior is reminiscent of that of the Jewish secular radicals in czarist Russia, who returned, after the trauma of the pogroms of 1881, to the Jewish community.

The "enlightened" Jews of the period, who had already begun to abandon religious observance, were the very ones who hastened to accept a religious definition of the Jewish polity in deference to the demands of the modern nation-state. The traditionalist Jews, on the other hand, insisted on a national or ethnic dimension in defining themselves as Jews.

Self-conscious and sensitive because for two centuries they were harassed for being both a religious entity and a nationality (and stateless to boot), Jews still tend to forget that this nexus of identity is not an exclusive Jewish property. Even today, Northern Ireland and the Indian subcontinent bear out Leopold von Ranke's observation of a century ago that "in most periods of world history nations were held together by religious ties alone." Nor could Arab nationalism muster any dynamism without the rallying power of Islam. Yet how many people in Ireland, Bangladesh, Syria, or Egypt fully believe in the teachings of their respective religions? Still, their religious loyalties remain, and it is these that shape and strengthen national identity.

So too with American Jews. The overwhelming majority of Jews in America today—all, except for a handful of unreconstructed secularists—define Jews as members of a religious faith, even if they regard that faith as merely a buttress to communal survival. This is in accordance with the American pattern of pluralism, which, as Will Herberg had occasion to write some years ago, is largely defined in religious terms. Efforts to retain a national/ethnic group identity without a religious framework have been singularly unsuccessful. Out of this understanding of America, American Jews have constructed a community which, although it may not hold true to all the particulars of the Jewish tradition, still has set the historic Jewish faith as the cornerstone of its existence.

5

MIDDLE-CLASS JUDAISM

In the quarter century between 1948 and 1973, Jackson Heights, a middle-class neighborhood in New York City's borough of Queens, turned markedly Jewish. It had once been the nearly exclusive domain of middle-class Old Immigrants and their children—the English, the Irish, the Germans. In 1930, some twenty years after the first Jews had moved in, there were no more than a thousand Jews in a population of 46,000. But after World War II, the Jews came in numbers and soon made themselves visible. In the mid-1970s, however, they began to leave when Jackson Heights, along with adjacent Elmhurst, was turning into a North American outpost of Bolivians, Colombians, and Ecuadorians.

Living in Jackson Heights during its "Jewish period," I became a participant observer of the Jewish community and an amateur historian of its past. Late in the 1950s, when nearly 30,000 Jews lived there, along with about the same number of Protestants and about 37,000 Catholics (Italians now among them), I began to visit the several synagogues, attending services and interviewing rabbis and laymen. I hoped that this exploration would reward me with an understanding of how middle-class Jews in the mid-twentieth century observed Judaism.

The growth of Jackson Heights in the postwar years was replicated in dozens of other places in Queens. After years of housing starvation (during the Depression and the war years), many young families in New York found that the great Queens building boom of 1948–1951 offered them a wide choice of modest apartments at modest monthly rentals from $75 to $140. Besides wanting a place to live at rents they could afford, these young people were fleeing from the changes in their old neighborhoods in Manhattan, the Bronx, and Brooklyn. They were looking for an inexpensive facsimile of the suburbs a half hour from Times Square.

A similar process characterized Jewish migration in most northern cities. Before settling in the suburbs, metropolitan Jews first began moving out of the old, central parts of the city into newer, less crowded neighborhoods at the fringes of the city limits. While the expanding Negro and Puerto Rican populations changed the character of the center city, the Jewish population changed the character of the outer urban ring.

Like the gentiles there, most Jews who lived in Jackson Heights were white-collar workers, professionals, and businessmen. About three-fourths of the people I interviewed had at least some college training; most, in fact, were college graduates who earned between $5,000 and $7,000 per year, then the median income of urban middle-class Jews and somewhat higher than that of the population as a whole.

Jews and gentiles in Jackson Heights very seldom mingled,

even though the once prevalent exclusionist policies had become a thing of the past. Most of the Jews I talked with assured me they got on well with their Christian neighbors, but it turned out that relations were apt to be formal and neutral, limited to polite greetings in the elevator or on the street. The only places where Jews and gentiles regularly encountered each other were at the political party meetings and in nonsectarian civic organizations like the League of Women Voters or the PTA. The familiar preference for finding one's recreation among Jews came up time and again: "It's more comfortable"; "There's less pressure"; "It's one barrier less between people."

To serve the social and religious needs of its 30,000 Jews, Jackson Heights had ten local branches of national Jewish organizations (including fraternal groups like B'nai B'rith, Zionist groups like Hadassah, and defense agencies like the American Jewish Congress) and five synagogues (three Orthodox, one Conservative, and one Reform). The full ideological spectrum, right to left, ultra-Orthodox to atheist, was represented. But it was often hard to distinguish one organization from another on the basis of their activities: the ideological outlook and ambitions of the great national Jewish organizations were seldom reflected in their local counterparts.

The five synagogues in Jackson Heights had a combined membership of about 1,300 families, or about 15 percent of the total Jewish population in 1959, when I surveyed them. Half were the kind of transients that passed through the synagogue only long enough for their children to attend its Hebrew school. A fair estimate is that about 40 percent of all the Jewish families in Jackson Heights belonged to some synagogue at one time or another. The two oldest and largest of the synagogues were the Jewish Center (Conservative), which grew out of a tiny *minyan* founded in

1919 by the first Jewish settlers of Jackson Heights and first housed in a little bungalow; and Adath Israel (Orthodox), dating from 1927, with 430 members (only males are counted). The other three synagogues were all established in the 1950s by dissidents whose dissatisfaction with the older synagogues was either social or ideological. The Elmhurst Hebrew Congregation had some 135 members— mostly Orthodox German Jews who had arrived in America in the late 1930s. The Young Israel of Jackson Heights, a congregation affiliated with a uniquely American version of Orthodoxy, had been founded in 1954 and by the end of that decade reached its peak of 175 male members. The Reform Temple Menorah, housed in a converted movie house whose marquee announced that every Wednesday was "Game Nite," had been established in 1947 and within three years had built up a membership of 200 families. Half had deserted in 1950 when the rabbi was found to have been involved in various Communist-front organizations. The congregation never recovered and became the ragtag of Jewish life in Jackson Heights.

Without giving it much thought, I had supposed that these different congregations would conform to the ordinary notions of Orthodoxy, Conservatism, and Reform. Orthodox Jews were in my mind associated with poor immigrants, Reform generally with wealthy third-generation German Jews. It turned out that in Jackson Heights many of the older and richer residents were Orthodox—the richest Jew in the community was a nationally known toy manufacturer who had long been affiliated with the Orthodox Adath Israel, and his four-figure contribution to the UJA was by far the largest single gift coming from Jackson Heights. By contrast, an active leader of Temple Menorah's Reform congregation was the owner of a local dry goods store which probably yielded a decent living only by dint of the hard work he and his wife put into it. These two instances may be regarded as constituting the not-too-extensive range between the well-to-do and the not so well-to-do in a community that was predominantly middle class.

The range in religious belief was hardly any wider. At one end was a small group of ideologically committed Orthodox Jews, like the leaders of Young Israel; at the other were some equally strongly committed Reformers. Most of the rest of the Jews in Jackson Heights, regardless of their formal affiliation, stood somewhere between. In such matters as Sabbath observance and *kashrut* there was very little difference among the various groups—excluding the Reform congregation, of course. A few among the Conservatives and the Orthodox were, indeed, strict observers; but most made their less rigorous individual adjustments. Melvin Kohn,* Adath Israel's first president, told me he thought about 85 percent of Adath's members could be classified as "Conservative" in terms of observance (of course, he meant nonobservance). In fact, their deviations were very conspicuous. For example, when Rabbi Diamond, who for almost three decades held the congregation formally within Orthodoxy, objected to the synagogue's Boy Scout troop joining weekend trips that were to start Friday afternoons, his congregation tried to talk him out of his objections. But when he insisted that the boys must wait till Saturday evening to set out, the laity finally solved the problem another way. As one member confided to me, "We began to sneak the boys out without the rabbi's knowledge. He never knew about the weekend trips."

Even the Orthodox German Jews of the Elmhurst Hebrew Congregation showed signs of relaxing. Observance among this group, who frequently obey the letter of the Law if not

---

* This, like all proper names used here, is a pseudonym.

its spirit, was no longer as rigid as it once had been in Frankfurt.

Nor did the three different seating practices in the various synagogues—total segregation in Young Israel, separation in Adath Israel and the Elmhurst Hebrew Congregation, and mixed seating in the Jewish Center—reflect individual beliefs or commitment. The convictions and practices of the Jews formally affiliated either with Conservatism or Orthodoxy—perhaps even with Reform—more closely resembled each other than they did the separate movements out of which they originally developed. Solomon Schechter and Isaac Mayer Wise would scarcely approve of what passed for Conservatism or Reform in Jackson Heights. For if the Jews in Jackson Heights—and this is true of middle-class urban Jewish communities everywhere—have put their unmistakable Jewish stamp on the community at large, they have also placed an American middle-class stamp on their own traditional religious beliefs and observances.

The Conservative Jewish Center of Jackson Heights provides a vivid and, I believe, representative picture of the religion of middle-class American Jews. The Center was the largest synagogue in the community, the oldest and the most stable, and in the course of its history encompassed both Orthodoxy and Reform. Its character was shaped to a considerable extent by the laity.

Its membership of 450 families and 150 individuals provided a yearly income of more than $80,000. On this budget the Center maintained a rabbi, a cantor and a sexton, a choir and an organist; a school principal and six teachers; a librarian and youth leaders; and office and building staffs. It boasted a sisterhood, a men's club, a couples' club, a teenage club, a *tallit* and *tefillin* club, Boy Scouts, a mothers' club, and youth groups. Its activities included lectures and discussions; bazaars, rummage sales, baseball pools, and sweepstakes; breakfasts, luncheons, dinners, and cocktail parties; dances, theater parties, fun and games. The Center was of course affiliated with all its national correlates in the United Synagogue of America: the National Women's League, the National Federation of Jewish Men's Clubs, the Young People's League, the Commission on Jewish Education. Alvin Spiegel, the Center's young and energetic rabbi, was a member of the Rabbinical Assembly; he reported periodically on the Center's activities in the pages of the various publications of the Conservative movement. The Center's school was affiliated with the Associated United Synagogue Schools of Queens and the Jewish Education Committee. The Center itself belonged to the Jewish Community Council of Jackson Heights and to the nonsectarian Jackson Heights Community Federation, a civic-improvement association.

Rabbi Spiegel made no complaint about his congregation's attendance at services. It was not unusual for the Center's synagogue, which seated about 350, to be filled to overflowing on festivals, even when these occurred on weekdays. On Friday nights, on an average, about 150 worshipers were there, mostly couples seated together—the sexes seemed about evenly represented. Decorum prevailed in dress and in manners. The service was marked by dignity and evoked a fairly high degree of participation during responsive readings and communal singing. Cantor, choir, and organist provided pleasant music. The rabbi's sermon was neither long nor taxing. The late Abraham Joshua Heschel might have been describing just such a Friday evening when he wrote, "Our services are conducted with pomp and precision. The rendition of the liturgy is smooth. Everything is present: decorum, voice, ceremony. But one thing is missing: Life."

If by life Heschel meant *kavanah*—direction, inspiration, an awareness of the meaning of prayer—there seemed to me to be little of this even on Kol Nidre night, the most solemn service during the High Holidays, or during *hakkafot* on Simhat Torah. Only the very elderly pleaded for forgiveness at Kol Nidre, and only the children generated excitement during *hakkafot*. But at a dedication of a Torah scroll which was being presented to the junior congregation, I did, finally, it seemed to me, find *kavanah*.

The dedication of a Torah scroll has never been set as a fixed observance. The ceremony, which evolved in Eastern Europe, is based on the notion that anyone who inscribes even one letter on a Sefer Torah earns a mitzvah, or good deed. Traditionally the scribe—the *sofer*—first outlines the letters of the opening and closing verses of the Torah; then the congregation sells these letters to individual purchasers who, on completing them, receive the *sofer*'s blessing. Parents at the Jewish Center bought letters for their children.

The *sofer* was a short, ruddy-faced, white-bearded Hasid from Rivington Street, on the East Side, where remnants of the old immigrant Jewish community still lived. As he approached the Sefer Torah to help the children fill in their letters, he seemed indeed to become transfigured into a living testimony of the joy in serving God. He guided each child's hand, asked in his Yiddish singsong the child's name, and blessed him. When all the letters were filled in, his glowing face grew redder still, his tempo, as he sang the *Toras-Emes*, became livelier and livelier. He infected the slower cantor with his own excitement, and the two men began dancing together. When all the Torah scrolls, dressed in their gold-braided satin and velvet mantles, with their silver breastplates, crowns, and *rimonim*, were taken from the Ark for the procession, the *sofer* reached a high stage of God-intoxication. Many of the adults were visibly moved. The children seemed amused, perhaps bewildered, perhaps even embarrassed at the sight of men dancing together.

The members of the congregation at the Jewish Center were not really convinced that the Torah is Divine Revelation. They regard it as a great religious and historical document. But the *sofer* from Rivington Street, in the midst of the congregation that night, believed the Torah to be Divine Revelation of the God of Abraham, Isaac, and Jacob. He blessed the children in the name of the God of Abraham, Isaac, and Jacob. Probably most members of the Jewish Center did not think of their God as different from the God of the Episcopalians, Lutherans, or Roman Catholics.

In the course of my visits, I talked to a good many Center members, some of whom even consented to a formal questionnaire interview. I asked them why they attended services and how important these services were to them. All expressed the notion that belief in God was essential to being a good Jew—but only two people agreed that attending services was a way of being brought closer to God. Almost everyone said that a good Jew must belong to a synagogue—but only one person declared that attending weekly services was essential to being a good Jew. The majority of those with whom I spoke said they attended services because it made them feel better, or because they enjoyed the atmosphere of the synagogue. But only one was able to follow the Hebrew prayers, let alone understand them. Most members of the Jewish Center considered themselves to be Conservative, and they felt they were authentically represented by a Conservative institution. Many of those I interviewed, brought up in Orthodox homes, defined Conservatism as a moderation of Orthodoxy's "fanaticism," a loosening of its "rigidity," a "realistic accommodation to the needs of the modern Jew." A few thought of Conservatism as a brake against headlong flight into Reform— practically apostasy, in their eyes. As one woman put it, "I never liked the strict old-fashioned Orthodox, and I'm a little afraid of Reform. It's too non-Jewish. Conservatism is just right for the middle class."

But not many members of the Jewish Center realized how many deviations from tradition and how many accommodations to the modern world they had accepted. Few noticed that they prayed in a synagogue without a *mehitzah* and without a *bimah*, a synagogue in which the rabbi and the cantor turned their backs on the Holy Ark as they faced the congregation, and where female voices joined in a choir accompanied by an organ. Years ago, however, the congregation had been in constant upheaval over just these changes.

The founding members of the Jewish Center had been split into two camps, the Orthodox and the "antis," the latter a highly diverse group whose common bond was the common foe. These "antis" included Jews who thought a Jew, even if he was not very pious, ought to belong to a synagogue; American-born Jews who had joined the synagogue for social reasons; East European Jews—Zionists and secularists—who hoped to turn the synagogue into a community center.

In 1925 the congregation hired Rabbi Hirsh Riegelman. Recently arrived from Austria, he was then attending Stephen S. Wise's newly established Jewish Institute of Religion "to get a little American polish," as a friend had advised. It was he who inspired the "antis" into the desire to make something worthwhile of the little "bungalow" synagogue. The synagogue president, Isaac Milman, had no ambition for the shul beyond its *minyan* and school; the secularists and socialites had more grandiose ideas.

There had not been enough room within the cramped confines of the bungalow synagogue for conflict, but the congregation's new two-story building, to which it moved in 1927, could easily hold a house divided against itself. The new restrictive immigration laws were in some sense responsible for the beginnings of the battle. One of the congregation's important donors had extracted a quid pro quo for his contribution to the new building: the synagogue was to hire his brother-in-law, a Polish rabbi, who would then be permitted to enter America as a nonquota immigrant. But when he arrived, Rabbi Greenstein turned out to have a long beard, to speak only Yiddish, and to be very, very Orthodox.

Many in the congregation resented attending services at which he officiated. Once having turned their backs on the Lower East Side, they hated to be reminded of their immigrant origins. Besides, going to shul was a social event, and the women insisted on equal rights: they wanted to sit with their husbands. The Orthodox Jews, naturally, strongly opposed any such thing. Finally, an arrangement satisfactory to both factions was reached. The Orthodox were to hold their services in the *bet midrash*—a small synagogue one flight down from the main floor—with women sitting in the rear and Rabbi Greenstein officiating. In the main synagogue, upstairs, where men and women sat together and the cantor faced the congregation with his back to the Ark, Rabbi Riegelman was to conduct what we would today call a "modern" or "liberal" Orthodox service. This was the classic compromise that started the transformation from Orthodoxy to Conservative Judaism everywhere in America.

The new arrangement did not long satisfy everyone who attended services in the main synagogue. Rabbi Riegelman, fresh from the Jewish Institute of Religion, decided to try further innovation. Using a meeting room on the third floor, he arranged a late Friday evening service with a string trio. Thus, in the fall of 1928, three different services were held simultaneously for the High Holidays: the traditional Orthodox service in the *bet midrash* with Rabbi Greenstein, the modern Orthodox in the main synagogue with a rabbi hired for the occasion, and a service that today would be best described as Conservative, on the third floor with Rabbi Riegelman.

Clearly, the "third floor" had become very popular, and the annual membership meeting that was soon to be held would have to decide once and for all what manner of services should be conducted permanently. The "main synagoguers" felt themselves caught in a squeeze between the Orthodox and the "liberals," while the "liberals," for their part, worried about being forced out by a combination of the modern and traditional Orthodox. Each group sent out feelers; finally, at a caucus of the "liberals" and modern Orthodox, a compromise was reached which the general membership subsequently adopted. Under this compromise, the old-fashioned Orthodox were to continue their Sabbath eve services in the *bet midrash*, while the main synagogue would hold a late Friday night service with music, thus accommodating the third-floor practices. But Saturday morning would revert to the modern Orthodox—a traditional Sabbath service without music. High Holiday services, it was agreed, would be Orthodox, and without music. Once again, the congregation adopted a classic formula on the road to Conservative Judaism.

At first, a small barrel organ replaced the string trio. But when Rabbi Greenstein's brother-in-law expressed a wish to do something for the congregation to make amends for the trouble he had caused, Rabbi Riegelman suggested the gift of a pipe organ and—no sooner said than done—a $1,500 instrument was installed. That was in 1929. Rabbi Riegelman, proud of his achievement, promptly hired a concert organist for that first late Friday service.

But no organ sang out that evening. Isaac Milman, former president and *baal-tefillah* in the *bet midrash*, had, with a zeal worthy of the Maccabees, slashed the pipes. The next morning Rabbi Riegelman descended to the *bet midrash*, calling for repentance. But the congregants openly applauded Milman, for it is said, "They that strive with the Lord shall be broken to pieces." Rabbi Riegelman felt he had no choice but to resign.

During the next ten years the organ was never used, not even for weddings. With Rabbi Riegelman gone, and the stock market in collapse, the reformers' zeal flagged. They had achieved a great deal—mixed seating, the use of English in the services, dissociation from the immigrant Orthodox. Around 1930 the Jewish Center joined the United Synagogue, the national congregational body of the Conservative movement, thus becoming officially Conservative. But the Center had little interest in its adopted parent, and little money in the bank. Each year it rejected the $250 quota the United Synagogue imposed, unanimously voting to pay only the annual $25 dues. In 1936 the sisterhood of the Center formally joined the National Women's League, the women's Conservative organization.

Time proved to be on the side of the Conservatives. The *bet midrash* congregants began to die out; and in 1937 the congregation's new rabbi, Samuel Levin, discussed with the board a plan to draft men from the main synagogue for the daily *minyan* in the *bet midrash*, so that the *minyan* could go on functioning. On High Holidays, the *bet midrash* continued to conduct a strictly Orthodox service for those Jews in Jackson Heights of whom Rabbi Mordecai Waxman has written, "Men and women who stayed away from the synagogue throughout the year wanted the shul they stayed away from to be a shul where people *davvened*."

The dues-paying members of the Jewish Center, however, were satisfied with the Conservative service. There were even some newcomers in the late 1930s who had Reform leanings. To satisfy them and himself, too (for he was a "left-winger" in the Conservative movement), Rabbi Levin proposed to repair the organ which had been standing mute in the choir loft for nearly ten years. On February 2, 1939, the board, six to three, authorized $90 for repairs. The organ was first used in February in a "dramatic play," and the organist was paid $5. It did not take long before the organ and its music were accepted as part of the service. Some members complained, a few resigned, until, on June 28, 1939, the board adopted a motion that it "favors the use of the organ at Friday evening services and authorizes the ritual committee to proceed with arrangements for such use." Now, too, a compromise had been effected, for having the organ made it more agreeable for the Reform-minded to wear their skullcaps.

The 1939 compromise was identical with the one of 1928–1929. But this time there were no bolts from heaven or its representatives.

In 1943, Rabbi Levin left Jackson Heights. He was succeeded by Rabbi Philip Goldstein, a "centrist" in the Rabbinical Assembly. Rabbi Goldstein's ten years at the Jewish Center coincided with a period of intensified organizational activity on the part of all Conservative institutions to strengthen Judaism among the laity. Postwar developments encouraged rabbinic leaders to set higher standards for practicing Judaism: more Jewish education for children and adults, more synagogue attendance, more observance. People were beginning to come to the synagogue in larger numbers than ever before. Perhaps the war had had this effect, or the Holocaust, or Israel, or the new exodus to the suburbs. Whatever the reason, it was important to do something for Jews once they were in the synagogue. The wish to do something expressed itself concretely during the years immediately following the war in a drive to give the children more Jewish education.

In 1941, Dr. Mordecai M. Kaplan, then chairman of the education committee of the United Synagogue of America, had said, "With very few exceptions, most of the congregations have to maintain a double system of schooling in order to meet the wishes of the two classes of members that are usually to be found in every congregation, namely those whose slogan is 'More Judaism,' and those who ask for 'Less Judaism.' "

It had been the practice of many Conservative synagogues to conduct both a Sunday school and a weekday Hebrew school; congregants could elect to send their children only to the Sunday school or, in addition, to the afternoon classes twice a week. In 1940 more than 200 children attended the Center's Sunday school, while only 75 were enrolled in the Hebrew school.

The Rabbinical Assembly continued to agitate for increased Jewish education, and its members in turn tried to influence their congregations in this direction. Finally, in 1947, Rabbi Goldstein succeeded in establishing the three-day-a-week Hebrew school in the Jewish Center. Parents could no longer choose between the Sunday school and the Hebrew school. Members with Reform leanings complained most loudly, and the conflict led to secession and the founding of the Reform Temple Menorah. This left the Center with an almost entirely homogeneous membership loyal to Conservative Judaism.

In the ensuing years, Conservatism became so entrenched that no one even noticed the last gasp of the *Kulturkampf* in the Jewish Center. One weekend in 1957, Rabbi Spiegel took twenty couples to Lakewood for a retreat. During the Saturday morning Torah reading, someone suggested, "Why not give a woman an *aliyah*?" A woman was called up. Later she admitted she had been uncomfortable. Her attitude coincided with the views of the majority in the Rabbinical Assembly's law committee, who felt it was "ill advised to change the *general* pattern of the traditional Torah reading procedure . . . let the ladies of the synagogue find blessing in the fact that the men take the *lead* in its rituals." This episode was mentioned in the congregational bulletin, but scarcely anybody paid attention. It was the sexton who told me about a very Orthodox old man who regularly had attended the daily morning and evening services, though he paid no dues to the Center. The old man, aroused by the story of the *aliyah* in Lakewood, stopped coming to shul.

The 613 commandments which, according to traditional belief, were transmitted by God to Moses have been widely breached, and it was hard to find any that were universally obeyed among the Center members I interviewed. Fasting on Yom Kippur, removing bread (but not other *hametz*) from the house on Passover, and lighting candles on Hanukkah were the three most observed commandments. One might think the Jews in Jackson Heights were paying heed to Rabbi Judah ha-Nasi's advice: "Be as attentive to a minor commandment as to a major one, for thou knowest not what is the reward to be given for the commandments."*

Kashrut survived in a mangled form: about two-thirds of those whom I interviewed bought kosher meat regularly, but even they did not all keep the meat and dairy dishes

---

* Lapses in observances and changed emphases in tradition are not unique among Jews—Catholics, too, have been seduced by urban industrial America. In *Dynamics of a City Church* (Chicago: University of Chicago Press, 1951), a study of an urban parish in the South, Father Joseph H. Fichter wrote that the diocesan Lenten regulations "admit such a latitude of interpretation that they seem to be observed more in breach than in practice." His comments on the unexpected popularity of Easter over Christmas and on the social function of confirmation and midnight Mass indicate that secularism made drastic inroads into the Catholic Church long before Vatican Council II.

separate. Scarcely anyone *kashered* the meat. Again, about two-thirds of the respondents never served bacon or ham, but these were not the same two-thirds who bought only kosher meat. Some who would not serve pork at home were willing to eat it elsewhere. The general feeling was that observance of dietary laws had no real bearing on whether a person was a "good Jew."

The vestiges of Sabbath observance were even fewer than survivals of *kashrut.* (A psychoanalyst could perhaps best explain the effectiveness of the taboos against forbidden foods.) The only Sabbath observance most of the people belonging to the Center still honored was the festive Friday night meal, with its candle-lighting ceremony. But perhaps only one out of every two families began the meal with the *kiddush,* the prayer recited over a cup of wine to consecrate the Sabbath. On the Sabbath itself, many people worked or did household chores; everyone smoked and rode. Hardly anyone was seen going to shul. The Jackson Heights Jews did not know and surely did not care that in 1950 the Rabbinical Assembly's law committee could not agree on whether to sanction riding to services on the Sabbath.

The Conservative rabbinate, like Gaul, is divided into three parts: right, center, and left. Although the right has the fewest practicing rabbis, its importance is enhanced by the Jewish Theological Seminary faculty, who command extraordinary prestige and whose position on questions of *Halakhah* is pervasive in the Rabbinical Assembly. The Assembly has tried to adapt the *Halakhah* to modern living, but it has done so slowly and with a heavy heart. Perhaps the slowness is intended to thwart the laity's unseemly haste in making changes. In 1938, twenty-five years after the United Synagogue was founded, the Assembly's law committee took the view that the Friday evening service was unobjectionable even when held at a late hour. It has not yet issued a formal decision on the use of the organ, even though about one-fourth of all Conservative synagogues do in fact use one at services.

The Rabbinical Assembly modified the *ketubah* (marriage contract); its law committee voted to permit using electricity for illumination on the Sabbath; and a majority sanctioned riding on the Sabbath in order to get to shul. Yet the laity has been riding everywhere on the Sabbath— except, it seems, to shul.

One rabbi complained at a meeting of the Rabbinical Assembly, "While we are discussing the trivialities and the minutiae, the very props of our Jewish life are disregarded, violated, and broken. Not five in a hundred of our members are Sabbath observers; not five in a hundred observe the dietary laws; not two in a hundred are *yodei sefer*; and not even one in a hundred cares about our decision, or, for that matter, the legalistic decisions of any group." To this charge, Rabbi Jacob Agus replied in the spirit that has characterized the Conservative rabbinate: "Manifestly, our central purpose is not to save the Halakhah. . . . We want to save the Jews."

The United Synagogue stopped trying to change individual behavior. Instead, it adopted a code setting forth an appropriate standard of congregational behavior on the synagogue's premises and at official functions elsewhere. Besides demanding the sanctity of the Sabbath and *kashrut* observance, the code attempted to guide congregations toward decorum and dignity in dress and behavior. The Jewish Center's Rabbi Spiegel, too, frequently addressed himself to raising the level of public taste at congregational functions. But his most important role, he believed, was to teach his congregation that Judaism was "a response to the most vital and immediate concerns of the Jew, what to do with his life and the days that make it up, and how to face suffering, setback, and death itself."

Rabbi Spiegel's attitude toward tradition did not differ much from that of older rabbis who argued that "out of the *naaseh* comes the *nishma*"—the doing precedes the believing. "Tradition," he once told me, "is the result of the Jews' encounter with the Divine. It is what has become public Jewish property after the 3,000-year cry after God." Though he held that both preserving and changing Jewish tradition were of deep concern to the Conservative movement, he thought it most important that Jewish tradition be returned to "proper perspective" and again be viewed "as the effect of Israel's dialogue with its Living God. Jewish tradition ought to be the means to help restore the religious dimension to the Jew, to expose him to the luminous throbbing world of faith." On another occasion he told me that "living as a Jew creates a sense of holiness in each person and increases his awareness of living in the sight of God."

Jewish public life in the last few decades has been monopolized by rabbis with such single-minded dedication to nationalism and social justice that we have become unaccustomed to rabbis who place God above His people. Under thirty-five then, and a postwar graduate of the Jewish Theological Seminary, Rabbi Spiegel had been in the rabbinate for ten years. His God-centeredness, like that of many of his contemporaries, had been molded by many elements: personal tragedy, the war, existentialism. His teachers had been Franz Rosenzweig, Martin Buber, and Abraham Joshua Heschel. Intellectually attracted to Reconstructionism under Mordecai Kaplan's powerful influence in his student days, Rabbi Spiegel later was convinced that the Reconstructionist movement offered no "compelling idea of God" which could satisfy his needs or those of his congregation.

Rabbi Spiegel hoped to teach his view of Judaism to his

congregation not by sermons, nor even by his enormous number of lectures, talks, discussions, reviews, and courses, but by personal example. Being a Jew, he said, was a joyous experience. Thinking of himself as part of the Hasidic tradition, he wanted to show his people that Judaism did not need to be morose, dogmatic, or ascetic. Did he succeed? Perhaps half the people I asked thought a rabbi should be "a source of inspiration and faith," in good times and bad, and a "counselor for guidance and advice." They looked to him for facts, guidance, information. They wanted to find a faith or formula that would help them cope with life, death, and suffering. A sisterhood parlor discussion about the Book of Job attracted many women, seeking an answer to the question "Why does God make suffering?"

These were the people who attended the pleasant services in the Center, the people who were looking for faith, peace, and comfort. Some hoped to find understanding in a discussion about Job, as they sought to find comfort in the service. They were worlds apart from the rabbi.

As to the question of the ethical element in Judaism, practically every single person I interviewed recognized that a "good Jew" must lead an ethical and moral life. (Whether an ethical and moral life meant belonging to a synagogue or supporting humanitarian causes the question-naire was not refined enough to establish.) About half my respondents thought it essential for a Jew to promote social justice by working for civic betterment, helping the under-privileged, and helping to achieve equality for Negroes. This response, it would seem, grew out of the mainstream of the Jewish tradition. For it is written that when man appears before the Throne of Judgment, the first question asked him is not, "Did you believe in God?" or "Did you pray and perform ritual commandments?" but "Did you deal honorably and faithfully with your fellow man?"

Yet the modern Jew's concern with social justice does not, I think, derive mainly from the ethical teachings of Judaism, which rise in turn from the religious wellsprings of belief— the belief that man was created in God's image and should imitate him in the ways of justice, truth, and mercy. The modern Jew's impulse to help the wronged and the oppressed springs, it seems to me, from the fact that he associates his own security with a democratic, liberal, and secular society. He looks upon a threat (even if not directed specifically against him) to any of these aspects of the society he lives in as an evil to be combated. To be sure, Jewish advocates of good deeds and social welfare draw upon the teachings of the Torah and the prophets to stimulate Jewish involvement. But chapter and verse merely serve to adorn the will to self-preservation.

The sense of group identity and the wish for group survival were the chief elements which shaped the Jewishness of the Jackson Heights Jews I talked to. Being Jewish was as real to them as being an American or an accountant or a mother. They were born Jews and reared as Jews. But the only way they could consciously express their identity as Jews was through the synagogue, even if most of them rarely attended its services, were ignorant or skeptical of Judaism's teachings, and failed to observe its laws. They no longer lived in a natural Jewish milieu; having rejected the culture of Eastern Europe and its American transplantations, they had no viable Jewish culture of their own. They spurned Yiddish, which today survives only in a few expressions and jokes. They were, at best, half-learned in the religious literature. The specifics of the Jewish ethos were dissolving, and only vague, haunting forms remained.

Fear of anti-Semitism persisted, no matter how good conditions then were. Such fear was either concealed in withdrawal and hypersensitivity or exposed in assertiveness and paranoia. When one observed the middle-class Jews of Jackson Heights week in and week out, the fear seemed groundless enough, but in the pitiless glare of Jewish history it was not totally irrational. And this fear had its counterpoise in the wish to remain Jewish and perpetuate Jewishness, in a refusal to elude the ineluctable Jewish fate. Every person I talked to said that accepting one's Jewishness and not concealing it was essential to being a "good Jew." It was an elementary, almost biological, expression of group survival.

Also, all but one of the group I interviewed thought a "good Jew" must marry within the Jewish faith. Their "explanations" were merely repetitions of their disapproval: "I'm a Jew; my boys are Jews and they should marry Jewish girls." Or: "I don't believe in ethnic exploration." Conversion was the unspoken horror of intermarriage, the symbol of a Jew's death at the hands of the Christian. In the classic story of intermarriage, Sholem Aleichem's *Tevye der Milchiker*, Tevye's antagonist is not his daughter Chave's Christian husband but the priest who converts her. In the case of an intermarried couple who stay away from both synagogue and church and give their children an Ethical Culture Sunday-school education, the Jewish loss is less poignant: the Jew who does not become a Christian remains a Jew.

Doubtless the most public and lavish expression of the desire for group survival was and has remained the feeling of loyalty to Israel—all my respondents expressed warm feelings for the State. Many referred to it as the "Jewish homeland," which they uniformly defined as "a place where Jewish refugees can find a home." Everyone was eager to help Israel—though no one had considered settling there. Raising money, all agreed, was the way to help Israel, yet no one thought Israel's needs should come before those of

American Jews. It was important, my respondents said, to influence American policy in behalf of Israel, but they insisted that we must protect America's interests too. Though all were very proud of Israel, none had thought to study Hebrew in order to keep up with Israel's culture. The very idea of this struck people as strange. What went on inside Israel seemed of less moment to them than what happened —perilously—around its borders.

Philanthropy, too, was an index of group survivalist feeling. Jackson Heights, so quintessentially middle-middle-class, was not a big-money neighborhood. In 1958 the United Jewish Appeal (UJA) raised $29,000 there, which would be about a dollar per Jewish head—though a good part of this money came by way of the UJA's business and industries division. But however slim the philanthropic pickings in Jackson Heights, the Jewish organizations took most of what the Jews had to give.

Finally, the most striking evidence of the desire for group survival was the stress the parents put on Jewish education for their children—most people joined the Jewish Center for that very reason. With two exceptions among the group I spoke with, the parents themselves had had a meager education. Only three adults knew Hebrew well enough to understand the prayers; about half knew Yiddish, but only one person, who had attended a Workmen's Circle school for three years, knew that Yiddish was more than an immigrant's language. In many homes the *Hadassah Newsletter* was the sole form of Jewish literature. But everyone wanted his children—particularly the boys—to have some Jewish education.

I was reminded of a tale about the rabbi of Kotzk, as told by Martin Buber. A man came to Reb Menachem Mendel of Kotzk to ask how he could make his sons devote themselves to the Torah. The Kotzker replied:

If you really want them to do this, then you yourself must spend time over the Torah and they will do as you do. Otherwise, they will not devote themselves to the Torah but will tell their sons to do it, and so it will go on. For it is written: "Only take heed to thyself . . . lest thou forget the things which thine eyes saw . . . make them known unto thy children and thy children's children." If you yourself forget the Torah, your sons will also forget it, only urging their sons to know it, and they too will forget the Torah and tell their sons that they should know it, and no one will ever know the Torah.

What about the children in Jackson Heights? Their parents, at any rate, were very optimistic. "Don't worry about the future"—that seemed to be a general motto. "Everything is getting better," a young woman assured me. "More and more young people are joining the synagogues. Maybe they're not as religious as their parents were, but they recognize they're Jews and they want to be with Jews." One mother said, "My son knows more about Jews and Judaism than I do. I know that he'll stay a Jew all his life." Many parents argued that they counted heavily on the rabbi and the Hebrew teacher, the professional transmitters of tradition and knowledge. "It's up to the rabbis and teachers to develop the young people into good Jews," said one of the Center's more active lay leaders.

The optimism about the Jewish future was ultimately grounded in optimism about America. "This is the best country in the world for Jews," one man said flatly. Another expressed his view of the bright Jewish future in these terms: "Life is getting better and easier all the time. Our children have more leisure than we did. They will have more time to rediscover Judaism's enduring values."

Here, then, was the Jewish way of life in America, the Jewish aspect of what Will Herberg once characterized as the American Way of Life—a way of life in which religion makes no demands on personal behavior. This religion, as it lends its moral sanction to mundane purposes, reflects a middle-class outlook, and it is therefore not surprising that American Jews—who belong predominantly to the middle class—should have embraced it so enthusiastically as their own.

6

WHEN REFORM
WAS YOUNG

As THE FOUNDER of American Reform Judaism and all its
institutions—the Union of American Hebrew Congregations, Hebrew Union College, and the Central Conference
of American Rabbis—Isaac Mayer Wise has been apotheo-
sized in a prodigious number of works. Bibliographically,
indeed, he outranks every historic figure of American Jewry.
To date, the most ambitious addition to the sacred writings
is a voluminous work by the son of one of Wise's first disciples and rabbi of the congregation Wise himself served
for nearly half a century.* Small wonder then that this
biography, with extensive selections from Wise's writings,
reads like Hasidic hagiography. Wise is *morenu, rabbenu*:
our teacher, our master, sainted scholar, prince of Torah,
one in a generation. Instead of a living man, peppery and

* James G. Heller, *Isaac M. Wise: His Life, Work and Thought* (New
York: Union of American Hebrew Congregations, 1965).

vitriolic, combative and vituperative, we are presented with a rabbinic Pollyanna embalmed in universal esteem.

Nor is this book, like its predecessors, illuminating about the rise and development of the Reform movement in America. By far the most interesting and important of the many questions raised by Wise's career is why the mid-nineteenth-century Reform movement enjoyed so phenomenal a success in America, far beyond its achievement in Europe. The question can be answered only by viewing Wise and his movement in the context of American religious life as a whole.

When Isaac Mayer Wise came to the United States from Bohemia in 1846 there were between 40,000 and 50,000 Jews here, forming compact communities in most of the large and some of the smaller cities of the Atlantic seaboard, the Middle West, and the South. These Jews were organized into about forty congregations, but they had only four, just recently arrived, rabbis among them. Jewish learning was at the time in rather short supply in America. Even among the German and Polish immigrants, knowledge of the Talmud was not very extensive, while among the earlier Sephardic settlers it was nearly extinct. Isaac Leeser, for example, the pioneer preacher and founder of the Jewish press in America, whom we think of as a pillar of traditional Judaism and learning in his time, had not yet completed his study of the Talmud when he arrived on these shores at the age of seventeen. The same held true for many other and lesser Jewish leaders.

Given the shortage of rabbis, the conduct of Jewish religious affairs was largely in the hands of laymen. Most of these were *baale-tefillah*—readers, cantors—while the more ambitious among them became "preachers," bestowing upon themselves the honorific title of "reverend." Two decades later, the writer Israel Joseph Benjamin (whose chronicles of life in far-flung Jewish communities earned him the sobriquet "Benjamin II") attributed the sorry state of Judaism in the United States partly to "rabbis and teachers who have knowledge neither of the Talmud nor of the literature of Judaism." "Not infrequently," he wrote in *Three Years in America*, "he, who at home enjoyed not even the benefits of a superficial education, in this country holds his head high and proud and makes a lot of noise, like an empty ear of grain."

Under these circumstances, responsible laymen tended to be suspicious of anyone who claimed rabbinical competence. Thus, in 1845, when three leading German congregations in New York agreed to employ Max Lilienthal as their rabbi, their contract stipulated that he must produce documentary evidence of his ordination, and once submitted, the document, particularly the ordaining rabbi's signature, was scrutinized by a committee for authenticity.

If Judaism in those days was in a somewhat wavering state, Protestant America was in the throes of religious upheaval. An indigenous American religion was coming into being whose primary impulse was a repudiation of the orthodoxies of European Christianity and the institutional authority of established churches. Despite basic theological differences, pietists and rationalists alike concurred in the view that Christianity had been corrupted by the churches and their priests, and that the true meaning of Christianity could be restored only by a return to the original religious source—the words of Jesus. The liberals regarded the New Testament as a nondoctrinal source of faith and morality that yielded readily to latitudinarian interpretation, while for their part the host of competing right-wing Protestant sects which were beginning to flourish on the American frontier considered the New Testament the chief symbol of their Christian authority and legitimacy. All sects claimed the right of "private judgment" in matters of faith and doctrine, validating their private judgments by their own reading of the Scriptures.

Into these surging currents of religious reformism, Reform Judaism flowed quite naturally. It, too, was in revolt against its European origins, standing in much the same relation to European Jewish Orthodoxy as the burgeoning Protestant frontier sects like the Baptists, Methodists, and Disciples did to their European forebears. In its attempt to decommunalize Judaism and make it a private matter, Reform was, like these frontier sects, in revolt against centuries-old tradition and institutionalized clerical authority. The fact that Reform discarded the Talmud and rabbinic tradition and recognized only the Bible as authoritative made it even more consonant, in style no less than in doctrine, with developments within American Protestantism: its service was frequently in the charge of men who had little more than the Bible in their hands, and who, like the frontier Protestant preachers, rejected traditions and practices which they had never even succeeded in mastering.

When one examines the origins of Reform Judaism in America, nothing strikes one more forcibly than the marginal relation of its earliest mentors to traditional Judaism. The first rabbi to settle permanently in the United States was Abraham Reiss (or Rice, as he later called himself), who arrived in 1840, at the age of forty; but Rice—reared and trained in Bavaria, and a finished product of European Orthodoxy—was distinctly an exception during this period in the development of American Judaism. In the next decade some half dozen or so young rabbis were to arrive, all in their late twenties or early thirties, and all scantily qualified by traditional standards. Notwithstanding Jacob Schiff's dictum that no one could be a good Reform Jew unless he had once been Orthodox, these fledgling rabbis were to lay the groundwork for Reform Judaism in America.

The European rabbinical experience of that same Max Lilienthal, the only one among the early Reform rabbis who could satisfactorily document his ordination, is a good illustration of this marginality. Lilienthal's first post had been with a prosperous, status-striving congregation in Riga, which allowed him free rein for the antitraditionalism that would soon bring him to the attention of Count Serge Uvarov, the czarist minister of education. Uvarov enlisted Lilienthal in his plan to eliminate the *hadarim* and *yeshivot* and to establish in their stead secular schools for Jewish children. These schools became the target of an extraordinary boycott by the traditionalist Jews, who believed their ultimate purpose to be the conversion of the Jews—as indeed it was. When Lilienthal suddenly learned what the Russian Jews had known all along, he fled Russia and came to America, where, at the age of thirty, unchastened by past experience, he once again set about reforming the Jews.

Isaac Mayer Wise arrived the following year. At twenty-seven, he was already a full-fledged modernist and a disciple of Moses Mendelssohn and Gabriel Riesser, having come under the sway of the Enlightenment as a youth of eighteen. Wise's rabbinic experience was limited to a few years as the green and unseasoned young rabbi in a Bohemian shtetl, where he early came into conflict with the traditionalist district rabbi. The rabbinical conferences of 1844 and 1845 at Braunschweig and Frankfurt, convoked by the modernists for the purpose of reforming Judaism, strengthened him in his rebelliousness, but it was left for America to provide him with the richest possible opportunity to revise the tradition without having to face the intractable opposition of established and prestigious rabbis.

The Jewish learning that Wise brought with him to these shores was not very extensive (indeed, his Orthodox critics charged he was better qualified for the stage than for the pulpit), and his secular education was hardly less meager and random. What Wise did bring in ample supply, however, were the visions and hopes of the Berlin *Haskalah* of a half century earlier. He was, as Jacob Rader Marcus put it in the shortest and best study of Wise yet published, "an 18th-century European liberal on 19th-century American soil."*

Neither theologian nor philosopher, at heart a man of action, Wise energetically promoted in the United States the reforms he had admired in Germany. There, as in other European countries with absolutist regimes, the Jews thought their political emancipation was conditional on the "modernization" of Judaism. Zealous to demonstrate their fealty to the state, to repudiate charges that they preferred the Kingdom of Heaven to (for instance) the Margravate of Baden, German Jewish reformers favored such measures as eliminating from the liturgy the prayers for the return to Palestine, for the restoration of the Temple sacrifices, and for the coming of the Messiah. This German Jewish super-patriotism Wise transported to America along with the whole package of German reforms, so that in his first year as rabbi at the Beth El Synagogue in Albany he introduced a choir and a violin into the service, abbreviated the liturgy, and excised the "objectionable" prayers concerning the Messiah, Palestine, and the sacrifices. He also eliminated the sale of *mitzvot* and *aliyot*, had the women's gallery moved down to the ground floor of the synagogue, and introduced the practice of confirmation. These "reforms" embroiled the congregation in ceaseless turmoil, lawsuits, and even physi-

* Jacob Rader Marcus, *The Americanization of Isaac Mayer Wise* (Cincinnati [priv. print.], 1931).

cal violence. Finally, in 1850, Wise was ousted, but not before taking with him a seceding faction of the congregation, which, reorganized as Anshe Emet, provided him with his next post. Here he augmented his previous innovations by the addition of pews and an organ for Sabbath and Yom Kippur services.

In his private life Rabbi Wise took even greater liberties. In 1849, after the death of his two-year-old daughter, he disregarded traditional mourning customs. A year later, in Charleston, he publicly proclaimed his skepticism about the Messiah's coming, about bodily resurrection, and, for that matter, about the doctrinal authority of the Talmud. Returning in triumph from his Charleston visit, Wise was tendered a banquet by his Christian friends, where the guests, as he boasted in his *Reminiscences*, consumed "oysters, champagne, and bananas in as great quantities as possible decently." That menu may have served as a model for the notorious *trefa* banquet of 1883.*

In 1854, Wise bettered his position by becoming rabbi of B'nai Yeshurun in Cincinnati, where he remained until his death in 1900. The congregation had undergone the traditionalist-modernist struggle some years earlier, with victory going to the modernists. Even so, Wise found much that was still in need of "reform." He abolished observance of the second days of festivals, introduced a hymnbook, initiated a late Friday evening service, and permitted uncovered heads in the synagogue; at last, in 1873, he dropped the observance of the second day of Rosh ha-Shanah as well. (Many years before, after B'nai Yeshurun had adopted Wise's abbreviated and modernized prayerbook, *Minhag America*, "Benjamin II" noted that the second section of the prayerbook, containing the service for Rosh ha-Shanah and

* See John J. Appel, "The *Trefa* Banquet," *Commentary* 41 (February 1966):75–78.

Yom Kippur, had not yet appeared, and that on those days the congregation adhered to the old ritual. "Perhaps," he commented, "they were afraid that God was awake on those days and they might be the worse for it in God's judgment.")

When Wise, following the German Radical-Reform belief that all Judaism was reducible to the Ten Commandments, declared that the only "external laws" were "those based on the principles expressed in the Decalogue," he became the first influential rabbi to permit, even to recommend, adapting Jewish law to the American way of life. There is no doubt that the uninhibited spread of Reform during this period in America was in large measure due to its do-it-yourself aspect. Wise provided a Jewish equivalent to the freewheeling Protestant sects of the frontier, a religion which Jewish peddlers could easily shoulder in their travels through the roaring West, and which Main Street merchants could readily follow without undue detriment to their fledgling businesses.

Conservative Judaism had its origins, as Marshall Sklare has shown us, in the struggle between a traditionalist rabbinate on the one hand and a largely nonobservant, status-striving laity on the other. Making all manner of concessions to the laity and to the times, the rabbis nevertheless held fast to the *Halakhah* so that Conservative Jews eventually came to expect their rabbis to observe the Law which they themselves disregarded; through their rabbis, therefore, they remained linked, however tenuously, to the normative Jewish tradition. But the pioneer Reform rabbis broke the chain of tradition, releasing themselves as well as the laity from the *Halakhah* and setting their rabbinic stamp of approval on nonobservance. The consequence was that the zealous young Reform rabbis—and Wise was among the most zealous—goaded part-observant Jews into nonobservance, and liberated the nonobservant from their guilt over abandoning the Law. (Some Reform rabbis, however, nurturing a private sense of guilt, later testily denied that the rabbis had fathered the Reform movement, insisting that the laity had done it all by themselves!)

Not only did the original Reform rabbis approve modifications and changes in the tradition, but eventually—in the Pittsburgh Platform of 1885—they went on to elevate nonobservance into a doctrinal antinomianism. The most radical Reform document ever issued, the Pittsburgh Platform declared obsolete all Mosaic and rabbinic laws governing diet, dress, and priestly purity. A leading Reform rabbi once described the document as "the Jewish Declaration of Independence," which led Orthodox opponents to ask the question, "Independence from what?"—and to answer it, "Independence from Judaism." More than fifty years later, in 1937, when Reform rabbis convened in Columbus, Ohio, to adopt a new statement of principles, it was clear that nothing had dated so rapidly as the "modernism" which the Pittsburgh Platform had promulgated. And since then, the thrust of the Reform movement, especially among its younger rabbis, has been in the direction of restoring part of the discarded tradition.

So far as his own theological views went, Wise was a man hard to pin down; to him, inconsistency was no hobgoblin. One thing was clear, however: he disliked Orthodoxy, whether Jewish or Christian, and never ceased attacking it for its "irrationalism," "supernaturalism," and "superstition." Probably he could best be described as a "liberal" in religion, without dogmas and constricting practices. On one occasion, according to his *Reminiscences*, he as much as identified himself as a Unitarian, describing a conversation he had with Daniel Webster in Washington in 1850:

I referred to Theodore Parker's conception of Unitarianism, and set over against this my conception of Judaism. This forced me to the conclusion that there was no essential difference in the matter of doctrine, but in historical development, which, however, did not enter into the question of doctrine. "It is well," said Webster, extending his hand to me; "you are indeed my co-religionist."

But five years later, when Wise called David Einhorn, leader of the Atlantic seaboard German Radical Reformers, "a Deist, a Unitarian and a Sadducee and an Apostle of deistical rationalism," he was being abusive, not admiring. Einhorn, who was challenging Wise's hegemony in the Reform movement, had declared that only the Ten Commandments were immutable laws of the Covenant, a view that Wise was himself insistently to proclaim only a few years later.

Wise intensely disliked the Germans (apparently both Jews and non-Jews) in and around Cincinnati who, he claimed, affected atheism because it was fashionable. In his *Reminiscences,* he accused "some wounded apostles of the atheistical stripe" for the failure of Zion College, a precursor of Hebrew Union College, and further charged them with having driven him out of the Republican Party, then being founded. One must, I think, treat this accusation with reserve, for on other occasions Wise charged these same "atheists" with being in sympathy with his Eastern opponents, the advocates of German Radical Reform, whose theology he nevertheless supported whenever it seemed politic to him.

In later years, Wise became more conservative in his attitude toward certain Jewish practices and more radical toward others, but he certainly did not become a *baal-teshuvah* in his old age, nor did he return to Orthodoxy. From reading his views on Judaism and on religion in general, I am convinced that he was stirred most of all by a vision of a universal religion (he once called it "Israelism") along the lines of the Hebrew theism of the Danish Jew, Meir Aaron Goldschmidt; the Bible Brotherhood of the Russian Jew, Jacob Gordin; and the Hillelism of the Polish Jew, Ludwig Zamenhof. All these men had attempted to create a nondogmatic religion that would unite mankind in brotherhood on the basis of the ethical principles underlying Judaism. However, Wise's messianism was, I think, somewhat more worldly than that of the others. (The American Constitution, he once said, is "Mosaism in action.") Moreover, he seemed to think that the messianic age would arrive momentarily in America.

Yet this ardent advocate of universalism, this apostle of liberty, equality, and justice, who looked forward to a universal republic, when "soon, very soon, all mankind will celebrate one Passover before the Lord," was not sufficiently compassionate or generous to include in his vision Negroes as free men, or Russian Jewish immigrants as his equals. Such was his vehemence against the Abolitionists that it inhibited his outrage against the conditions of Negro slavery. He blamed Abolitionist "Protestant priests" for causing the Civil War. They would rather, he claimed, "see this country crushed and crippled than discard their fanaticism or give up their political influence." As for immigrants, Wise demanded of American consulates in Europe that they send only "useful" ones, instead of the "cripples, beggars, work-and-light shunning loafers who crowd together, particularly in the dirtiest streets of New York and Chicago." In his paper, the *American Israelite*, he editorialized that it was "next to an impossibility to associate or identify ourselves with that half-civilized orthodoxy which . . . gnaws the dead bones of past centuries." The only time he approved of the Zionist idea of restoring Palestine as the Jewish homeland was when it offered the possibility of diverting the Russian Jewish immigration from the United States.

Wise's favorite expression, we are told, was "the spirit of the age." But he mistook both spirit and age, thinking they were still those of the short-lived Enlightenment in France and Prussia. In the United States, Christian theological liberalism was rapidly losing ground in its struggle with the resurgent Protestant orthodoxies: it was the heyday of revivalists, evangelists, Bible-quoting enthusiasts, and sectarians. But though this spirit permeated most of American society, Wise ceaselessly and vigorously denied its existence. All his life he fulminated against the notion that the United States was a "Christian nation" and that Americans were a "Christian people." (Alexis de Tocqueville showed himself more perceptive when he wrote two decades earlier that Americans "combine the notions of Christianity and of liberty so intimately in their minds that it is impossible to make them conceive of one without the other.")

Arguing on constitutional grounds against the incorporation into law of the sentiment that America was a Christian nation, Wise arrived at the position that because the United States was not a Christian nation de jure, it was not, nor could it be, a Christian nation de facto. On that failure to distinguish the legal from the social reality he based his ideas about the separation of church and state in America, ideas which became the sanctified heritage, preserved intact for a century, of Reform Jews, Conservative Jews, and even some Orthodox Jews. In recent decades many of Wise's synagogal reforms have been abandoned and his theological views discarded in favor of a return to Jewish traditionalism and a restoration of the distinctively Jewish elements in prayer and ritual. On the other hand, his ideas about church and state are now accepted more than ever, and have become as ossified and resistant to change as the most inflexible Orthodoxy.

We often think that the more traditionalist Jews are in matters of religion, the more conservative they are in politics. In European countries, the Orthodox community usually followed a policy of accommodation toward the state, avoiding open opposition. Reform Jews, whose philosophy of Jewish existence was almost always identified with liberal political philosophies, nevertheless frequently pursued a policy not of accommodation but rather of submission to the modern state. Modernist Jews often bought political emancipation at the price of religious emancipation, but in the end paid also with slavish patriotism. No Germans were as patriotic as the Reform Jews. Similarly, American nationalism and American patriotism flourished among Reform Jews. Thus, Wise was prepared to discard from Judaism whatever he thought inappropriate to Americanism: "Whatever custom, law, doctrine or practice can be justified before the tribunal of reason, if it collides with American sentiments, is doomed to perish; and what is left, that is American Judaism, or Judaism transformed to correspond to American sentiments, feelings and thoughts."

This passion to assimilate Judaism into Americanism provides yet another instance of the conformity of Wise's sentiments to the prevailing Protestant trend. It was during Wise's lifetime that the Protestant denominations added the finishing touches to a Christianity whose God was manifestly directing America's destiny, and who had set a providential course for America.

Among Jews, the effect of this Americanization of Judaism was to reinforce assimilatory trends and to provincialize Jewish religious culture. Here, then, was yet another way in which American Reform Judaism came to resemble American Protestantism, sharing its optimism and its identification of America as the chosen land.

7

FROM PAST TO PAST:
Jewish East Europe to Jewish East Side

For many American Jews the East Side was the world of
parents and grandparents. Its demise has enshrouded it in
nostalgia and sentimentality. A hardheaded approach may
bring us closer to the reality, to see it as it really was.

The Jewish East Side was, at the start, Jewish Eastern
Europe transplanted. But America added one new element,
a catalyst that transformed Old World Jews into New
World ones, into American Jews. Its effect was unpredictable—sometimes it produced gold, sometimes trash. It
created fantastic new possibilities for Jews, but it also
undermined traditional modes and values. It created and
destroyed. That element was freedom—freedom to build
and freedom to destroy.

For the Jews who came from despotic czarist Russia,
from the autocratic Hapsburg Empire, and from the bru-
tally oppressive Kingdom of Rumania, the freedom they
found in America—in that one square mile on the East Side
that was their America—overwhelmed them. That freedom

liberated them from the tyrannies of the past. To this Jacob
Zvi Sobel, a Hebrew-Yiddish poet, testified in 1877:

> Now here am I already in this free land,
> Where equal rights exist . . .
> Where there are no slaves,
> No barons, no counts.*

But America was also a land of freedom abused, which
swept many immigrants from their moorings and loosened
their restraints from interior authority. Isaac Rabinovich,
another Hebrew-Yiddish poet from Lithuania, who came to
New York in 1893, wrote back home:

> The Jews become much more demoralized here than any
> other immigrants. The spirit of freedom, which they inhale
> on their arrival in this new country, is changed into a
> destructive spirit. And Jeshurun waxed fat—and trampled
> on everything holy, on all sacred traditions.

The Jews who came to America and settled in the East
Side were hungry for freedom, for political liberty, and for
basic human rights: the right to live (and live in safety), to
work, to study, to vote. These rights and liberties they pursued intensely in that crowded, overcrowded square mile
on the East Side.

Most highly they valued political freedom—the right to
vote, to determine their political fate. That Jews are today
the most compulsive voters in the nation is their East Side
heritage, and that, in turn, is the consequence of earlier
political deprivations in Eastern Europe. The East Side

* This and the following quotation have been translated from Shlomo
Noble, "Dos bild fun dem amerikaner yid in der hebreyisher un yidisher
literatur in amerike (1870–1900)," *Yivo-bleter* 38 (1954):50–77.

Jews registered and voted in greater proportion than any other immigrant group, except perhaps the Irish, and Jews treated the franchise with greater seriousness than any other group, especially the Irish. At the turn of the century, it was observed that "neither pleasure nor business exigency" prevented Jews from voting, nor did the Jewish voter succumb to "the curious inventions of the Bacchanalians" on election day: ". . . the Russian Jew does not drink anything stronger than tea before he votes and after he has voted he goes about his business without celebrating or rioting."* In the main, immigrant Jews voted the Jewish interest, and that interest they associated, more often than not, with the Democratic Party, the party of immigration.

But the East Side also inherited another political tradition from Eastern Europe—the politics of revolution. Czarist oppression and Christian anti-Semitism had bred a Jewish brand of political radicalism, a socialist world view of a universal people and of a cosmopolitan society from which no one would be excluded and in which no one would be depised because of his religion or nationality. This millenarian hope fostered, in Jewish Eastern Europe as on the Jewish East Side, a profound and passionate idealism, but it also encouraged a radical brand of Jewish self-hate and a precipitous flight from Jewish identity, alienation from the Jewish community, and ignorance about one's own roots and origins. That political outlook, too, still persists. We see it today among the young Jews active in the splinters of past radical movements, who regard politics as a conflict of pure principle, and compromise as a moral sellout.

As important to Jews as political freedom was the freedom to live and make a living. In Pobedonostzev's long-range

---

* Emanuel Hertz, "Politics: New York," in Charles S. Bernheimer, *The Russian Jew in the United States* (Philadelphia, 1915, reprint ed., New York: A. M. Kelley, 1971), pp. 264–265.

tripartite "solution" to the "Jewish problem," one-third of the Jews of Russia were destined to die of hunger. As for Galicia, it was too impoverished and industrially too backward to permit its Jews more than bare subsistence. But America was *di goldene medine*, the golden land, and the streets of New York were paved with gold. Jews were free to work at whatever they wished to work at. The seriousness which Jews applied to politics matched the seriousness which they applied to making a living. Unrestricted from working here or there, in this trade or another, the East Side Jews devoted themselves to making money where they could. The freedom to make money became an obsession. To be sure, it was for *tachles*, a useful purpose—money to bring up the children, to spare them the misery of the sweatshop, to provide for the future, to make life better and easier in time to come. But for some this desire to make a living, to accumulate money, to be secure, became an end in itself. Their family life was neglected, community was disregarded, tradition abandoned. Jacob Riis, no particular friend of the Jews, put it this way:

> Thrift is the watchword of Jewtown. . . . It is at once its strength and its fatal weakness, its cardinal virtue and its foul disgrace. Become an overmastering passion with these people who come here in droves from Eastern Europe to escape persecution, from which freedom could be bought only with gold, it has enslaved them in bondage worse than that from which they fled.[*]

In Eastern Europe, in contrast, successful businessmen seldom managed to evade their familial responsibilities and communal duties. Conforming to older traditions and pat-

[*] Jacob A. Riis, *How the Other Half Lives: Studies among the Tenements of New York* (New York: Sagamore Press, 1957), pp. 78–79.

terns, they were motivated by a sense of noblesse oblige. A rich man gave not just money but time to communal affairs, even if he was common and greedy; for only that way could he win position, prestige, honor. But on the early East Side, none of these counted.

Freedom to get an education, to go to school, was high on the list of rights which the Russian Jews pursued as avidly, energetically, and single-mindedly as making a living. In Eastern Europe the quest for general education accompanied the gradual breakdown of traditional society. Among the upwardly mobile Jewish middle classes—big businessmen, merchants and entrepreneurs, contractors, holders of vast land leases, government concessionaires, doctors and lawyers—education was the key to economic success. These people regarded general secular education as a necessity, not a heresy. But at the other end of the East European Jewish social scale, among the Jewish working-class radicals, rebels against Judaism, the quest for education, not revolution, was the real heresy. Julius Martov, who was to become a leader in the Russian Social Democratic Party, discovered this early in his career when he tried to organize Jewish workers in Vilna: "The idea of employing the class struggle to transform the uncultured environment itself . . . was still alien to them . . . They considered self-education . . . the alpha and omega of the socialist movement."

In America, lavish with its freedom to learn, the Jews' quest for education and self-education became intensified and magnified. The public schools were wide open and hospitable. There was no need to bribe government officials to enroll in high school, and no need to convert to be admitted to a university. "The public schools are filled with little Jews," wrote Hutchins Hapgood. "The night schools of the east side are practically used by no other race. City College, New York University, and Columbia University are graduating Russian Jews in numbers rapidly increasing." City College, where the enrollment in those days was about 75 percent Jewish, used to be called Jews College. That American Jews are today as well educated as the high-status, old-stock Episcopalians whose ancestors came on the *Mayflower*—that they owe to their ancestors, most of whom came by steerage in the ships that plied between Bremen, Hamburg, Rotterdam, Antwerp, and New York.

In addition to these freedoms, America also offered freedom of expression—freedom of speech, press, assembly, thought. Having escaped the stifling czarist censorship, immigrant Russian Jews rushed to exploit their freedom to write, to talk, to congregate. Between 1885 and 1900 nearly 100 Yiddish papers were founded in America, and in New York alone there were nearly 20 Yiddish dailies between 1885 and 1917. "The Yiddish newspaper's freedom of expression," a Jewish editor remarked, "is limited by the Penal Code alone." The Yiddish press had a violent and extremist tone, whether politically conservative and Orthodox or radical and antireligious. The irresponsible tone, with slashing accusations directed against government, capital, Jewish institutions, or competing papers, was due partly to the license spawned by American freedom and partly to the lessons learned from the yellow journalism that William Randolph Hearst was then cultivating.

This untrammeled freedom of expression hatched and multiplied writers, journalists, pamphleteers, poets, speakers, orators, and actors. The period before World War I witnessed an explosion of freedom rather than of talent. Morris Rosenfeld, the sentimental lyricist of the sweatshop, and Jacob Gordin, the prolific playwright, are the great literary monuments of that era, but upon closer examination they appear like Hollywood foam-rubber boulders, illusions created by distance and accepted as real because of condescending and indulgent literary standards. The Yiddish theater and Yiddish poets like Rosenfeld fascinated outsiders who were captivated by the energy and intelligence of the Jewish immigrants. No doubt they felt much like Samuel Johnson about a woman preaching—observing that it was not done well but surprised that it was done at all, like a dog walking on its hind legs.

David Pinski, who in time liberated the Yiddish drama and stage from their tawdriness and sensationalism, inveighed against the cheapness: "The Yiddish theater has come to denote tomfoolery, clownishness, and degeneracy—the caricature of Jewish life."[*] As for that early East Side Yiddish literature, at best it testified to the powerful persistence of folk poetry among the Yiddish-speaking folk. After World War I, Yiddish writing in America emancipated itself from the Rosenfeld–Vinchevsky–Edelshtat primitivism of form and message; the sentimentality and lugubriousness of the earlier era were wrung out, and Yiddish writing was transmuted into literature.

The freedom of immigrant life also spawned social demoralization, more pernicious than second-rate verse and third-rate theatricals. The Jewish immigrants were largely a youthful group; many were adolescents and men and women in their early twenties, many single and without parents, with perhaps only an older brother or sister in loco parentis. They were free—free from parental supervision, from religious obligation, from communal authority. Among some this freedom generated crime and corruption, prosti-

---

[*] David Pinski, "The Yiddish Theatre," in *The Jewish Communal Register of New York City, 1917–1918* (New York: Kehillah of New York, 1918), p. 576.

tution and vice, bohemianism and free love. Communal anarchy and the inability of existing Jewish organizations to cope with these social diseases became shamefully public in 1908 when New York Police Commissioner Theodore A. Bingham charged that half the criminals in New York were Jews, though Jews were only a quarter of the population. Four days later the first steps were taken toward creating the Jewish Community, the *Kehillah* of New York City.* It was an attempt to create authority, discipline, and self-control among people intoxicated by freedom—especially religious freedom, by which I mean the antireligious arrogance of Yom Kippur balls, for instance. In tyrannical Russia, where Jews had been persecuted for being Jewish and rewarded for turning Christian, no Jews made Yom Kippur balls.

If Commissioner Bingham's charge was the direct cause of the *Kehillah's* founding, the lack of religious authority was one of its basic and underlying causes. In his second annual report to the *Kehillah* in 1911, its president, Judah L. Magnes, stressed that "the problem of religious organization is largely the problem of restoring to the Rabbis their authority in matters affecting Judaism as a religion."

Among the immigrants who settled on the East Side, many (how many we do not know—perhaps half, or even more) had been bitten by the bug of modernity. Though they knew nothing of Aristotle or Philo, or of the Rambam's proofs of God's existence, they knew that religion was the opiate of the people. They knew that back in the Old Country the keepers of Judaism had been unmoved by the upheavals in the world, which indeed had made them even more repressive and inflexible. Cutting one's earlocks, wear-

* See Arthur A. Goren, *New York Jews and the Quest for Community: The Kehillah Experiment, 1908–22* (New York: Columbia University Press, 1970).

ing a coat shorter than the prescribed traditional style, reading "modern" books—these had been the greatest heresies. Consequently, in America, where in those days rabbis were few and unheeded, the immigrants seized their religious freedom. Observant East European Jews knew that while America was a *goldene medine*, it was also a *treyfene medine*, an unkosher land. After all, the Slutsker rabbi had publicly declared that anyone who emigrated to America was a sinner. *

To be sure, the fault was not entirely with the immigrants, or with their willingness to be seduced by America's freedom to live and work and become educated. The fault was also, here as there, with the rabbis who mistook custom for divine law; who, withdrawing from the real world, sheltered themselves in Talmudic study. They resisted even the introduction of English into the services (perhaps sermonic words of exhortation might have helped—who knows?), and they made no effort to reach out among the young to halt the drift into indifference, immorality, or crime. Yet, looking back, we see the rabbis themselves were not to blame. They came here, late in life, finished products of another culture, often baffled by the complexities and inconsistencies in American society. Here is one poignant example: when the Association of American Orthodox Hebrew Congregations began looking for a chief rabbi, one of their most promising candidates asked whether the position would be recognized by the government as an official, permanent position.† How could they have understood America?

* Moshe Davis, *The Emergence of Conservative Judaism: The Historical School in 19th Century America* (Philadelphia: Jewish Publication Society, 1963), p. 318.
† Abraham J. Karp, "New York Chooses a Chief Rabbi," *Publication of the American Jewish Historical Society* 44 (1954–1955):129–198.

In America too, as in Eastern Europe, the rabbis resisted change in the traditional forms of Jewish education, though not so adamantly. After all, here the alternative was obvious: Jewish children could do without any Jewish education at all, and in fact most did. Less than one-fourth of the Jewish children in New York before World War I had any Jewish education. In Eastern Europe, as late as 1905, Rabbi Isaac Jacob Reines was the first to combine rabbinic and secular studies in his yeshiva at Lida. The change came sooner in America, under the pressure of the religious left. Just as the Reform movement affected the Conservative movement, so the Conservative movement affected Orthodoxy. The Yeshiva Etz Chaim in 1886 and then the Rabbi Isaac Elchanan Theological Seminary—later to merge and become Yeshiva University—paired secular studies with Jewish studies.

The Young Israel movement too was a product of American and Jewish tensions. The founders of Young Israel were the children of pious and inflexible Hasidim, who would not let their clean-shaven, English-speaking sons conduct services or receive an *aliyah*. For these young men, East Side radicalism and atheism were as repulsive as the idea of conversion. They too seized their religious freedom and made an accommodation to America. They shaved their beards and wore modern dress. To differentiate themselves further from their parents, they listened to English sermons, and made a virtue of decorum in the synagogue.*

For decades the East Side lived off the emotional capital of revolutionary Europe. Heine had once observed that

* *Young Israel Synagogue Reporter*, 50th Anniversary Issue, March 3, 1962; David Stein, "East Side Chronicle," *Jewish Life* (January–February 1966):26–39; interview with Rabbi Ephraim H. Sturm, National Council of Young Israel, May 1967.

"liberty is a new religion, the religion of our age." The Jews of the East Side took a long time to learn that the religion of liberty often turned into idolatry, that the radicalism and atheism which were expected to liberate the human spirit instead suppressed and obliterated it. After the abortive revolution of 1905 a new kind of immigrant started coming to America and gradually began to change (read: improve) the quality of immigrant life. After World War I, that qualitative change became quantitative as well. Maturity, stability, responsibility—personal, familial, communal—came back into style.

East Side Jews created a transitional, one-generation immigrant culture that had in it more past than future. Standing now at a distance from the East Side, American Jews ought to admire and perhaps envy the enormous energy that their parents expended to overcome, control, and change their environment. But admiration ought not to slide into sentimentality and nostalgia.

8

THE JEWISHNESS OF
THE AMERICAN JEWISH
LABOR MOVEMENT

NEARLY 90 PERCENT of American Jews in the labor force today are white-collar workers, while less than 10 percent are blue-collar craftsmen and operatives. But once, only a half century ago, those proportions were very different. Not only did Jewish blue-collar workers then outnumber Jewish white-collar workers, but in centers of Jewish immigrant concentration, Jewish workers were actually a plurality in the total industrial labor force. Many of the Jewish aged, now living in sunbelt retirement communities, were in their youth factory workers, union members, veterans of picket lines, demonstrations, and strikes, the rank-and-file of the Jewish labor movement.

They were among the 1.5 million Jews who were part of the great stream of immigrants that expanded and transformed the industrial and commercial structure of the United States. In the Old Country they had been artisans or merchants, but in America most of them became shopworkers, primarily in the clothing industry. (The fact that

German Jews owned most of the clothing factories in New York City made it easier for Russian Jews to find employment in them.)

From 1881 to 1910 nearly 18 million immigrants arrived in America. These were the New Immigrants, those who came from Southern and Eastern Europe—the Italians, Slovaks, Croats, Poles, Ruthenians, Greeks, Hungarians, and Jews. The Old Immigrants—the English, Scottish, Welsh, Irish, Germans, and Scandinavians, who had come before the Civil War from northwestern Europe—had been assimilated into the native population.

The New Immigrants began to replace the Old Immigrants and native Americans in the coalfields and in the steel mills. They crowded America's great manufacturing and mining centers—New York, Detroit, Chicago, Pittsburgh, Buffalo, Cleveland—bringing their own ethnic flavor, linguistic variety, religious practices, hostile prejudices, and political traditions, which still linger, giving each urban community its unique character. Each wave of New Immigrants followed their compatriots into the same neighborhoods of the same cities and into the same industries, where they clung together for comfort and aid in alien urban America. Tensions multiplied between them and both the Old Immigrants and the natives. Old-timers resented alien newcomers speaking foreign tongues, who displaced them on the job, underbid them in wages, worked longer hours, and were, in addition, full of dangerous ideologies.

The early labor movement incorporated its members' prejudices, sharing their nativism, xenophobia, and even anti-Semitism. Narrowly construing its interests, organized labor vociferously opposed free immigration. It was foreseeable then that the Jewish immigrants from Eastern Europe, long habituated to social, political, and economic exclusion and to the separatism of their own institutions, should have set about forming their own "Jewish" unions.

The United Hebrew Trades, organized in 1888, was a natural outgrowth of the inhospitality on the American labor scene to immigrant Jewish workers. Even a quarter of a century later, the formation of the Amalgamated Clothing Workers Union as a split-off from the United Garment Workers reflected the unabating tension between Jewish and non-Jewish workers in the men's clothing industry. Among the hat workers, too, the Jewish and non-Jewish unions developed in mutual hostility for more than thirty years. Not until 1934 did the two hatters' unions combine, the conflicts between the Old and New immigrants having finally subsided.

These Jewish unions in the garment trades, born in the struggles of the Jewish immigrant workers to find their place in America's industrial society, eventually helped shape an enlightened trade unionism in America. In addition, they served as a way station on the road to acculturation. Fortuitously, these unions became the vehicle through which the Jewish immigrant workers expressed their values and transmitted their traditions. Blending Russian radicalism with Jewish messianism, these unions sounded an alien note on the American labor scene at the turn of the century. They were too radical for the American Federation of Labor and its head Samuel Gompers—an English Jew—who feared that the Russian Jewish socialists forever chanting about a better world were jeopardizing the here-and-now of pure-and-simple trade unionism. But the ideological vocabulary of the Russian Jewish radical movement, with its thick overlay of German philosophy, French political slogans, and English economic theories, obscured its true underlying emotional impulse and its fundamental character.

Since the French Revolution the European Jews had identified themselves with the political left. (The same political upheavals converted the Catholics into the strongest supporters of the right.) In the struggle for emancipation it became clear to the Jews that the political right was committed to a model of a Christian society in which only Christians were deemed fit to govern. From such governments and social orders the Jews knew that they could expect few rights and many wrongs. Little wonder, then, that though traditional in their own communities, Jews supported the left and sundry political groupings which strove to change the established order. It was natural, for example, that Rabbi Dov Berish Meisels, elected to the Austrian Constituent Assembly in 1848 from Cracow, should have adhered to the Polish nationalist oppositional bloc. When asked by the Assembly's incredulous president how an Orthodox rabbi could support the left, Rabbi Meisels is said to have replied, *"Wir Juden haben keine Rechte,"* a play on right and rights.

The Jewish identification with the left persisted as long as autocratic and despotic rulers persecuted the Jews and deprived them of elementary human and political rights. The autocracies in czarist Russia and in the Hapsburg Empire by their very illiberalism forced the political struggle for constitutional liberties and national/ethnic rights into a revolutionary mode. Consequently, the apparent Jewish proclivity for the political left was long mistaken as an expression of class interest and radicalism rather than as a striving for individual political rights and national acceptance.

For at bottom, the revolutionary passion of the Jews originated in their situation as Jews in a gentile world. In Russia, anti-Semitism, pogroms, and discrimination had alienated the Jews from the established order. By participating in the revolutionary movement, the Russian Jews protested against Russia's tyranny, its denial of the common humanity of all men and particularly of Jews, and its refusal to grant those basic political rights already commonplace in most of Western Europe—freedom of speech, press, and assembly, the right to vote and to elect representatives to a legislative assembly, and freedom from arbitrary arrest. The economic goals of the radicals were in fact modest: the right to organize, to work only a twelve-hour day, for a living wage to be paid each week. The Jewish radicals in Russia were engaged not so much in a class war against a ruthless industrial capitalism, for such a capitalist system hardly existed there, but rather in a revolutionary enterprise to establish a constitutional state providing political equality for all. These Jewish radicals embraced a liberal-humanitarian utopianism, rational and this-worldly, in contradistinction to the chiliastic utopianism of the Hasidim, who computed the coming of the Messiah by the extent of Jewish suffering.

In America, where they found most of their political utopia already in existence, the East European Jewish immigrants directed their revolutionary energy toward creating an economic utopia. They talked in class-war terms about redistributing the wealth and taking over the means of production, but in practice they fought on the barricades only for union recognition. That was the American equivalent of the struggle for the dignity of man, the dignity of the worker, and his parity with the boss as a human being.

To be sure, the leftist parties on the scene in New York's East Side once attracted a substantial body of voters, but never a majority. Indeed, the only socialist who made it politically in New York was Meyer London, three times elected to Congress from the Jewish East Side, but only by a plurality of votes in a three-way contest. London's political success was accounted for not so much because of his allegiance to socialism but because of his devotion and loyalty to the East Side and the East Side Jews.* In fact, Morris Hillquit, an unsuccessful socialist candidate in the same neighborhood, once characterized that congressional district inhabited almost entirely by immigrant Jews from Russia this way: "Geographically it is located in the slums; industrially it belongs to the sweating system; politically it is a dependency of Tammany Hall."

In their political behavior the immigrant Jews demonstrated that they were not nearly so class-conscious as they sounded. Nor did they perceive their own position in the class structure in Marxist terms. *Tachles*, the purposeful striving for improvement, impelled them far more than any notion of class struggle. Not content to remain proletarians, many sweatshop workers quickly became entrepreneurs—from worker to subcontracter, to contractor, to jobber, to wholesaler, to manufacturer. No group had a more fluid class structure than the immigrant Russian Jews. They soon outranked all other immigrant groups in attaining, in their own generation, a socioeconomic status as high as or higher than third-generation Americans.

Still, not all Jewish immigrants succeeded in escaping from the sweatshop. Those who remained concentrated on educating their children for something better than the shop. They formed a one-generation working class, being "neither the sons nor the fathers of workers."† For themselves they sought dignity and community in their unions and the institutions associated with Jewish labor. In Russia the Jewish community had been an organic whole, and most Jews,

---

* See Arthur Gorenstein, "A Portrait of Ethnic Politics: The Socialists and the 1908 and 1910 Congressional Election of the East Side," *Publication of the American Jewish Historical Society* 50 (March 1961):202–238.

† See Will Herberg, "The Jewish Labor Movement in the United States," *American Jewish Year Book* 53 (New York: American Jewish Committee and the Jewish Publication Society, 1952). This is still one of the best studies on the subject.

however alienated, found their place within it, whether they were traditionalists or secularists. In America, however, Jewish communal life was atomized, and the immigrant had to recreate a community of his own. The Jewish labor movement and its institutions became the secular substitute for the old community. In many ways, the Jewish immigrant workers looked upon the institutions of the Jewish labor movement—the unions; their fraternal order, the Workman's Circle; their Yiddish daily newspaper, the *Forverts*— as their vehicles of Jewish continuity. They brought Yiddish into their unions and sustained a Yiddish labor press for many decades. They were the consumers of a "proletarian" literature in Yiddish (largely revolutionary didacticism tempered with self-pity). They established Yiddish schools with a labor orientation. The labor movement was their means of preserving Jewish values and traditions as they understood them.

François Guizot once wrote that peoples with a long history are influenced by their past and their national traditions at the very moment when they are working to destroy them. In the midst of the most striking transformations, he said, they remain fundamentally what their history has made them, for no revolution, however powerful, can wipe out long-established national traditions. The Jewish revolutionaries who fled czarist prisons and Siberian exile to come to America rejected the Jewish religious tradition, shattering what they regarded its constricting mold. Yet they themselves had been shaped by that mold. David Dubinsky, at a convention of the International Ladies Garment Workers' Union (ILGWU) in May 1962, when he was reelected president, conjured up his youthful dreams, in which Jewish messianism and the perfect society appeared in a Jewish Labor Bundist guise. "I was sent to Siberia," Dubinsky said, "because I dreamt at that time of a better world. I dreamt of being free, of not being under the domination of a czar and dictatorship." He then recalled that his father, a religious man, used to read to him from the Bible on Saturday afternoons. In reading, his father used to stress that "a good name is better than precious oil." He had heard it so often, Dubinsky confessed, that it became part of him and of the movement with which he was identified: "When we saw the labor movement imperilled because of lack of ethics, I realized a good name is better than all the riches and all the offices to which one could aspire." Like many other Jewish labor leaders, Dubinsky had lived only briefly with the Jewish tradition he wistfully recalled and had rebelled against it. Yet this Jewish tradition, discarded and unacknowledged, affected him, thousands like him, and indeed the way the entire Jewish labor movement developed.

In America, shortly after World War I, the Jewish unions pioneered with their social welfare programs: medical care, housing, unemployment insurance, health insurance, vacations (and vacation resorts), and retirement benefits. They were the first to develop educational programs and the first to make philanthropy a union practice. Such activities became accepted in the general labor movement only after the New Deal. That welfare, education, and philanthropy became union concerns in Jewish unions demonstrated the ways through which the Jewish workers transferred the social responsibilities of the East European Jewish community to the labor movement. In the Jewish world of Eastern Europe, the community took care of its sick and its poor, its old and needy, and created the institutions to administer this care. This tradition the Jewish unions took over. It was only natural, then, that the ILGWU started the first union health center in 1916 and the Amalgamated started the first loan society in 1923. The Amalgamated Bank was not the first labor bank; a few labor banks had been established a little earlier in the hope that banking might yield large profits and make the unions independent. But the Amalgamated Bank was the first to offer union members low-interest loans, without collateral, which they could not get elsewhere. This was the sort of *zedakah* which Maimonides might have designated as the highest degree.

In 1927 the Amalgamated built the first cooperative houses in New York, to provide some of its members with housing that was not only decent but also attractive. Thirty years later other unions followed that example. Probably the most paradoxical episode in union housing occurred in 1957, when the ILGWU lent a corporation headed by Nelson A. Rockefeller $2.6 million to help finance a workers' housing development in Puerto Rico.

The Russian Jews' passion for learning had been satisfied in the Old Country by the revolutionary movement, which had been teacher as well as agitator, publisher of popular science and philosophy as well as political tracts. In America, Jews had more educational opportunities, and they embraced the public schools and public colleges with more enthusiasm than any other immigrant group. For those who did not go to school, there were the classes, lectures, and debates at the settlement houses, at Americanizing agencies like the Educational Alliance, at Cooper Union and the Rand School. Still, the immigrant workers continued to look to the labor movement for learning. And so the Amalgamated and the ILGWU gave courses in English and economics, history and philosophy. They were indeed labor colleges. It took another quarter century, during Roosevelt's New Deal, for other unions to sponsor labor education.

Philanthropy, too, as the Jewish unions practiced it, demonstrated the pervasiveness of Jewish tradition. For many decades, a small portion of union dues has been set aside for donations to labor organizations, health and welfare agencies, educational and cultural institutions, civic and political causes, and finally to the ethnic beneficiaries—Jewish organizations, Italian charities, and later, as a consequence of ethnic succession, Negro and Puerto Rican causes. During the Nazi period and in the immediate postwar era, the unions distributed colossal sums of money for relief and rescue, mostly for Jews but also for non-Jewish labor leaders and unionists. Jewish causes—the Jewish Labor Committee and the United Jewish Appeal being the top beneficiaries—enjoyed the support of the ILGWU. The Histadrut and many Israeli labor projects have been the richer for gifts from the Jewish labor movement.

The Jewish influence has perhaps been most lasting in the realization of industrial peace in the garment industry, though industrial peace was not particularly a Jewish idea. The National Civic Federation, founded at the turn of the century, had brought together representatives of labor, capital, and the public to head off strikes by mediation and to use conciliation to settle disputes. But the Federation had limited success, being accepted, at best, on a temporary basis by some segments of capital and labor, because labor for the most part suspected that cooperation meant sellout, and capital thought conciliation meant surrender. But the situation was different with regard to Jewish labor and capital in the clothing industry.

In 1910 the Protocol of Peace settled "the Great Revolt," an eight-week strike of some 60,000 cloak makers in New York. The strike involved mostly Jewish workers (with a substantial minority of Italians) and nearly all Jewish manufacturers. The mediators were Jewish community leaders, many associated with the Ethical Culture Society. The most active in the settlement were Louis D. Brandeis, distinguished Jewish lawyer and political liberal; leading Boston merchant and Ethical Culturist A. Lincoln Filene, who was also a member of the National Civic Federation; pioneer Jewish social workers like Meyer Bloomfield in Boston and Henry Moskowitz in New York; and the most prominent of Jewish community leaders, Jacob Schiff and Louis Marshall, of the American Jewish Committee. The manufacturers and the union alike were torn between the militants and the compromisers. Yet a precedent-setting settlement was reached which, besides increasing wages and decreasing hours, also established a preferential union shop, a union-management joint board of sanitary control in the factories, a grievance committee, and a board of arbitration. The arbitration board was to consist of one representative from the union, one for the manufacturers, and one for the public. To be sure, the Protocol of Peace broke down, was repaired, and broke down again after some years. But most scholars agree that its influence was lasting.

Several months thereafter, a four-month strike in Chicago of some 8,000 workers at Hart, Schaffner and Marx, the world's largest men's clothing manufacturer, was settled by establishing a three-man arbitration board. As in New York, most of the workers were Jews and nearly all the manufacturers were Jewish. That settlement started a tradition of such harmonious labor-management relations between Hart, Schaffner and Marx and the Amalgamated that, in 1960, the late Meyer Kestnbaum, then president of the company, spoke at the Amalgamated's convention commemorating fifty years of collective bargaining.

Exceptional in this history of cooperation between labor and capital have been its liberal, humanitarian qualities. The unions did not sell out their workers, nor did they compromise their ideals. On the contrary, they succeeded in enlisting the employers' support for economic and social programs once considered eccentric and visionary, turning these into commonplace realities.

How did this come about? I believe that Jewishness was the determinant. The existential Jewish situation, Jewish workers and Jewish bosses in a gentile world, must have had an effect, entangling them in one community. They could not extricate themselves, even if they chose, from each other's fate. Nor could they divest themselves of the habits and outlooks of centuries-old traditions. This is not to minimize the special character of the garment industry—the multitude of small shops in an industry that had not quite reached the factory stage; the cutthroat competition of highly individualistic employers; the industry's seasonal character, in which a strike meant unemployment for the worker and financial calamity for the employer.*

Still, the Jewish differential remains. Because they were Jews in a gentile world, both workers and bosses felt responsible for one another despite class differences. The wealthy Jews may have been more sensitive to the Jewish situation, feeling their position and prestige imperiled by the flow of immigration from Eastern Europe. They were ashamed of the appearance, the language, and the manners of the Russian Jews, aghast at their political ideologies, and terrified lest the world crumble by the mad act of a Jewish radical. (The fear was not entirely unfounded: a crazy Polish anarchist had assassinated President McKinley.) Unhappily and involuntarily identified with the immigrant community, the American Jews sought to restrain and tranquilize the revolutionary temper of the immigrant workers with Americanization programs and traditional Jewish education. Afraid to be accused of burdening the

---

* See Selig Perlman, "Jewish American Unionism, Its Birth Pangs and Contributions to the General American Labor Movement," *Publication of the American Jewish Historical Society* 41 (June 1952):297–337.

public charities with immigrant Jewish paupers, they contributed to Jewish relief societies and welfare and educational institutions. But they knew that employment and labor peace were better guarantees against economic hardship than was charity. In the long run, it may have been cheaper to pay higher wages than make bigger donations.

Furthermore, labor unrest hurt the reputation of Jewish employers. The dignity of man and the dignity of labor were as high in the system of values of the Jewish capitalist as of the Jewish worker, for it was Judaism itself which endowed labor with divine attributes ("Israel was charged to do work on the six days, just as they were ordered to rest on the seventh day"). Louis Marshall, who had not much sympathy for radical ideologies, nonetheless had a deep sense of the dignity of labor and the workingman. Some months after the Protocol of Peace had been signed, he chided a manufacturer whose workers had struck:

> So long as the manufacturer considers his employees as mere serfs and chattels, so long as they are considered as unworthy of being brought into conference or consultation, so long as their feelings and aspirations as human beings are lost sight of, so long will labor troubles be rampant and a feeling of dislike, if not of hatred, will be engendered against the employer in the hearts of the employees.[*]

The practice of Judaism, as well as its principles, helped to bridge the gulf between worker and boss. Sholem Asch's Uncle Moses, who brought his whole shtetl over to work in his factory, prayed with his workers at the evening services, if only to encourage them to work overtime. Lillian Wald

---

[*] Louis Marshall to Samuel Stiefel, August 28, 1911, in *Louis Marshall: Champion of Liberty*, ed. Charles Reznikoff (Philadelphia: Jewish Publication Society of America, 1957), vol. 2, p. 1129.

told a story about a Jewish union leader who met Jacob Schiff. At first the union man was uncomfortable about his shabby clothing, but this was forgotten when, arguing an issue, both he and Schiff began to quote Bible and Talmud, trying to outdo each other. This kind of familiarity reduced the workers' awe for the boss and made discussion between them not only possible but even likely.

The Jewish situation had made well-to-do American Jews receptive to liberal and humanitarian ideas. They befriended the pioneering social workers of their day and were willing to learn from them about the conditions of the industrial poor. Lillian Wald in New York City taught Jacob Schiff. Judge Julian W. Mack and Jane Addams educated Julius Rosenwald in Chicago. Little wonder, then, that Schiff used to contribute anonymously, through Lillian Wald, for the relief of striking workers and sometimes even to a union treasury. Back in 1897, during a garment workers' strike, he asked Miss Wald, ". . . is it not possible that representatives of workers, contractors, and manufacturers meet to discuss ways and means in which a better condition of affairs could permanently be brought about?"

The question may have seemed novel or naïve in those days of labor's unrest and capital's indifference. Yet in a short span of time, radical Jewish unions, conservative Jewish community leaders, and profit-seeking Jewish manufacturers answered Schiff's question affirmatively. Perhaps the most curious milestone on this path was erected in 1929, when three great Jewish financiers and philanthropists— Julius Rosenwald, Herbert H. Lehman, and Felix Warburg —lent the ILGWU $100,000 to help the union's reconstruction after its locals had been recaptured from the Communists.

The Jewish tradition of arbitration and conciliation had cut a broad swath. Originating in Talmudic times, incorporated in the *Shulhan Arukh*, practiced for centuries in all Jewish communities, these principles of compromise, arbitration, and settlement were familiar and venerable to worker and boss alike. The rabbi and *dayanim* decided in the *bet din*, the religious court, but disputants frequently took their cases to communal leaders who acted as arbitrators, *borerim*. The procedure must have seemed commonplace to most Jewish workers, not long from the Old Country and the old culture. As for the manufacturers, they too were responsive to the teachings that peaceful compromise was preferable to the humiliation of a court and that Jews should settle their disputes within the Jewish community.

Jewish solidarity and the Jewish tradition, albeit secularized, bred innovations in the institutions of modern American labor. The Jewish situation itself—the Jew poised on the margins of gentile society, in an existential *Galut*—created the energy and the impetus for those innovations. That tension of Jews living in a gentile world has accounted for much of Jewish creativity in modern society. The Jewish labor movement too shared in that creativity.

III

Heritage: The World of Yiddish

9

YIDDISH: Past,
Present, and Perfected

IN 1961 THE FIRST VOLUME of a projected ten-volume *Great Dictionary of the Yiddish Language* appeared in New York. Its editors explained in their introduction that they wished to create "a monument" to the centuries of Ashkenazic Jewry's creativity: "We have not forgotten for one moment what happened to our language at the bloody hand of the murderer and in the tempests of linguistic assimilation. We consider our task to be not just linguistic, but social and moral." Under the pressure of an importunate history, the editors saw their responsibility as primarily to preserve the Yiddish language for the historical record, and only secondarily, as lexicographers, to set standards and define its usage as a living language. When the second volume appeared in 1966, Judah A. Joffe, the elder editor and lifelong Yiddish linguist, died at the age of eighty-seven. The third volume appeared in 1971, and a fourth volume was ready for press in 1975, when the surviving editor, Yudel Mark, Yiddish scholar and stylist, died at the age of seventy-eight. Who is there to complete the work which they felt obliged to begin?

The outlook for Yiddish as a living spoken language is melancholy, yet never has the language's status been higher. Yiddish is taught at many universities; Yiddish writers, in translation, are in vogue; adult education courses in Yiddish and Yiddish literature have by now a predictable popularity. The Yiddish novelist Isaac Bashevis Singer, commenting on this phenomenon, formulated the law of Yiddish status: the fewer its speakers, the greater its prestige.

Nearly 3 million people—less than one-fifth of all Jews—speak Yiddish today or know it well enough to speak. Perhaps half as many more understand it. Before the Holocaust, Yiddish had nearly 7 million speakers, or 40 percent of all Jews. Back in 1900, over 60 percent of all Jews spoke Yiddish. Nowadays most Yiddish speakers are bilingual, knowing and speaking also the language of the country they live in, but Yiddish was once the primary spoken language of most Jews. Statistically, English has displaced Yiddish: twice as many Jews speak English, and English has twice as many Jewish periodicals published all over the world (not counting Israel) as Yiddish. In the United States, where, according to the 1970 census, more than 1.5 million persons said they regarded Yiddish as their mother tongue (over 25 percent of American Jews), the *New York Times* has many more Jewish readers than the nearly 46,000 who buy the city's only surviving Yiddish daily.

The decline in the number of Yiddish speakers and the ascendancy of English are easily explained by the great migration from Eastern Europe at the turn of the century and by the enormous Jewish losses during World War II. It is unlikely that any language would long survive both the worldwide dispersal of its speakers amid alien tongues and the destruction of its linguistic base. That Yiddish has survived at all under such conditions illustrates its adaptability and the persistence of its speakers. This determination to hold onto Yiddish is one of the ways in which Yiddish speakers have tried to win acceptance and status for their language.

Almost every language has, at some stage in its history, aspired to political recognition and social acceptance. The struggle for recognition of the native languages in Lithuania and Latvia symbolized the peasants' defiance of the Polish- and German-speaking landowners. In Finland and Norway the native languages fought for emancipation from foreign rule. In Norway the conflict persists between Riksmaal, the official Danish-derived language, and Landsmaal, the modernized standardized form of Norwegian dialects. In Sri Lanka the 2 million Tamil-speaking Hindus are still in revolt against the government's decision to make Sinhalese, the language of the Buddhist majority, the official language. Hindi is still seeking status as the national language of India, competing with the high prestige of English and the multiple claims of the regional languages. Most modern languages have suffered the disabilities of their speakers, in class, caste, religion, or nationality, but none, I think, has ever had so large a share of disabilities as Yiddish.

Yiddish developed as a vernacular among Jews, under a double disability. It was despised as faulty German by those who did not discern its distinctive character. And as a written language, it had the lowliest status, being a substitute for Hebrew among women and the most uncultivated men. Early Yiddish books were addressed to "women and the common people who cannot study Torah." (The *Tsene-Urene* was renowned as the "women's Bible.") The status of Yiddish has been reflected in some of the more common epithets applied to it: *taytch* ("translation" or "explanation"), meaning Yiddish as intermediary between the learned texts and the common people; *mame-loshn* (literally "mama-tongue"), meaning one's own language, with emphasis on the woman and mother; *prost-Yiddish* ("plain Yiddish"), pointing to Yiddish as connected with the common and uneducated; *zhargon* ("jargon") and *shifha* ("maidservant"), both embodying contempt.

The struggle of most vernaculars for recognition has frequently been a class conflict. In Europe the lower classes spoke the vernacular and the upper class, the nobility and the educated, spoke Latin, French, German, or whatever the prevailing cultural style was. In eighteenth-century Russia, after Peter the Great's reforms, when French culture flooded the upper classes, Russian was looked upon as "the language of lackeys and of all common people." Just so, among Jews Yiddish was associated with the lower classes. It was offensive to the educated upper class, and despised by the middle class aspiring to gentile society, where German, Polish, or Russian were spoken. While most vernaculars have gained status with the emergence of the middle class as an influential factor in society, the emergence of a Jewish middle class in the main spelled doom for Yiddish. (One exception: the very Orthodox among middle-class Jews were a highly significant factor in halting linguistic assimilation.) So intent were these modern skeptics, the newly educated middle-class Jews, on integration into gentile society that they even blamed anti-Semitism on Yiddish, as a particularly objectionable aspect of Jewish separatism. At the beginning of the nineteenth century, German Jews appealed to Polish Jews to discard Yiddish: "How long will you continue to speak a corrupt German dialect instead of the language of your country, Polish? How many misfortunes might have been averted by your forefathers had they been able to express themselves adequately in the Polish tongue before the magnates and kings!" Disdain for the language of the Jewish masses is quite old. Long after Aramaic had spread as the vernacular among Jews, Rabbi Judah ha-Nasi protested, "Why should the Syriac language be used in Palestine? Either Hebrew or Greek!"

Most of today's Yiddish speakers were born in Eastern Europe, though only a small percentage still live there. (Nearly 400,000 in Russia gave Yiddish as their mother tongue in the 1970 census; about 150,000 Yiddish speakers remain in Rumania, Poland, and Hungary.) Transported and transplanted to many countries of different cultural climates, Yiddish has flourished or withered, to complete the metaphor, according to the fertility of the soil and the care and skill of the gardener. Its fate has been inextricably bound up with each immigrant community, and with the way in which the community has adapted itself to the host country. The steadfastness of Yiddish has varied from place to place for the widest variety of objective reasons: the continuing immigration of new Yiddish speakers, the general cultural level of the non-Jewish milieu, the nature of the school system and particularly the existence of Jewish day schools, the segregating tendency in many countries of the prevailing Catholic culture, the absence of a native middle class and the entrepreneurial function of Jews in industrially and commercially underdeveloped countries, the unreserved acceptance of cultural pluralism and multilingualism.

The subjective reasons that have kept Yiddish alive, far from its Ashkenazic base, are fewer but perhaps more potent than the objective ones. National consciousness, national will, and religion—old-fashioned Orthodox Judaism—have been the dominant factors in preserving Yiddish, admittedly among a relatively small number of Jews. In the United States, the survival rate has been rather low.

America had much to offer the Yiddish-speaking East European Jewish immigrant: civic and political equality, unparalleled economic opportunities, unlimited educational advantages. In return, America demanded Americanization, or Anglo-conformity, as Stewart G. Cole termed this traditional pressure of the majority on the minority to conform to the basic cultural pattern. Anglo-conformity, long before its vulgarization, was considered a virtue by the Founding Fathers. John Jay wrote in the *Federalist*:

> With equal pleasure I have as often taken notice, that Providence has been pleased to give this one connected country, to one united people, a people descended from the same ancestors, speaking the same language, professing the same religion, attached to the same principles of government, very similar in their manners and customs. . . .

Since 1788 the American ethos has repeatedly expressed itself in open and often violent hostility to foreignness, whether cultural, linguistic, religious, or racial. The Anti-Masonic party, the Know-Nothing movement, the American Protective Association, the Chinese Exclusion Act, the Ku Klux Klan, and the "national origins" quota system describe an unmistakable pattern of how America demanded conformity to its dominant Anglo-Saxon culture. The immigrants' retention of the Old Country's language, religion, and customs was viewed by the natives (sometimes justly) not merely as habitual and nostalgic but also as ideological and political, and therefore a threat to American unity.

Partly in reaction to the pressure of Americanization, exerted formally through the public school and the already Americanized Jewish community and informally in the street and factory, and partly in an overwhelming response of love to America, Jews jettisoned Yiddish very rapidly. The 1940 census showed how rapidly. Yiddish ranked fifteenth of eighteen groups in the percentage of its third-generation speakers. Only 3 percent of those who gave Yiddish as the language spoken at home in their earliest childhood were third generation, while one-third of Spanish and French speakers were third generation, and about one-fifth of Dutch and German speakers. Most who claimed Yiddish as their mother tongue were the foreign-born, whereas among other groups the largest percentage admitting a foreign language as mother tongue generally came from the second generation. These figures show, starkly and shatteringly, how few Jews have valued Yiddish enough to pass it on or even to claim it. The comparatively high rate of linguistic retention among Germans, despite their much earlier immigration and their high level of acculturation, suggests that the conscious effort to maintain the national language—a product of nationalism or self-esteem—was a vital factor in that retention.

In its transplanted immigrant existence, Yiddish has been cultivated only by two groups of immigrants, for whom it has expressed the cultural or religious commitments of their past. The first group were the nonreligious (once antireligious) socialist and Zionist radicals, the second, the most traditionally Orthodox Jews.

Most of the radical immigrants were ideological Yiddishists; Hebraists among them were few. Coming to America from Eastern Europe at the turn of the century, these Yiddish-speaking masses created not only the American clothing industry but also a host of institutions—the Jewish labor movement, the Yiddish press, the Yiddish theater, Yiddish schools, *landsmanshaftn*, massive fraternal and communal organizations—through which they accommodated themselves to America and which, ironically, served perhaps more as Americanizing agencies than as preservatives of the old culture. Sharing the revolutionary traditions of prerevolutionary Russia, they were divided on their particular Jewish ideologies (Diaspora nationalism or Zionism), but they agreed that Yiddish was the language of the Jewish masses. They were the heirs of a tradition that went back to the late decades of the nineteenth century, to the *narodnichestvo* —Russian populism, going to the people.

This movement had had a great impact on Jewish enlighteners and radicals alike, opening their eyes to the possibility that Yiddish, the language they despised and loathed, might be used as a vehicle for their propaganda. The Westernized *maskilim*, who thought the benighted Yiddish-speaking Jews needed secular education and Western culture, finally agreed that enlightenment, transmitted even in what they considered an unworthy language, was better than no enlightenment at all. As for the Jewish radicals, it soon became obvious to them that they could preach socialism, revolution, and labor unity to the people only in the language of the people. Few of the leaders among the radicals knew Yiddish, and many had to learn it while teaching revolution.

Both the *maskilim*, often believing Jews, and the revolutionaries, nonbelievers, propagandized against the fanaticism and rigidity of degenerating Hasidic courts, against the rabbinic narrow-mindedness that kept the people fettered in superstition. They succeeded in the long run, reinforced by larger processes of modernity, in attenuating the adherence to Judaism. Thus, wherever the secular teachings prevailed, Yiddish was often the one element of a Jewish culture that was regarded as an acceptable Jewish heritage to be taught and transmitted to the next generation. The vernacular became the hallmark of Jewish identity and the symbol of Jewish national self-consciousness.

It was this kind of linguistic nationalism among Jews that Ahad Ha'am particularly detested. In the tradition of the Russian *maskilim*, for whom rational humanism and high culture were the greatest desiderata, Ahad Ha'am considered the ideological Yiddishists a threat to the survival of Judaism. He wrote in 1909 to Simon Dubnow, the Jewish historian and architect of cultural autonomism:

> If after thousands of years the Jewish people is to start developing its culture from the very beginning, if it is to fashion for itself a new literary language and new "literary and cultural values" which are nothing more than a pale reflection of other cultures; if it is to be just like the Lithuanians and the Ruthenes and so forth: then I can see no point and no purpose in a national existence on so low a level.

Dubnow, also a *maskil*, was a lukewarm partisan of Yiddish as the basis of linguistic nationalism. In answer to Chaim Zhitlowski, who had become the ideologue of Yiddishism, Dubnow wrote, "Yiddish is dear to us and we must use it as a uniting force for the greater half of our people in the coming generations." But he argued against erecting a Jewish national culture on "Yiddishism," for that would mean casting off "millions of Jews who do not speak this language and to prepare millions of others for bankruptcy at a later time."

In another essay, replying to Ahad Ha'am's views, Dubnow compared the Jews to a cripple with one natural leg, Hebrew, and one artificial leg, Yiddish. "On these two legs our people has stood and survived for many generations," he wrote, "just as in former years it stood on the linguistic dualism of Hebrew and Aramaic."

That was a period when nationalist ideologies flourished and when no one questioned the then popular notion that language and nation were inseparably fused. Pan-Germanism and Pan-Slavism provoked small nations to seek a new national mystique through the elevation and cultivation of their own national languages. The Jews shared in this nationalist ferment and ideological explosion, and in the long run the Yiddish language was the beneficiary. The *Jewish Daily Forward* (*Forverts*) in New York City, the Montreal Jewish Public Library, the Colegio Israelíta de México, the Workmen's Circle Yiddish schools are all part of the heritage of that period, however remote the ancestry may now seem.

Yiddish has had a more direct line of continuity among the Orthodox, particularly the Hasidim. The tradition of *targum* is an ancient one among Jews, dating back to the Septuagint. Aramaic, as the language most widely spoken by the Jews, became the language of translation par excellence in the Talmudic period. The rabbis prescribed that a pious Jew should read the weekly portion on the Sabbath twice in Hebrew and once in translation. As the Jews in the course of centuries migrated away from the Aramaic-speaking Near East, the Aramaic *targum* became unintelligible, but tradition had enshrined it as a semisacred language, and it has persisted as such. (It is an amusing commentary that the Yiddish expression *targum-loshn*, literally "language of translation," means something unintelligible, the equivalent of "It's Greek to me.")

The Baal Shem Tov, the founder of Hasidism, urged his followers to use Yiddish because that way they could achieve spontaneous expression. The marvelous tales of Nahman of Bratslav, the sayings of Dov Ber, the preacher of Mezritch, the prayers and poems of Levi Yitzhak of Berditchev—these gave Yiddish a sanction far transcending its function as a vernacular. In a Yiddish textbook used in the Orthodox Beth Jacob schools for girls in interbellum Poland, a poem described Hebrew as the language of holiness and of the Torah. It was paired with a poem identifying Yiddish not

only as the language of millions of Jews but also as semisacred, the language of Reb Levi Yitzhak and Reb Nahman
of Bratslav.* In elevating the common and uneducated man,
in teaching that the unlearned man was the equal in God's
eyes of the scholar, that fervor and faith could compensate
for ignorance, the Hasidic rabbis succeeded in elevating not
only the common people but also their language, lending
it the dignity of intercourse with God. In some Hasidic-based
Talmud Torahs and yeshivot, Yiddish still remains the
language of translation and interpretation and is, I suspect,
more effectively mastered than in some secular Yiddish
schools. The reason may be—though I am surely simplifying
—that among the Hasidim Yiddish still fulfills a real function
in the transplanted but living culture. For they believe a
Jew must speak Yiddish; otherwise he speaks "goyish," that
is, any non-Jewish language. They have no need to ideologize
Yiddish, for it is part of an organic whole, where the whole
person and the whole Jew are identical. But this is scarcely
true of most secularists, among whom Yiddish has shrunk
from an ideology into a cult or, even worse, a sentimentality.

That sentimentality is, in a way, endemic to Yiddish.
Languages have their characteristics. German has been
described as the language in which to give orders, Russian
the language to swear in, French the language of elegance.
Yiddish is the language of tenderness and endearment; it is
indeed a *mame-loshn*. I recall a vivid illustration of this in
a Swiss movie about refugees from Nazism, *The Last Chance*,
in which many languages were used. A grandfather spoke

*Two of the verses read: *Yidish loshn, hartsik loshn/fun milyonen
brider,/Reb Yitskhok-Levi hot mit dir/geshafn frume lider,/S'hot Reb
Nakhmen mayselekh oyf yidish undz gegebn./ Yidish loshn, mame-loshn/
freyd fun undzer lebn.* (Yiddish language, tender language of millions of
our brothers. Reb Levi Yitzhak composed devout poems in Yiddish. Reb
Nahman gave us stories in Yiddish. Yiddish language, mother tongue, joy
of our life.)

Yiddish to his little granddaughter, Chanele. The Yiddish dialogue between them touched me more than anything else in the film. I cannot remember now whether it was the poignancy of the situation or the evocative power of Yiddish that called forth from me tears for the destroyed Jewish world of Eastern Europe. For Yiddish, originally the expression of a culture and its way of life, became first a symbol and then a substitute for that culture. Today, it has become the embodiment of a tragically lost past. That is why the *Great Dictionary of the Yiddish Language* was so important as a national cultural enterprise, for had its editors lived to complete their task, the dictionary would have contained the complete wealth of Yiddish, offering, in place of sentimentality and tears, words and meanings.

The editors had estimated that upon completion the *Great Dictionary* would contain about 180,000 words. In comparison with Webster's 450,000, Yiddish may seem poor, but not in comparison with other major European languages like French, Russian, Spanish, or Italian, whose total vocabularies are estimated to range from 140,000 to 210,000 words. But though Yiddish is undoubtedly not what the linguists call a "sociologically complete" language, being deficient in scientific, technical, and military vocabularies and meager in botanical, zoological, and agricultural terms, it is nevertheless linguistically abundant in other areas of expression— religion, personal and social relations, morality, ethics, intellect, and feeling.

For the first time in the brief history of Yiddish lexicography, the *Great Dictionary* has given, in its three published volumes, each word's complete record. Stress is shown and pronunciation given for Hebrew words (Yiddish is phonetic). Each word is grammatically described: part of speech, gender for nouns, verbs characterized as transitive or intransitive, with inflectional forms for nouns and verbs.

Etymologies are given for basic words. Substandard borrowings from other languages are indicated (Germanism, Slavism, Americanism, Hispanism); regional and local dialects are indicated (Lithuanian dialect, Ukrainian localism). Special labels are used to indicate subject matter (mathematics, music, trades, and professions); other labels identify the vocabulary by particular user—the speech of the *talmid khokhem* (the religiously learned man), the language of the ghetto and concentration camp, thieves' argot. Status and usage labels are also given: archaic, neologistic, rare, ironic, slang, vulgar, coarse. Definitions are extraordinarily precise and subtle in their distinctions. *Oyg* ("eye") has thirty-four different meanings; *agude* ("union") has six. *Ibergebn* ("to hand over" and "to transmit" are its more common meanings) has seventeen definitions; *onvarfn* ("to pile up" or "to impose") has thirteen possible meanings.

All this is topped off by an extraordinary richness of quotation, drawn from folk usage and literary sources. Elijah Bahur's *Bovo-bukh* of 1541, the *Mayse-bukh* of 1602, the statutes of the *kehillah* of Cracow of 1595, and a contemporary Yiddish account of the Turkish siege of Vienna in 1683 are among the early literary sources. The recent ones include the Yiddish press of New York and Buenos Aires and contemporary Yiddish writers all over the world. Between them is the incredibly rich treasure of Yiddish literature: not only the preclassical *Haskalah* and Hasidic writings; not only the three modern fathers, Mendele, Sholem Aleichem, and Peretz; not just fiction and poetry; but also the scholarly, historical, linguistic, political, journalistic, and philosophical writings that appeared at a time when Yiddish was flourishing.

How does one decide which words go into a dictionary? Who defines their status? The practice varies. In France, the French Academy; in India, the government's Language

Commission; in England, the *Oxford English Dictionary*; and in the United States—at least until the publication of the Third Edition—*Webster's Unabridged.* But whatever the source, the basic criticism is universal: the standardizers are attacked either for being too conservative, for not admitting new words, new usages, new definitions; or for being too radical, for not protecting the language against corruption and vulgarity.

The makers of dictionaries, like the interpreters of Jewish law, may be put in two categories: *mekilim*, lenient interpreters, and *mahmirim*, strict ones. In the United States, for instance, the editors of Webster's Third Edition were avowed *mekilim.* They were following an old lexicographical tradition which Oxford linguist Archibald H. Sayce summed up, "The sole standard of correctness is custom and the common usage of the community."

The editors of the Yiddish dictionary shared this outlook. They defined as a word in the Yiddish language "every word used by a group of Jews, thinking and speaking in Yiddish." They were obviously *mekilim*, and as such they incurred the wrath of the *mahmirim.* Standardization is difficult enough in all tongues, even for so high status a language as English, as the controversy over Webster's Third Edition demonstrated. What about Yiddish then? It has no country, no government, no academy, no permanent dictionary committee, no ministry of education, no geographical limits, no higher education to speak of—just words and speakers.

The first attempt to standardize Yiddish was the Yiddish Language Conference held in Czernowitz in Rumania in 1908. It was initiated by Nathan Birnbaum, one of the great (and unjustly neglected) personalities of the recent Jewish past, who wanted to have Yiddish proclaimed as the "national" Jewish language. The specific purposes of the conference were to deal with standardization of spelling and grammar and the compilation of a dictionary. But little was accomplished, because the conference became a platform for quarrels between Yiddishists and Hebraists. Time was short, and the ideologically charged atmosphere was not conducive to the laborious and tedious tasks of linguistic standardization. The conference adopted the position that Yiddish was *a* (not *the*) national language of the Jewish people: this, like most compromises, satisfied no one. (Yitzkhok Leibush Peretz, who took a leading role at the conference, had argued that Jews had no national language: Hebrew was no longer the national language, and Yiddish, aspiring to it, had not yet attained that status.)

No progress in standardization of Yiddish was made until after World War I. Only then were modern school systems established in which Yiddish was the language of instruction. (The Polish Minorities Treaty had guaranteed cultural or national minorities the right to schools in their own languages.) A new university-educated intelligentsia arose, identifying itself, like the earlier populists, with the Yiddish-speaking masses. They helped to create a wide network of institutions which made it possible for Yiddish to aspire to high culture. One of these was the Yiddish Scientific Institute —YIVO (an acronym based on its Yiddish name), founded in 1925, which became for the Yiddish-speaking world an academy and university in one, bringing to Yiddish a luster and prestige among educated people that it had scarcely ever before enjoyed.

The rise of the Yiddish school systems in Poland, Lithuania, and Latvia after World War I, the rapid growth and proliferation of the Yiddish press and book publishing, and the unique authority of YIVO made possible some standardization where cultural anarchy had been rampant. YIVO and the Yiddish schools in Poland agreed in 1936 on 150 rules for simple, hyphenated, and compound words, plurals, abbreviations, spelling, and punctuation. But the rules were not universally accepted: those that seemed too radical, departing too much from tradition, were often disregarded. Most of the daily press resisted standardization, modernizing its spelling with the speed of glaciers. Even today, the orthography of the Yiddish daily press is far from consistent and scarcely correct by modern standards.

Both editors of the *Great Dictionary of the Yiddish Language* had been closely associated with YIVO for a long time (Yudel Mark had been editor of YIVO's periodical *Yidishe Shprakh* for more than twenty years), yet both felt that a few rules should be reviewed. They decided, on the basis of replies to a questionnaire from some 200 Yiddish writers, linguists, teachers, editors, and journalists, to retain the silent *alef* (which YIVO had eliminated) between combinations of *vov* (generally when the double-*vov*, the consonant, followed or preceded the single-*vov*, the vowel) and *yud* (as vowel, semivowel, and diphthong). The other important difference from the old YIVO standards concerns the spelling of compound words or phrases (whether separated, hyphenated, or as one word). The editors concluded that meaning must determine the word unit: for example, in the new dictionary *farayorn* ("last year") is one word rather than three, *far a yorn*, as the YIVO rule requires. These deviations deprived the dictionary of YIVO's imprimatur.

Of course, most of the words in the Yiddish dictionary are like words in any language. *Ober* is a conjunction like "but"; it is also an adverb and even a substantive, used in precisely the same sense as "But me no buts." But Yiddish is, I think, more Jewish than English is American. Yiddish has recorded and reflected Jewish history and Jewish dispersion. The etymologies of the words and the labels affixed by the editors reveal the spread of Yiddish from the Rhineland eastward and then outward: Western Yiddish, Hungarian Yiddish; then the Ukrainian, Lithuanian, White Russian, and East Galician dialects; the later subversive penetrations from German, Russian, Polish, English, and Spanish; the exotic kinds of Yiddish in Alsace and in nineteenth-century Jerusalem under Turkish rule.

Ordinary words are permeated with Jewish history and tradition. *Oysshnaydn* ("to cut out," "to carve") seems an ordinary verb, yet, unexpectedly, it contains a chunk of Jewish folklore. In defining the word, the editors quoted Peretz: "The famous forest looms darkly in the corner of the sky; on these trees our ancestors carved the names of the tractates of the Talmud which they finished studying on their way." The reference, the editors explain, is to a legend about Jewish settlement in Poland. The first Jews who came to Poland stopped in a small forest near the town of Laszczew, where they carved the names of the Talmud tractates they had studied on their long wanderings. Then they heard a voice: *"Po-lin"* (Hebrew: lodge here). That is where they settled and the way Poland got its name.

Then there are the special words. Take a place-name, *Odessa*, for example. It is defined this way:

Geographical name. Large city on the Black Sea, the Ukraine. In 1797—246 Jews; in 1914—165,000, a third of the population. Nicknames: Odessa hoboes, free-livers, crooks, pickpockets, knaves. To live like God in Odessa = to live in comfort. Explanation: No one bothers God in Odessa, no one asks anything of him, people leave him alone; parallel to: to live like God in Paris. Proverbs: "Odessa is Little-Paris." (Mendele, *Fishke the Lame*: "Odessa is Little-Stanislavchik," *ironic*.) "Hell burns ten miles around Odessa" (it is a very sinful city). "God protect us from Kamenetzer helping hands and Odesser rakes." Saying: "Don't belittle the Odessa moon" (*ironic,* when someone describes the wonders of the big city). "An Odessa moon"—a beautiful woman (Ukrainian and White Russian Yiddish expression). "The wise men of Odessa" = the scholars and writers of Odessa in the Haskalah period and at the beginning of the 20th century (Mendele, Ahad Ha'am, Dubnow, etc.). "Odessa Yiddish" = full of Russian words.

A miniature social and cultural portrait emerges, reflecting the ambivalence of the folk about the well-to-do, secularly educated, *Haskalah*-minded, skeptical Jewish community of Odessa.

Oysleyzgelt ("ransom") is another example of a word given specific colorations to all its meanings by Jewish history. The definitions and quotations refer to *pidyon ha-ben,* the ceremonial redemption of the first-born; to *pidyon-shevuyim,* ransom for a prisoner or money paid to ward off persecution or avoid great peril, with citations from medieval history through the Nazi occupation; to money paid to avoid conscription in czarist times; and, finally, to German restitution ("atonement payments").

The dictionary is indeed more than a collection of words and definitions. It is a vast repository not only of the Yiddish language but also of Jewish customs, folkways, and history. I once predicted that, when completed, the *Great Dictionary* would stand beside Sholem Aleichem, Peretz, Mendele, and Yehoash's translation of the Bible as one of the great achievements of Yiddish. But, alas, that is no longer likely.

The dictionary, too, is a marvelous witness of how Yiddish has preserved Hebrew. The words and expressions from the Bible and Talmud which are extensively used in Yiddish, particularly in the speech of the *talmid khokhem,* have here received their formal acknowledgment. The definitions of *ahavas-yisroel* ("love of Israel"), for example, encompass a Jewish tradition, beginning with the Pentateuch and going through the Talmud, the Rambam, the Kabbalists, and down to the present:

1. Love of Jews for the Jewish people, for all Jews, expressing itself in constant readiness to help Jews, to seek and find merit in Jews. Derived from the commandment to love one another "Thou shalt love thy neighbor as thyself" (Leviticus 19:18) and from Rabbi Akiba's saying "This is a great principle in the Torah." Maimonides ruled that *ahavas-yisroel* was a positive commandment of the Torah. Before praying pious Jews used to resolve to love Jews as themselves: "I am prepared to take upon myself the positive commandment to love thy neighbor as thyself" (*Kavaanat ha'Ari*). "The *ahavas-yisroel* spark in each Jew should be kindled" (Joseph Isaac Schneersohn, *Likute Diburim*).

2. Trait of loving Jews even with their faults; interceding on behalf of the Jewish people and arguing with God about how wonderful the Jewish people are (reflected especially in hasidic writings and folklore, in stories about Reb Levi-Yitzhak of Berditchev, Reb Moshe Leib of Sassov, Reb Abraham Yehoshua Heschel of Apt, and others).

3. Love of a non-Jew for the Jewish people, for Jews. *Ahavas-yisroel* of the pious among the gentiles. "From love for the daughters of Israel he came to love of Israel"—said about a non-Jew who converts to Judaism for love of a Jewish girl.

Hebrew, of course, has a particular vitality in Yiddish. Without Hebrew, Yiddish appears dull and listless. Yehoash once said that the Hebrew words wore top hats. They have dignity, style, tradition, elegance. These qualities they bring into Yiddish. Their absence impoverishes the language, cutting it off from the culture, the religion, and the very traditions that shaped it.

For, in the final analysis, the religious culture created the Yiddish language. The religion and the way of life it imposed on its believers separated the Jews from their neighbors in medieval Germany. It determined the vocabulary and from the very inception made Yiddish different from German. Later on, other factors came into play, strengthening and supplementing the role of Judaism in shaping Yiddish: residential separation and occupational differentiation; governmental and popular anti-Semitism and the persecution of Yiddish itself, which, in fact, only reinforced the language; restriction of educational opportunities and discrimination in employment; and finally, national consciousness—most nearly a substitute for Judaism—and the will to maintain Yiddish. Today, it appears that only the most old-fashioned kind of Judaism, national consciousness, and national will remain as effective agents to perpetuate Yiddish.

In a small way, national consciousness has manifested itself among some young American Jews, most of them third generation, for whom Yiddish does not have the association with ignorant immigrants which their parents felt so intensely. For the most part, these third-generation Jews do not know Yiddish. A study of an eastern seaboard Jewish community some years back showed that among parents, two-thirds of whom were second generation, about half could speak Yiddish, while among their children, nearly all native-born, less than 10 percent could speak it. A study of a midwestern community was even more depressing. Over half of the parents, mostly native-born, had heard Yiddish spoken at home when they were children, but only a little more than a third could speak it, and even fewer could read. Among their children, a bare 5 percent could speak it, and nearly all only poorly.

For those who know a bit, Yiddish serves as a form of

Jewish identification in a broader group—the use of a word or expression helps to locate other Jews, or perhaps merely kindred spirits. Sometimes it is the object of curiosity, and occasionally Yiddish becomes the discovery of roots. Marcus Lee Hansen, the historian of immigration, once formulated "the principle of third-generation interest": "what the son wishes to forget the grandson wishes to remember." In their quest for their origins, and for that background which gives their Americanness specificity and value, many young Jews are curious and sometimes eager to know where their grandparents came from and what their culture was like. Yiddish is something they would like to know or, at least, know about.

Yiddish can help give the individual access to his past, the world from which his parents came and whose culture, however attenuated its form, has had some influence on him. Yiddish is also important for the group past. Ahad Ha'am, sharp-sighted and penetrating as he was, was nevertheless mistaken when he predicted that no one would ever claim for Yiddish as for Hebrew "that it must be studied as a matter of national duty." Today, the importance—sometimes the crucial importance—of Yiddish for an understanding of the history and culture of Ashkenazic Jewry for the last 500 years has been generally acknowledged. Hasidism, the Jewish labor movement, Zionism, the Agudas Israel movement—none can be understood without Yiddish. The scholar will need Yiddish for his work, and his Yiddish, in time to come, will have to be learned. We should be grateful even for the three volumes of the *Great Dictionary of the Yiddish Language.*

10

YIDDISH AND ITS TRANSLATION

JEWS, IT MAY BE SAID, are cultural universalists par excellence. Even when residing within their own linguistic jurisdictions—Yiddish in pre-Holocaust Eastern Europe, Hebrew in present-day Israel—they have always been, and remain, avid consumers of the published products of Western civilization. Hence the enduring Jewish practice of translation. In Eastern Europe this practically amounted to an industry, as popular scientific and philosophical works, histories, political tracts, fiction, and what have you were rendered into Yiddish and traditional Hebrew for the edification of a reading public hungry for enlightenment. The tradition continues in Israel today, where translations from foreign languages account for about one-third of all adult books published. (It would seem that the contemporary reader in Israel has more in common, insofar as his cultural tastes are concerned, with a Jew in Poland of fifty years ago than with his counterpart in the United States, where translations constitute a mere 10 percent of trade-book publication.) As for the Jews in the English-speaking Diaspora, translations are as much a requirement, but here a reverse process obtains. Jews in the United States, Canada, South Africa, and Australia have ready linguistic access to Western culture, but they are for the most part ignorant of the languages which contain their own people's religious texts, historical records, and literary creations. For such Jews, translations *from* the Hebrew and Yiddish are what is needed—and it is good to report that their number is increasing—in order to overcome the handicap of estrangement rather than insularity.

Given its historic preeminence, to say nothing of its special sacred character, Hebrew has enjoyed a longer tradition of translation than has Yiddish, a comparative newcomer to the family of Jewish languages. Moreover, Yiddish, for much of its history, was denigrated by the intelligentsia as the "jargon" of the masses and its literature regarded as unworthy of serious consideration, let alone translation. Indeed, it was not until 1898 that the first translation from Yiddish into English appeared, when Leo Wiener, professor of Slavic languages at Harvard, produced a prose rendition of Morris Rosenfeld's sweatshop poems. Since that pioneering effort, the status of Yiddish literature has continued to rise, in generous measure owing to the accomplishments of Maurice Samuel (1895–1972), a prolific and witty writer on Jewish historical and literary subjects and the prince of Yiddish translators.

In Praise of Yiddish, Samuel's last book, was a capstone to his career as translator and Jewish cultural mediator. It should serve as an enduring guide not just to those who wish to learn the art of translating from Yiddish but to all who would penetrate the real character of the language. Maurice Samuel's special talent, to quote Robert Alter, was "to explain a world alien to Western readers by locating it on cultural coordinates familiar to them."* This ability was displayed to striking effect in his now classic works *The World of Sholom Aleichem* and *Prince of the Ghetto*, which have served to introduce generations of nonreaders of Yiddish to the culture of East European Jewry. In his last work, Samuel continued in his role as cultural mediator, taking the reader into the inner laboratory of the language and unraveling a good many of the complexities peculiar to the development of Yiddish. For Yiddish, more than most languages, blends a variety of strains and cultures, and the resulting mix can often confound the would-be translator, as well as the student and the ordinary reader.

Through informal discourse, interspersed with apposite doses of history and folklore, etymology and personal anecdote, Samuel set himself the task of "convey[ing] to the English reader the inside feel of Yiddish." Beginning with a description of the character of Yiddish, Samuel noted that Yiddish was the *goles* (exile) language of the Jewish people. Indeed, it is the most important of all exile languages, having endured longer than either Aramaic or *Dzhudezmo* (Judeo-Spanish)—thus far, for a thousand years—and having been spoken by more Jews at any one time than any other Jewish tongue. Within living memory, before the near total destruction of East European Jewry, Yiddish was still the day-to-day language of nearly 10 million Jews.

Yiddish, moreover, embodied the migrations of its speakers over the centuries and thus became a repository of European Jewish civilization. The oldest stratum of the language is the Hebrew/Aramaic, associated largely, though not exclusively, with the sacred system of the Jewish com-

* See Robert Alter, "Maurice Samuel and Jewish Letters," *Commentary* 37 (March 1964):50–54.

munity. The second layer, and the thinnest, derives from Old French and Old Italian. Here Samuel regales the reader with examples—for instance, *tsholnt*, the Sabbath dish of meat, potatoes, and beans, set in the oven on Friday and kept there until the Saturday meal, harks back, etymologically speaking, via Old French, to the Latin *calens* ("to be hot") and is related to the French *chaud* and *chaleur*. *Bentshn*, the recitation of the blessing after meals, has its source, by way of Old Italian, in the Latin *benedicere*. *Yente* (Yiddish for a busybody, but also a respectable female name) originates, curiously enough, in the French *gentille*. The third stratum, and a very substantial one, is formed by German, specifically Middle High German, the language spoken in the Middle Rhine basin in the ninth and tenth centuries. From that region Yiddish spread, over the following 200 years, throughout the entire German-speaking territory, receiving a strong infusion from the various German dialects, but principally from the High German of southern and central Germany. By the middle of the thirteenth century the Yiddish orbit extended well beyond the Danube into the Slavic East, a development that had an indelible effect on the linguistic structure of Yiddish and contributed yet another important stratum to the language. Here, in the next 250 years, Yiddish was formed.

Yiddish, like most languages, is a product of the historical encounter of its speakers with different cultures and of the fusion of the linguistic components of those cultures. Yet, even after many centuries, the specific cultural origins of the components, or strata, of Yiddish remain distinguishable. Speaking of the Hebrew/Aramaic words and phrases that have found their way into Yiddish, Samuel remarks that they are "as fresh today as when they were minted." That is partly because Yiddish itself has evolved distinctive sig-

nals whereby the various components announce their identity. For instance, written Yiddish retains the original
spellings of its Hebrew/Aramaic component, and, as Roman
Jakobson has pointed out, spoken Yiddish has assigned a
penultimate stress to words of Hebrew origin to distinguish
them from simple Germanic and Slavic words, which are
accented on the first syllable. Furthermore, despite the
workings of the fusion process, Yiddish speakers have always retained a "component-consciousness," a term coined
by Max Weinreich to describe the awareness on the part
of most Yiddish-speaking Jews of distinct etymologies that
constitute the language. This sensitivity may be accounted
for partly by the fact that most Ashkenazic Jews were to
some degree bilingual and even trilingual, familiar not only
with Yiddish and Hebrew but also with at least one of the
"coterritorial" languages, Russian or Polish.

Samuel suggested, somewhat tentatively, that the various
components of Yiddish fulfilled specific functions. He characterized words of the Slavic component as "homey and
intimate," nearer to the "folk" than their Germanic equivalents. The Hebrew element was reserved largely for the
ritual and religious culture; and it was widely believed that
a Yiddish liberally sprinkled with rabbinic Hebrew elements
reflected the speaker's Talmudic erudition. It turns out, however, as Marvin I. Herzog has indicated in his study of
Yiddish dialects,* that the presence or absence of a rabbinic
Hebrew vocabulary is determined not so much by the extent of the speaker's learning as by regional distribution patterns. "Market women in one area," Herzog notes, "make
free use of words and phrases that a scholar elsewhere might
cite and understand, but which he would no sooner con-

---

* Marvin I. Herzog, *The Yiddish Language in Northern Poland: Its
Geography and History* (Bloomington, Ind.: Indiana University Press, 1965).

sider Yiddish than he would accept 'foreign' words." In fact, the Hebrew component has served to furnish many words for certain rude concepts, ranging from elegant euphemisms to outright vulgarities. For instance, "hands" in Yiddish is the Germanic *hent*, but the Yiddish word for clumsy, brutish hands is *yodayim*, Hebrew for "hands." The Yiddish for "toilet paper" is *asher-yotser-papir. Asher yotser* ("who hast fashioned") are the first two operative words of the blessing recited after bodily elimination.

Samuel estimated the Germanic element of Yiddish at 80 percent; Leo Wiener put it at 70 percent; the Yiddish poet, lexicographer, and Bible translator Yehoash gauged both the Germanic and the Slavic elements at 80 percent. But the componential numbers game is a treacherous exercise. Calculations are wildly conjectural, and different styles and different texts yield different proportions. The only scientific investigation ever made of the frequency of the Hebrew component showed an immense range in sixty different style categories, from 1.5 to 16 percent. Altogether, componential statistics reveal little about the nature of any language—this is perhaps especially true of Yiddish—for the general practice is to count only word roots, while prefixes, suffixes, constructions, and inflections are often overlooked. But, as we have seen, though the lexicon of Yiddish is largely derived from Middle High German stock, the growth and development of the language has been predominantly within the Slavic orbit. In addition, as Roman Jakobson has observed,[*] geographically adjacent languages which find themselves in social contact, even though unrelated linguistically, will significantly influence each other's phonemic and grammatical structures and even displace the

---

[*] In his (Yiddish) essay "The Sound Structure in Its Slavic Environment," in *Yuda A. Yofe bukh* (New York: YIVO, 1958).

earlier effects of the original language family. This, he felt, also held true for Yiddish, as witness the Slavic-Yiddish symbiosis.

Samuel illustrated this theory in a chapter entitled "What Is Not German," in which he analyzed a series of compound Yiddish words whose individual parts—prefix and root verb—are of German stock but whose structure and meaning derive from the Slavic. For example, *unterzogn* ("under" + "tell") in Yiddish means "to prompt," but the German *untersagen* means "to forbid." The true parallel is to be found in the Polish and Russian: the Polish equivalent is *podpowiadać*, "to prompt," and is made up of *pod* ("under") and *opowiadać* ("to tell"); in Russian, the word is *podskazat*, the product of a similar combination. "To eavesdrop" in Yiddish is *unterhern* ("under" + "hear"), but in German it is *horchen* or *belauschen*. The Polish and Russian forms, however, correspond to the Yiddish: *podsłuchiwać* and *podslushivat*. The list could be extended indefinitely.

The Slavic influence on Yiddish, Samuel observed, extended beyond the linguistic: "The melancholy of the steppes echoes in Chassidic melodies, and there is a kinship between the mystical religious yearnings of certain Russian and Jewish types." The Yiddish-Slavic affinity was confirmed in an interesting study which compares English, German, Hebrew, Russian, and Ukranian translations—all of uniformly high caliber—of a Sholem Aleichem story.[*] The Ukrainian rendition turned out by various objective standards to be the most successful in terms of fidelity to the letter and spirit of the original; the Russian version was a

---

[*] Theodore Gutmans, "Sholem Aleichem in the Stock Languages: Notes on Translations of 'Dos Tepl' into Ukrainian, German, Hebrew, English, and Russian," in *For Max Weinreich on His Seventieth Birthday: Studies in Jewish Languages, Literature, and Society* (The Hague: Mouton, 1964).

close second. The English translation was awarded the lowest mark (it was *not* a Maurice Samuel translation). This should come as no great surprise, for of the five languages in question, English has the least in common with Yiddish —no common territory or even geographic adjacency, no common stock vocabulary, no common religion or culture. The study dramatized the particular hazards of rendering Yiddish into English and served to confirm Maurice Samuel's own enormous contribution in making Yiddish and East European Jewish culture more readily accessible to English-speaking readers.

In Praise of Yiddish, as I have noted, should prove useful to every would-be translator of Yiddish; indeed, it can very well serve as a handbook for translators and students alike.*
For besides conveying "the inside feel of Yiddish," the work also constitutes, in effect, a kind of discursive Yiddish-English dictionary of more than 1,000 words, idioms, and phrases. These are not merely translated but defined and fully explicated, with appropriate examples. Samuel provides social and cultural microhistories for individual words and word-clusters, including terms relating to marriage, philanthropy, poverty (in all its economic and linguistic variations), and Jewish scholarship. He is perhaps at his best in suggesting equivalents that are particularly apt. The following examples—only two out of many such—are typical of the Samuel method of translation:

> *Akhtsn un draytsn,* literally, "eighteen and thirteen," etymologically not Hebraic but Germanic, belongs among

---

* I take this opportunity to call attention to a truly indispensable Yiddish lexical work and one that Maurice Samuel referred to frequently in his own book: the *Modern English-Yiddish Yiddish-English Dictionary* (New York: YIVO, 1968), by the late Uriel Weinreich. Each section contains over 20,000 entries, and the enterprise altogether meets the most exacting standards of dictionary making.

Hebraisms by way of content. The numbers eighteen and thirteen add up to thirty-one, for which the Hebrew notation in letters is *lamed alef*, which make up the word *loy*, "no." But the negative content of the phrase *akhtsn un draytsn* seems to have different meanings in different localities: (1) as an introduction to a negation, (2) as compelling someone to return to a subject he wishes to evade, (3) as introducing a discussion of money matters: *ober vos hert zikh mikoyekh akhtsn un draytsn*, "But what about that matter we were discussing?" or "What about the money side of the question?"

Klots, "a wooden beam," as applied to a person, is "heavy, doltish, lumpish," but when this Germanic word is combined with the Hebraic *kashe* in *klots-kashe*, we get something for which there is no English equivalent, and which has to be described at some length. If in the midst of a sophisticated discussion someone simple-mindedly harks back to an elementary question to which the answer has long been tacitly assumed, he is offering a *klots-kashe*. We must imagine a high-level conference of Madison Avenue executives, and someone asking earnestly, artlessly, "But gentlemen, is advertising a good thing?"

There is a renewed interest in Yiddish. Thousands of students are enrolled in Yiddish courses at a score of American colleges and universities, to say nothing of the host of adult-study groups throughout the country. Maurice Samuel observed that the phenomenon may be ascribed to the trauma of the Holocaust; and it may indeed very well be that for many young Jews, in the United States and Israel, learning Yiddish has become a way of bearing witness, of affirming Jewish existence and of refusing to permit Ashkenazic culture to die. For such Jews, Maurice Samuel's work is required reading.

11

MAX WEINREICH:
Scholarship of Yiddish

MAX WEINREICH's death on January 29, 1969, brought to a sad close the era of East European Jewish scholarship, uniquely associated with Yiddish, the language of East European Jews. A founder of the Yiddish Scientific Institute—YIVO (now called YIVO Institute for Jewish Research), Weinreich was its chief architect, animating spirit, and standard-bearer. As YIVO's head, first in Poland and then in America, he, more than any other man or institution, succeeded in gaining for Yiddish prestige and status it had never before enjoyed.

A distinguished linguist in the international community of linguists, Weinreich did not choose the prestigious academic career that his professors at the University of St. Petersburg had predicted for him, their most outstanding student. Instead, he chose to associate himself with Yiddish. It became his life's goal to fashion from this folk language a refined and supple instrument, a tongue fit for learned discourse, and to win prestige for it among Jews and non-Jews. This he achieved.

His life story reflects the history of upheaval and change which distinguished the age into which he was thrust. Max Weinreich was born April 22, 1894, into a middle-class merchant family in Goldingen (now Kuldiga), Latvia, a town of 10,000 people, a quarter of them Jews. Like most Jews influenced by the prevailing German culture of that region, the former Baltic Duchy of Courland, his family was lukewarm in their religious observance and preferred German instead of Yiddish. His first school was a *heder*, though a somewhat secularized one. When he was nine years old, his parents, ambitious for their precocious son, the youngest of ten children, enrolled him in a *gymnasium* (high school) attended mostly by children of Baltic German nobility and Latvian gentry. In 1908, after five years in this upper-class *gymnasium*, with a bare handful of Jewish pupils, he withdrew because of its anti-Semitism. He continued his studies in a private Jewish *gymnasium* in Dvinsk (now Daugavpils), Latvia. When he was about twelve, he became friends with a boy who was a member of the *Kleyner Bund* (Junior Jewish Socialist Bund). That friendship was to affect the future course of his life. Perhaps the repressive and intolerant atmosphere in the *gymnasium* had made him especially receptive to the warm friendship of a lower-class Jewish child. Perhaps it was the spirit of the times.

Czarist Russia was in revolutionary ferment, and the great wave of demonstrations and strikes that swept Russia in 1905 reached the Baltic cities and towns. Goldingen, too, witnessed a stormy demonstration in January 1905 in which the Bund took a leading role. The exhilaration of the revolution and its consequent brutal suppression affected the young Weinreich and drew him into the Junior Bund. A brilliant child, fluent in Russian and German, he now began to learn from his young comrades not only revolution and conspiratorial techniques but also Yiddish, the language of the common people. At thirteen he began his journalistic career as correspondent for a Bundist Yiddish daily in Vilna. When he was fifteen, his first Yiddish translations of European literature were published, and at sixteen his first articles on Yiddish appeared.

Distinctly and distinctively, Max Weinreich's identity began to be shaped in his youth. The scope of his interests was to grow and expand, his ideas to mature and deepen. Politics—the Bund, that is—brought him to Yiddish, but Yiddish eventually displaced politics in his scale of values.

At eighteen Weinreich entered the University of St. Petersburg, where he made a name for himself because of his scholastic brilliance. Yet he shared his passion for linguistics with politics. The spirit of revolution was alive at the university: Weinreich joined a Bundist student circle and wrote for Bundist publications. After the Bolshevik Revolution of November 1917, he left St. Petersburg and moved to Vilna, where he edited a Bundist daily. When the war was over, Weinreich went to Germany to continue his studies. In 1923 he received his doctorate from the University of Marburg for a dissertation on the history of Yiddish linguistic studies. He returned to Vilna, where he married Regina Szabad, of a distinguished Jewish family.

In 1923 some 56,000 Jews lived in Vilna, about one-third of the city's population. Despite the havoc of World War I, the flight and death of thousands of Jews, the succession of governments, and finally the capture and forcible incorporation of the ancient capital of the Grand Duchy of Lithuania into the new Republic of Poland, the Jewish community in Vilna remained intensely and vibrantly Jewish, as it had always been. Napoleon, it is said, dubbed Vilna "the Jerusalem of Lithuania" (Weinreich thought the epithet actually originated in the seventeenth century). The historic citadel of rabbinic Judaism, Vilna was also a center of Jewish secularity and a metropolis for Yiddish and its literature, press, theater, and school system.

In this Vilna, Max Weinreich began his adulthood. He taught Yiddish language and literature at the Yiddish Teachers Seminary and was an editor of Vilna's Yiddish daily *Der Tog* and a correspondent for the New York *Jewish Daily Forward* (to which he remained a regular contributor until his last years). He was active in educational and communal institutions.

In 1924 he received from Nahum Shtif, a Yiddish linguist then living in Berlin, a pamphlet proposing the establishment of a Yiddish academy. Such an academy would be a center for research and study in Yiddish linguistics and literature, Jewish history, social studies, and pedagogy; it could serve also as the authority for standardizing Yiddish usage, grammar, and spelling. A Yiddish academy, Shtif hoped, could systematically diffuse through the Yiddish school system, Yiddish press, and other cultural institutions whose medium was Yiddish the new scholarship being produced in that language. The academy would thus improve the quality of Jewish cultural life and enlarge the community of educated Yiddish-speaking Jews. These, in turn, would become consumers of the academy's high scholarship and culture.

Ideas for Jewish intellectual renewal were widespread in Berlin, then a haven for Jewish writers, scholars, and journalists who had fled Russia and Poland. But Berlin could not fulfill Shtif's plan. Vilna could—and did—because of Max Weinreich's initiative, determination, and passion. Yiddish was a sociopolitical reality in Vilna, and Weinreich held strategic positions on the Yiddish Teachers Seminary faculty and as chairman of Vilna's Central Jewish Education

Committee. He succeeded in winning community support for a Yiddish research institute. Thus, in 1925, YIVO was established, organized into four research sections: (1) Yiddish linguistics, literature, and folklore; (2) history; (3) economics and statistics; and (4) psychology and education.

YIVO's largest single asset was Weinreich's willpower, his strong-mindedness and his capacity to work for what he believed. That was a psychological, perhaps even a metabolic, characteristic. Determination, he held, could move worlds, could make something out of nothing. He used his willpower to realize a vision of scholarship in the service of the Jewish people. His youthful passion for politics was replaced, as he grew older, with a passion for scholarship. He envisaged YIVO as a vital center that would knit the work of individual scholars together with the needs of the Jewish community. Weinreich's concept of scholarship as a tool to clarify and serve the Jewish community's sociocultural needs inaugurated a new phase in modern Jewish scholarship.

For more than a century, secular Jewish scholarship had been shaped by the apologetic concepts underlying the *Wissenschaft des Judentums.* When Leopold Zunz and his friends founded the Verein für Kultur und Wissenschaft der Juden in 1819 to cultivate and disseminate knowledge of Judaism and Jewish culture with contemporary methods of scholarship, they wanted to demonstrate that the cultural level of the Jews was not inferior to that of Germans. That would prove that Jews deserved to be emancipated. Scholarship was thus a means to a political and social end. These scholars were not convinced of the viability of Jewish existence or of Jewish culture: most of the Verein's members abandoned Judaism within a few years. Only Zunz retained his commitment to Jewish scholarship as a way to preserve the past of a culture whose possibility of future existence he doubted.

In the mid-nineteenth century *Wissenschaft des Judentums*

was reorganized and continued under a variety of auspices into the beginning of the twentieth century. Though Jewish scholars today are less likely than those of the immediately preceding generations to belittle the accomplishments of *Wissenschaft des Judentums,* many of those earlier criticisms were justified. The movement focused on Judaism rather than the flesh-and-blood reality of the Jewish people, and its subject matter was usually antiquarian. Its orientation remained basically apologetic, in response to the so-called "scientific" anti-Semitism of Treitschke, Rohling, and Lagarde, and to the biblical scholarship of Wellhausen and his disciples. Furthermore, East European Jews, who then constituted two-thirds of the world Jewish population, seldom figured in the elitist scholarship of *Wissenschaft des Judentums,* or, if they did, only as objects of contempt and derogation.

The first East European Jewish scholarly group came into being in 1891 when young Jewish lawyers in St. Petersburg, under the influence of Simon Dubnow's epoch-making pamphlet *On Studying the History of the Russian Jews and Establishing a Russian Jewish Historical Society,* formed the Jewish Historical Ethnographic Commission. Like the institutions of *Wissenschaft des Judentums,* the Commission was elitist, its subject matter somewhat antiquarian, and its approach apologetic. Jewish historical societies were then being formed in Europe and the United States largely for apologetic purposes—to demonstrate the antiquity of Jewish settlement in those countries and to testify to Jewish loyalty and patriotism.

If *Wissenschaft des Judentums* began and long continued as an instrument to bring German Jews political emancipation, Weinreich conceived YIVO as the instrument to bring cultural emancipation to Yiddish-speaking Jews. On YIVO's tenth anniversary he said:

Our contribution in the struggle of the common Jewish people . . . for their cultural emancipation can be expressed on one foot, in a few numbered sentences: We want to fathom Jewish life with the methods of modern scholarship and, further, whatever modern scholarship brings to light, we want to bring back to the Jewish masses.

"Jewish life" means *all* Jewish life, its present as well as its past. This must be stressed, for it is the mark distinguishing our institution from those Judaistic institutes—with all due respect to them—which the German Jewish scholars started putting up and which their followers in other countries copied. For us the present is not less important than the past; for us the distant past is not rated more highly than the recent past; for us all study of the past is mainly a means of better understanding the present. The YIVO investigates all aspects of Jewish life—not only rabbis, scholars and writers, but also the social life of the common people; not only economic life, but also the language, the literature, the mind and spirit of the Jews.

Max Weinreich was a twentieth-century enlightener, a neo-*maskil*. He wanted to improve and uplift the East European Jewish community. He proposed to do this through research and study, by applying Western methods of critical scholarship to East European Jewish history and to Yiddish language, literature, and culture. Research and study were to be of the highest scholarly quality, but they were also to serve the intellectual needs of Jews, to increase their self-understanding, to fortify them intellectually against anti-Semitism and self-depreciation, and to help them develop a healthy sense of self-esteem.

The most concrete way to do this was to use scholarship to raise the social and intellectual prestige of Yiddish and, consequently, of its speakers. On one of his trips abroad, Weinreich noted that in the ship's first-class accommodations, despite the many Jewish travelers, Yiddish was not seen or heard; in second class, on the other hand, he saw Yiddish signs and heard Yiddish spoken aloud. Weinreich wanted Yiddish to be first-class, and he intended to do that by making Yiddish the language of cultivated men, a medium for discourse on the most abstruse, complex, and subtle subjects in all disciplines.

The standardization of Yiddish, with normative usage, grammar, and spelling, was one of his ambitions. Without an authoritative academy to set standards, without a scholarly tradition in secular Jewish matters, Yiddish spelling had been subject to the arbitrariness of its users. Indeed, the Jewish community's physical and political dispersal discouraged uniform usage. After years of consultations with scholars, writers, journalists, and teachers throughout Europe and in the United States, YIVO adopted a set of orthographic rules in 1936. These, somewhat modified after a consultative conference with the Central Yiddish School Organization in Poland (CYSHO), were published early in 1937 and instituted in all YIVO and CYSHO publications and taught in all CYSHO schools. Weinreich hoped that Jewish writers and publishers would voluntarily submit to the discipline of these rules and accept YIVO's authority. Until his last days he was active in this effort.

Max Weinreich was a true polymath, and no field of scholarship was alien to him—above all, languages and linguistics. He wrote on erudite, often recondite, subjects which only a handful of scholars could appreciate. A dedicated practitioner of high scholarship, he nevertheless also popularized. He translated many literary and scholarly works into Yiddish. He edited an immense number of works about linguistics, language, and style: on the history of literature, on folklore, on history and social psychology. His

productivity and breadth of interest are reflected in the
bibliography of his writings: 377 items, including books,
pamphlets, studies, book reviews, newspaper articles, and
translations.* Before he was forty, he had published several
books on Yiddish grammar and orthography, had edited
three volumes of linguistic studies published by YIVO, and
was an editor of *Yivo-Bleter*, a bimonthly scholarly journal
initiated in 1931.

In 1932, Weinreich left Vilna for Yale University, where
he spent two years as a Rockefeller Foundation fellow at the
International Seminar on the Impact of Culture on Personality. At a time of life when most men settle into a
comfortable routine or move ahead in predefined paths,
Max Weinreich turned his innovative energy in a new
direction. In pursuit of new knowledge, he went to Vienna
in 1934 to study with Dr. Siegfried Bernfeld, a pupil and
disciple of Freud. Psychoanalysis offered dazzling possibilities
for investigating the impact of culture on personality and
for expanding the therapeutic function of research.

At Weinreich's initiative, YIVO gathered, through com-
petitions, more than 300 autobiographies written by young
Jews. These provided the raw data for his path-breaking
book, *Der veg tsu undzer yugnt* (The Way to Our Youth:
Elements, Methods, and Problems of Jewish Youth Research).† In this work Weinreich applied the advanced
methodologies of diverse disciplines—psychoanalysis, social
psychology, anthropology, statistics—to illuminate the problems of Jewish youth growing up in a society that legitimated
anti-Semitism. Thereafter, when speaking of the social uses
of research for the Jewish community, Weinreich also

* Leybl Kahn, "Bibliography of Max Weinreich's Writings," in *For Max Weinreich on His Seventieth Birthday: Studies in Jewish Languages, Literature, and Society* (The Hague: Mouton, 1964).
† Published by YIVO in Vilna in 1935.

stressed this psychological component: Jews needed research and study to help them learn self-esteem, to help heal the sociopsychological wounds inflicted by society on personality, to create whole individuals and whole Jews.

In 1935, YIVO inaugurated its research training program (*aspirantur*) to train Jewish researchers and scholars. Weinreich believed that while the universities should provide the basic academic training an aspiring researcher required, only a Jewish institution, steeped in Jewish learning, could provide the right training for Jewish studies. In Poland, as elsewhere in Eastern Europe, Jews were subjected to a *numerus clausus* in the universities. Even those Jews who gained entrance had little opportunity for advanced Jewish studies. At the University of Warsaw, Jewish students, if they wished, could study ancient Jewish history and Hebrew with Professor Moses Schorr or modern Jewish history with Professor Maier Bałaban. The Institute of Judaic Studies in Warsaw, founded by Professor Schorr, also provided facilities for Jewish scholarship. Nevertheless, Weinreich's plan for the *aspirantur* was unique. He was not satisfied only to train university graduates for Jewish research by equipping them with a critical approach and methodological tools; he also wanted to imbue them with a sense of the social purpose of scholarship. Furthermore, in the *aspirantur* young scholars could learn from each other, developing an interdisciplinary outlook and overview, beyond the confines of their own specialization.

The *aspirantur* existed for only three years in Poland. In America, Weinreich again turned his attention to a center for training Jewish scholars. That was his last great institutional project. Chartered by the Board of Regents of the University of the State of New York in 1968, it began functioning in September 1969 as the Max Weinreich Center for Advanced Jewish Studies.

In the summer of 1939, Weinreich and his older son, Uriel, left Vilna to attend the International Conference of Linguistics in Brussels. The outbreak of the war precluded their return home. Early in 1940 they arrived in New York, where they were soon joined by the rest of the family.

Weinreich undertook to continue in New York what he had begun in Vilna, despite the gloomy prognosis about America's inhospitality to foreign tongues and foreign-language cultures. At the annual YIVO conference in 1941, he told his American audience about the magic of willpower. Inertia alone did not account for the success of Yiddish in Poland. Yiddish there had benefited from propulsion and thrust: "The question is not one of numbers or place. The question is: Do we have enough vitality, enough resistance?" Two years later, in the midst of the greatest catastrophe the Jews ever endured—though its full dimensions were not yet known—he returned to this theme: "All that is required is willpower. The responsibility of every communal institution is to strengthen the will of its people." The responsibility to survive became a moral one: "We have an obligation to ourselves, an obligation to our overseas brothers and sisters in the grip of the hangman, an obligation for the entire future of the Jewish people."

If the fate of the Jews under German occupation obsessed him, the role that German scholars and German scholarship played in the methodical murder of 6 million Jews tormented him. For him, scholarship had been an instrument for Jewish survival, but the Germans had turned it into a tool for Jewish death. This perversion of scholarship led him to write *Hitler's Professors* (New York: YIVO, 1946), a report on the role of German scholarship in Germany's crimes against the Jewish people—still another of his innovative accomplishments.

In the last two decades of his life, Weinreich worked on

his *Geshikhte fun der yidisher shprakh* (History of the Yiddish Language), a monumental work which he had virtually completed just before his death and which appeared in 1973 in four volumes. Largely linguistic in methodology (i.e., employing the techniques of the science of language), Weinreich's history is no narrow specialist's book. He used linguistics to illuminate the history of Ashkenazic Jewry, to illustrate the rise and flowering of Ashkenazic culture, and to explore the sociocultural relations between Jews and non-Jews. His wide-ranging scholarship and interdisciplinary approach, which had become hallmarks of his craft, found their consummation in this massive monument to Ashkenazic Jewry.

In Weinreich's definition, *Ashkenaz* was the Jewish community, with its language, literature, and culture. Born some 1,100 years ago in the Middle Rhine–Moselle territory, *Ashkenaz* had, over the course of centuries, slowly moved eastward. Until 1500 its metropolises were in Central Europe: Mayence, Worms, Ratisbon, Prague. Thereafter, *Ashkenaz* shifted to Eastern Europe: Cracow, Lublin, Mezbizh, Vilna, and Warsaw. Consequently, as Weinreich put it, *Ashkenaz* became "freed of its territorial connotations; geography, as it were, has been transformed into history." The Yiddish language was the most striking result of the encounters between Jewish culture and the non-Jewish cultures that the Ashkenazic community encountered in its eastward migration.

Yiddish, Weinreich writes, came into being as the linguistic vehicle of a community set apart from the outside world by its religion:

The principal cultural determinant in the history of Yiddish is the fact that Ashkenazic Jewry came into existence as a community defined by *yidishkayt* [Judaism]. On the basis of evidence uncovered it can be firmly stated that *yidishkayt* shaped not only the conceptual world of the Ashkenazic community but its language as well. Moreover, although Yiddish never was a language of religious expression only and, in recent centuries, in growing measure has become a medium of "secular" endeavors, too, the master pattern of Yiddish as the language of a community defined by *yidishkayt* has not changed.*

Ashkenazic culture rested on Hebrew-Yiddish bilingualism, but not on the dichotomy of sacred and profane. Weinreich rectified the popular misconception that relegated to Yiddish merely the expression of secular Jewish life. Not so, Weinreich proved abundantly, reclaiming for Yiddish a central place in traditional Jewish culture in a major and magnificent chapter of his last work entitled *"Di shprakh fun derekh ha-shas."* Weinreich used the phrase *derekh ha-shas* to mean Jewish social life as defined by the culture of rabbinic Judaism, *shas* being the acronym for the six orders of the Mishnah. In that chapter Weinreich richly documented how Yiddish absorbed the culture of traditional Judaism, reflecting its pervasiveness in the daily life of Ashkenazic Jewry.

In "Ashkenaz: The Era of Yiddish in Jewish History," a paper read at a YIVO conference in 1951, Weinreich concluded:

> In the culture and language of Ashkenaz are wonderful transcendental values from both a Jewish and universal viewpoint. It would be a cultural catastrophe for our children and children's children if these values vanished in the blood and ashes of the Jewish Holocaust in the Second World War.

* Max Weinreich, *"Yidishkayt and Yiddish,"* in *Mordecai M. Kaplan Jubilee Volume* (New York: Jewish Theological Seminary of America, 1953), p. 514.

Max Weinreich preserved Yiddish for his children and children's children and transmitted it to them as a living tongue. His son Uriel turned his father's hopes and dreams into reality. He grew up an eminent linguist; his chosen field was Yiddish, and his scholarship brought distinction to the name of Weinreich and to the study of Yiddish. But in March 1967, Uriel, at the age of forty, died of a cruel disease. Uriel left, besides his other work, a lasting monument to Yiddish, *The Modern English-Yiddish Yiddish-English Dictionary.* The Lord gave, and the Lord hath taken away.

In New York, Max Weinreich concluded what he had begun in Vilna. He found the YIVO in New York housed on the Lower East Side, alongside the Hebrew Immigrant Aid Society, small and shabby, surviving in an immigrant milieu. He left the YIVO housed on upper Fifth Avenue, in a former Vanderbilt mansion, its name and influence extending beyond the immigrant Jewish community, reputed in the academic world for its scholarship and publications. It had been his goal to elevate Yiddish intellectually and socially. He lived to see that goal fulfilled. To how many men is such grace given?

12

PICTURING THE PAST

THOUGH WORDS HAVE always counted for more than pictures in the Jewish tradition, when photography came to Eastern Europe—a bit late, like everything else—the Jews, like everyone else, began to have their pictures taken. The earliest of these photographs are of the high bourgeoisie—the great Jewish bankers of Warsaw and St. Petersburg, the counselors to the czar, and even some of the more prestigious big-city rabbis and communal leaders, a few of whom sat for the camera as early as the 1860s.* (Many others, mindful of the biblical prohibition against sculptured images, avoided it for years.) In those early days, photographs were strictly

---

* A stunning photograph of Jacob Gesundheit comes to mind. It was taken in 1870, when he became rabbi of Warsaw. The rabbi, in a long satin robe with a velvet head covering, sits on an ornate and finely carved high-backed armchair, upholstered in deep plush. He is posed, pen in hand, at a table with a splendidly embroidered damask cloth; several tomes, *seforim*, are at his elbow. It is a photograph that bespeaks the status and prestige of Warsaw's chief rabbi and does honor to the Jewish community.

for important people on state occasions, but as knowledge of photographic techniques became more widespread and supplies became cheaper and more readily available, young Jews of the middle class who were too status-conscious to do manual labor began taking up photography as a genteel occupation. Soon there were photography studios in most areas with a sizable Jewish population, and middle-class and lower-middle-class Jews too began having their pictures taken on important occasions.

Mass immigration to America, beginning in the 1880s—at about the time when photography had begun to penetrate Jewish social life—further accelerated its diffusion among even the poorest Jews. Families separated from one another for long periods turned increasingly to the new technique as a way of bridging space and time, of compensating in part for the lost presence of husbands or children. There were few Jewish households in Eastern Europe that did not boast a collection of family photographs, prominently displayed, of loved ones who had gone off to America or South Africa. Photographs became the symbol and substance of family solidarity.

With the German occupation of Poland during World War I, photography became mandatory, for every document used for purposes of identification was required to show its bearer's likeness. Weeping and wailing, the Hasidic Jews, who had been the last holdouts against the camera's legitimacy and who regarded the German regulation as an evil decree, nonetheless obeyed the law of the land. Even the *rebbes*—heads of the various Hasidic dynasties—betook themselves to the local atelier, where, tense and anxious, they looked into the camera's evil eye.

Photography among Jews consisted at first mainly of portraiture, for the East European tradition placed little value on the natural beauty of the outdoors, and Jews for the most part did not own great estates or precious works of art that might lend themselves to preservation on film. Photography as art, photography in the service of science—these were not yet Jewish métiers. Early in the 1900s, however, Jews in Eastern Europe began turning to the new technique for purposes of historical and legal documentation. Many pictures are available, for example, of the pogroms of 1905 and 1906—of the wounded, the dying, and the dead, as well as of their grieving families. These were probably taken not only for their news value (the East European press published pictures with some frequency) but also to serve as evidence in the legal cases which the Jewish community, as part of a concerted project undertaken by newly organized self-defense groups, was just then beginning to mount against its persecutors. The camera was also used in this period for quasi-anthropological purposes. In 1912 the Yiddish dramatist S. Ansky, best known as the author of *The Dybbuk*, organized a Jewish ethnographic expedition into the Ukraine. Two of its members were able to travel about the Ukrainian hinterlands taking pictures for almost three years—well into the war—before being arrested late in 1914 and charged with spying.

Curiously enough, it was that same German occupation of Poland (from 1915 to 1918) which first revealed the "artistic" possibilities inherent in Jewish subject matter. The Germans came to Poland not only as military conquerors but also as tourists, fascinated by the strange peoples and alien cultures they encountered in the eastern areas of their conquest. Strangest and most picturesque of all—and hence most photogenic—were the Jews, especially the religiously observant ones, in their long coats and wide-brimmed hats, with their bushy beards and curled sidelocks. No fewer than three picture albums of the city of Vilna—featuring many views of the city's Jewish quarter, its synagogues, and its "types," as the text put it—were published under German auspices during the years of German occupation, and these in turn stimulated a further rash of picture books about the city when the war was over. The Germans, with the fresh perspective of outsiders, had shown the natives that their town's familiar and commonplace landmarks were worthy of record and even had glamour.

Jewish photographers thenceforth became connoisseurs of beauty, transforming the worn cobblestones of crooked alleys into austere compositions of light and shade, the iron scrollwork of synagogue gates into striking visual arrangements. Imbued with modernist and populist ideas, they turned away from the high and mighty and began training their lenses on more humble subjects: the water carrier, the street musician, the engaging village idiot. Aesthetic considerations merged with a growing social consciousness to attract photographers in increasing numbers to the lower depths of the shtetl. Focusing their cameras on the distress and wretchedness that had hitherto been hidden from view, they called public attention to the sufferings of the Jewish poor. (Some of the finest photographs we have from this period were commissioned by a Jewish philanthropic organization in the United States to spur fund-raising campaigns.) By the late 1920s a number of master photographers of East European Jewish life had emerged: Moritz Grossman (ca. 1885–1941), Menachem Kipnis (1878–1942), Alter Kacyzne (1885–1941), and most distinguished of all, the noted microphotographer Roman Vishniac, who was born near St. Petersburg in 1897 and now lives in New York.

By 1939, thousands upon thousands of photographs had accumulated, comprising a documentary history of East European Jewry. Perhaps the best source for this material was the *Jewish Daily Forward* in New York, whose Sunday rotogravure section, begun in 1923, devoted a full page every week to photographs of the Old Country. Today, the YIVO Institute for Jewish Research has a vast collection of photographs of the Jewish populations of some 600 cities and towns of prewar Poland, as well as countless other places in prerevolutionary Russia. With the German destruction of Jewish Eastern Europe during World War II, these pictures —taken in the course of ordinary human pursuits and for ordinary human purposes—have become the artifacts of a vanished civilization.

Can photographs succeed at all in rendering East European Jewish life and culture, which were so quintessentially a matter of mind and spirit? East European Jewry had no architectural glories like Greece's, no monumental grandeur like Rome's. Its monuments were wooden synagogues and tombstones; its greatness lay in its human relations, in its moral values and religious commitment, in its abstract intellectuality and the sheer pulsating will to live, which animated every aspect of its existence. Can the camera capture such intense inwardness? And even if the inner being of a single individual can be so rendered, can the same things be done for a group, for a whole community? A number of recently published picture books of Jewish life in Eastern Europe suggest the problems involved in such an enterprise.

Abraham Shulman's *The Old Country: The Lost World of European Jews* (New York: Scribner's, 1974) illustrates some of the technical difficulties involved. A collection of over 200 photographs with an introductory essay on the shtetl (in fact, a good number of the photographs were taken not in small towns but in the major cities of Warsaw, Lublin, Lodz, Odessa, and Vilna), the book's contents are drawn entirely from the old *Forward* rotogravure section, where they were published during the last three decades. These rescreened, "second-generation" reproductions have darkened considerably, losing much of their original clarity. The resulting lack of definition has been further aggravated by having both photographs and text printed in brown rather than black ink. The sky in these pictures is always overcast, the subject of the photographs is half-hidden in darkness, and the pictures are oppressively melancholy and monotonous.

Turning these pages, and growing more and more depressed, one realizes that the flaw is not merely technical. The pictures seem to have been chosen to gratify the most self-flagellating kind of nostalgia, enshrining that stereotype of the East European shtetl which I have characterized (in *The Golden Tradition*) as "forever frozen in utter piety and utter poverty." Picture after picture conveys the same sense of unrelieved deprivation: the outdoors is endlessly signified by muddy stretches of unpaved road or cobbled pavements; the dimly lit interiors transmit a sense of imprisonment. The pictures also exude an air of vagueness and unreality, further compounded by the author's failure to identify most of them as to specific time or place, as though all these streets and houses were the same and therefore interchangeable. This view of East European Jewry is simply too lopsided to pass for history.

To take just one example: there is a single photograph in the present collection which is identified as being from Cracow. In this ancient and beautiful capital of the historic Kingdom of Poland, some 25,000 Jews lived at the turn of the century, when the city was part of the Hapsburg Empire. During that period, Jewish representatives sat in the Austrian Reichsrat, Jews served in the city's chamber of commerce, and Jewish professors taught at the university. Jewish Cracow, moreover, was a center of the modernist Hebrew revival. Yet all that Shulman shows us of Cracow is a photograph of two barefoot children pumping water from a town well. His book conveys neither the immense diversity nor the striking wholeness of East European Jewish culture, capable as it was of tolerating and finally reconciling within itself the most violently opposed cultural impulses. (One need only recall the great struggles between traditionalism and modernity, between Zionism and anti-Zionism, between Hasidism and rabbinic Judaism.) None of this ferment is evident in Shulman's book.

The overdrawn heritage of poverty and backwardness which he has presented panders to the contemporary taste for nostalgia. But nostalgia is to history what kitsch is to art. When nostalgia embraces an unexperienced past, imagined without memory, authentic sentiment degenerates into sentimentalism. It has been suggested that it is precisely this quality which appeals to American Jews, since it gratifies their sentimentalism for the past and their self-satisfaction with the present, giving them a moral warrant, as it were, to enjoy their fleshpots. But I think that surely their children, who reject those fleshpots anyway, will react otherwise. Seeing in these pictures only the mud and the poverty, they will not comprehend the vibrancy of East European Jewish life, from which millions drew moral and creative sustenance. These young people will be glad not to have been born in the shtetl, and glad to turn their backs on it.

A more ambitious and professional work is *The Jewish Family Album: The Life of a People in Photography* by Franz Hubmann (Boston: Little, Brown, 1974), an Austrian photographer who has previously done pictorial histories of the Hapsburg and Wilhelminian empires. The book consists of over 300 photographs which have been assembled from a great variety of state, public, private, and communal archives in Austria, Germany, Czechoslovakia, France, England, the United States, and Israel. It is not limited to Eastern Europe, but attempts a panoramic presentation of

Jewish life in modern times; accordingly, it is divided (rather unevenly) into four sections: East European Jewry (mistitled "Ghetto and Shtetl"); West European Jewry ("The Emancipated"); American Jewry ("The New World"); and pre-1939 Palestine ("The Promised Land"). A ten-page history of the Jews plus short introductions to each of the four sections (by Miriam and Lionel Kochan) complete the somewhat procrustean design.

Aesthetically, the volume is flawless. The large-size format is pleasing, the quality of reproduction and printing first-rate. The original values of clarity, distinctness, sharpness, and contrast have been marvelously preserved—and perhaps even enhanced—in the black-and-white plates. The layout is spacious and at times even elegant, and the pictures are more varied and more interesting than those in Shulman's volume.

Hubmann, too, sees the Jews of Eastern Europe as mainly poor and pious, though they are not so wretched and depressed as Shulman's. There is a rather heavy concentration on pictures of Galician towns, many taken during World War I; Eastern Poland by contrast is rather sparsely represented, though four plates of wooden synagogues (one exterior and three interiors) are impressive. The Jews of Eastern Europe are shown for the most part in the course of their daily pursuits—at work, in conversation, in religious study, and in the war zone. From the viewpoint of social history, perhaps the most interesting single photograph is one of a Galician family at the Seder table in 1915. There are eight at the table, which is set, as the camera reveals, according to Passover specifications: the festive cloth, the candlesticks, the ceremonial plate, the wine, the matzos, the *Haggadot*, the dishes, and the holiday cutlery. More interesting than these, however, are the two uniformed soldiers of the Austrian Imperial Army seated at either end of the table.

One wonders who they are. Family members home on furlough for the Passover holidays? Out-of-town Jews stationed in the town and invited to share in local hospitality? Like a number of other pictures in this section, this one lingers in the mind.

Yet for all the charm, interest, and character of the sixty-odd pictures which make up this section, it is inadequate as a portrayal of the social diversity of the teeming Jewish community of Eastern Europe. But perhaps, indeed, such a portrayal was not intended, for Hubmann's perspective on this material seems to have been shaped entirely by one cliché of Jewish sociology: the contrast between the poor and pious Jews of Eastern Europe and the affluent, emancipated Jews of Western Europe. (The section on America, too, follows through on this basic scheme, with the pictures neatly divided between humble East European immigrants and rich German Jews.) This particular dichotomy is a very orderly one, but it is no less a stereotype than Shulman's, and perhaps even more distorting.

In any case, "The Emancipated" dominate the entire album, with two or three times as many entries as any other category. The ambiguities of this section, one might say, begin with the subtitle itself, for it is never quite clear whether it is civic inequality or Judaism from which these Jews have been emancipated; the inclusion of a number of converts from Judaism only adds to the puzzlement. Those whom Hubmann has chosen to typify the community of Western Europe include philanthropists like Sir Moses Montefiore and Baron de Hirsch, statesmen like Benjamin Disraeli, and members of the great Jewish banking families of Central and Western Europe like Todesco, Wertheimer, Rothschild, Schey-Koromla, Péreire, Camondo, and Sassoon —to name just the most outstanding. The list from the world of culture and entertainment is even longer, and contains in addition to Jews a good number of ex-Jews. Interspersed among photographs of such stars as Gustav Mahler and Arthur Schnitzler, Arnold Schoenberg and Sarah Bernhardt, Marc Chagall and Franz Kafka, Gertrude Stein and Ernst Lubitsch, are also a few run-of-the-mill assimilated German Jews, along with a scattering of lower-class Prague Jews and Hasidim living in Vienna's Leopoldstadt—included, one cannot but feel, to point a contrast to the luminaries.

Shulman shows us the Jews as poor and downtrodden; Hubmann, as prosperous and triumphant. Both volumes distort reality in one way or another. Are we to conclude that picture books simply cannot render the institutions, values, traditions, and culture of the Jewish community? Are these simply too elusive to be captured by the eye of the camera?

A third work, *Jerusalem of Lithuania* (New York, 1974), a beautiful photographic history of Jewish Vilna, demonstrates that an authentic Jewish pictorial history is indeed possible, although this particular one was twenty-five years in preparation, required the services of dozens of devoted volunteers in addition to the editor, Vilna-born Leyzer Ran, and takes up three massive volumes. There have been hundreds of *yizkor* (remembrance) books to memorialize communities which perished in the Holocaust, but none to equal the present work in scope and profusion of detail, extending as it does from the earliest settlement for which visual documentation was available to the final extinction of the Vilna Jewish community. Volumes I and II—folio-size and bound in red cloth—contain over 3,000 reproductions of photographs, paintings, illustrations, documents, maps, and tables, a selection garnered from communal and private collections all over the world. Volume III, octavo and paperbound, contains indices to 1,500 subjects and 4,000 persons, an exhaustive multilingual bibliography on the

history of Jewish Vilna, and a listing of picture sources. The
several introductory essays and all of the captions are in
Yiddish, Russian, English, and Hebrew.

The Vilna immortalized here occupied a unique position
among Jewish cities. Though lacking the energy and bustle
of Warsaw, Odessa's cosmopolitanism, Lodz's enterprise, and
Cracow's elegance, it was indeed—as Napoleon is supposed
to have exclaimed on first seeing Vilna's Great Synagogue
in 1812—the "Jerusalem of Lithuania." With a Jewish population in the nineteenth century that fluctuated between
60,000 and 100,000, accounting for about a third of the city's
total population, Vilna was a center, and often a pioneering
outpost, of every major Jewish cultural and social movement.
It was the home of the most celebrated Talmudist of modern
times, Elijah ben Solomon (the Vilna Gaon), and hence the
most authoritative locus of rabbinic Judaism. It was the
cultural seat of the *Haskalah* and of the revival of Hebrew
literature, and was also home to the proto-Zionist movement
Hovevei Zion (Lovers of Zion). The Jewish socialist movement was born in Vilna, and the Jewish Labor Bund held
its founding conference there in 1897. The Romm Hebrew
printing and publishing house, whose editions of the Talmud
were renowned throughout the world, flourished in Vilna
for 150 years, and the fame of Vilna's *yeshivot* matched the
repute of its secular Hebrew and Yiddish teachers' seminaries.
Along with all this went a great profusion of newspapers,
magazines, and journals of every conceivable kind, most of
them in Yiddish, for Yiddish was the language of Jewish
Vilna, both of its marketplace and of its high literary and
scholarly culture.

Small wonder, then, that the story of this city should
have taken so many pages to tell. The first volume of
Jerusalem of Lithuania opens with reproductions of fifteenth-
century documents and of a 1606 woodcut showing Vilna's

main Jewish street and synagogue. The second volume closes with photographs of the destruction of Vilna Jewry and of the war-crimes trials of the Germans responsible for that destruction. Between the spare beginning and the irreversible end, the editor and his colleagues have given us a stunning profusion of pictures in which every facet of the Lithuanian Jerusalem is captured and preserved.

Is the reader interested in Vilna's political life? An 1869 photograph shows ten members of a Vilna Jewish commission appointed by the czarist government and headed by Vilna's eminent chief rabbi, Jacob Barit. A 1906 photograph shows the Jewish electors for the first Russian Duma. There is a whole series of individual and group portraits of Vilna's representatives in the Sejm, the city council, and the *kehillah*, as well as of the leaders and members of Vilna's countless political movements, caught in turbulent street demonstrations, with flags and banners aloft, or stiffly posed before the camera.

Is the reader interested in Vilna's communal institutions? There is a fascinating series of pictures of an old-age home, with its residents in both formal and informal poses, and another series on communal health facilities, ranging from the traditional bath house and the *hevrat bikur holim* (society to visit the sick) to the most modern of hospitals and clinics. My own favorite, in the section on philanthropic activities and societies, is a marvelously detailed portrait of one Deborah Esther Gelfer (1817–1907), a charitable dowager, obviously ill at ease before the camera, who sits clutching the tie-string bag from which she habitually doled out gifts and loans to the needy. (A later photograph, posed before her rather ostentatious gravestone, shows a man reciting the prayer for the dead to an assemblage of heavily shawled women—perhaps Madam Gelfer's beneficiaries, feeling the pinch of her demise.)

So far as Vilna's economic life is concerned, there are copious illustrations of street trade and town markets, and examples of mercantile enterprise ranging from secondhand dealers to Zalkind's sumptuous department store. The water carriers and woodcutters of shtetl mythology are here, but so also are the tailors, carpenters, glaziers, smiths, painters, upholsterers, porters and drivers, tanners, mechanics, bookbinders, bakers, and brewers, as well as men at work on lumber rafts, in plywood factories, and in pulp mills. A 1913 photograph of a Vilna beggar out-beggars all the wretched Jews in Shulman's collection, and contrasts with the complacent portraits of Jewish factory owners and members of manufacturers' associations. (An accompanying table informs us that two-thirds of Vilna's industrial enterprises and 60 percent of its commercial businesses were Jewish-owned.)

Finally, there is Vilna's academic and cultural life, with an array of photographs of *yeshivot* and secular schools, of children in the classroom and at play, of athletic contests and scholarly activities all the way from kindergarten to *gymnasium*. Vilna's cultural elite are also pictured here—its scholars and intellectuals, poets, journalists, cantors, composers, conductors, musicians, opera stars, child prodigies, dancers, actors (the famed Vilna Troupe), painters, and sculptors.

All of Jewish Vilna, in short, is in these pages, and also everyone of note who ever visited the city. There is a splendid photograph of Theodor Herzl seated in a droshky, with the driver standing at attention like a royal guardsman, and there are pictures of such other distinguished visitors as the Zionist leaders Nahum Sokolow and Vladimir Jabotinsky, the Yiddish classicists Mendele, Sholem Aleichem, and I. L. Peretz, the poet Chaim Nachman Bialik, the historian Simon Dubnow, and the novelist Sholem Asch.

Turning the pages of *Jerusalem of Lithuania* one has the illusion of looking through a kaleidoscope, or watching a kind of slow-motion film. But then ones comes, perforce, to the last section—the war, the German occupation, the ghetto, the killings, and the killers. One cannot go on turning these pages, so one goes back, to an earlier place, to a point where the 60,000 Jews of Vilna were still alive, and starts all over again from there.

The Jews of Vilna are gone now, missing from its pictured streets, ". . . pressing their vacancy/Against the walls . . . ," as Irving Feldman puts it in his haunting poem "To the Six Million." But in *Jerusalem of Lithuania*, Ran has given them a ghostly reincarnation, a life eternal in pictorial history. In place of mere nostalgia we have the true gift of historical remembrance.

IV

Torment: Anti-Semitism and the Holocaust

13

CAN ANTI-SEMITISM BE MEASURED?

> With regard to anti-Semitism I don't really want to search
> for explanations; I feel a strong inclination to surrender
> to my affects in this matter and find myself confirmed in
> my wholly non-scientific belief that mankind on the average
> and taken by and large are a wretched lot.
>
> —SIGMUND FREUD, IN A LETTER TO
> ARNOLD ZWEIG, DECEMBER 2, 1927

IN AN AGE when sociological scrutiny extends into the most
obscure corners of our experience, it may come as a surprise
to learn that the phenomenon of anti-Semitism—one of the
more enduring of social phenomena and, needless to say,
one of special significance in our own time—has received
scant attention from American social scientists. The apathy
of the sociologists has been matched by the indifference of
the great foundations, whose general view has been that
anti-Semitism is (or should be) a parochial concern. Be that
as it may, it is to the American Jewish organizations that we
are indebted for whatever studies of consequence exist. The

latest studies, sponsored by the Anti-Defamation League (ADL), have appeared in a series called *Patterns of American Prejudice,* undertaken in conjunction with the Survey Research Center of the University of California at Berkeley.

The ADL series evokes resonances of the past. In the late 1940s the American Jewish Committee (AJC) sponsored another series, the five-volume *Studies in Prejudice,* whose research was conducted jointly by the University of California Berkeley Public Opinion Study (no connection with the present Survey Research Center) and the Institute of Social Research, then at Columbia University, in exile from its original home in Frankfurt am Main. That entire series and most notably its now renowned centerpiece, *The Authoritarian Personality* (whose senior author was the late Theodor W. Adorno), exercised a remarkable influence on the social sciences, with regard to both methodology and conceptualization. The one historical volume in the series, Paul Massing's *Rehearsal for Destruction,* a study of political anti-Semitism in Imperial Germany, has still not been superseded. In the intervening years between the appearance of that AJC-sponsored series and the ADL series, no other serious work on anti-Semitism in the United States was published, with the exception of *Jews in the Mind of America,* by Charles Stember and others (1966), also sponsored by the American Jewish Committee.

The joint ADL–Survey Research Center project has produced seven volumes in the course of a decade, all published by Harper & Row. More are still to come. The first of the series, *Christian Beliefs and Anti-Semitism,* by Charles Y. Glock and Rodney Stark (1966), probed the opinions and attitudes of 3,000 church members in a metropolitan area of northern California, concluding that one-fourth of those professing anti-Semitic attitudes based their prejudices on what they took to be Christian teaching. The second volume,

The Apathetic Majority: A Study Based on Public Responses to the Eichmann Trial, by Charles Y. Glock, Gertrude J. Selznick, and Joe L. Spaeth (1966), undertook to determine whether public interest in the Eichmann trial bore any relation to anti-Semitism. In the summer of 1961 the authors interviewed 460 residents of Oakland and discovered that although 84 percent had heard of the trial, only 59 percent knew that Eichmann was a Nazi and only 33 percent knew that 6 million was the standard estimate of the number of Jews killed by the Nazis.

The third volume, *Protest and Prejudice: A Study of Belief in the Black Community*, by Gary T. Marx (1967), was a by-product of the riots in the Negro slums during 1964. The Survey Research Center had not originally envisaged an investigation of black anti-Semitism, but the seemingly anti-Jewish features of the riots, directed, as they appeared to be, against Jewish merchants in the ravaged communities, prompted the addition of this study to the series. The fourth work was *The Tenacity of Prejudice: Anti-Semitism in Contemporary America*, by Gertrude J. Selznick and Stephen Steinberg (1969); conceptually a more ambitious work than the previous studies, it was based on lengthy interviews conducted in October 1964 with about 2,000 respondents— a representative sampling of Americans by age, sex, education, income, race, religion, and region. This work sought to gauge the extent of anti-Semitic feeling in the United States.

The fifth study, *The Politics of Unreason: Right-Wing Extremism in America, 1790–1970*, by Seymour Martin Lipset and Earl Raab (1970), developed out of the authors' long involvement in studying the radical right in America. The authors treat anti-Semitism marginally, as a manifestation of right-wing extremism, and devote to it barely 50 pages of their 547-page work. Concentrating on right-wing political attitudes and voting behavior in the 1960s, this volume distinguishes itself from the others in the series by its attention to history through an analysis, cursory and superficial to be sure, of the cyclical recurrences of right-wing extremism in America's past.

The sixth study, *Wayward Shepherds: Prejudice and the Protestant Clergy,* by Rodney Stark, Bruce D. Foster, Charles Y. Glock, and Harold E. Quinley (1971), an unanticipated spin-off of the earlier *Christian Beliefs and Anti-Semitism,* was based on interviews conducted in 1968 with 1,580 Protestant ministers from California churches. The investigators found that though clergymen were less likely than the laity to be anti-Semitic, their anti-Semitism was rooted more in religious factors than in secular ones. The seventh study, *Adolescent Prejudice,* by Charles Y. Glock, Robert Wuthnow, Jane Allyn Piliavin, and Metta Spencer (1975), investigated the attitudes of teenagers in three communities within a radius of 200 miles from New York City. Analysis of the data, which had been gathered in 1963, showed that anti-Semitism and racial prejudice were more prevalent among the poor and the stupid (the study characterized them euphemistically as "the economically and academically deprived") than among "the privileged."

These studies, as I have said, have been carried out for the ADL by the Survey Research Center at Berkeley. Survey research (or survey analysis, as it is more commonly called) can briefly be described as the technique of interpreting data gathered from interviews. It endeavors to identify and isolate the significant causal factors (independent variables) of a given phenomenon and to determine how these affect the pattern of behavior under examination. To examine the effectiveness of survey analysis in studying anti-Semitism and to explore the premises underlying this research, I have chosen to concentrate on two volumes in this series—*The Tenacity of Prejudice* and *Protest and Prejudice.*

To study the extent and prevalence of anti-Semitism in America, Selznick and Steinberg drew up a series of negative statements about Jews. From these they constructed an "Index of Anti-Semitic Belief" which they submitted for comment to the 2,000 respondents. Included were such questions as: Are Jews "clannish"? "dishonest in business"? "disloyal to America"? "powerful in finance and government"? One-third of the respondents denied that Jews fit any of the unflattering descriptions. Another third subscribed to only a few of these commonly held anti-Semitic notions (Jewish clannishness proved the most popular). The final third, endorsing varied clusters of the proffered opinions, checked in with a pronounced strain of anti-Semitism. Nevertheless, most people who registered high on the index did not express any appreciable approval of political anti-Semitism.

Selznick and Steinberg then proceeded to locate anti-Semitism according to population patterns. Young people, they found, tended to be less prejudiced than their elders, native Americans less than foreign-born. "Liberal" Protestants (Congregationalists and Episcopalians) and Catholics proved less biased than "conservative" Protestants (Presbyterians, Methodists, Baptists, Lutherans). Geographically speaking, the greater concentration of anti-Semitism, it was discovered, was in the rural South and Midwest, regions with the least educated and most fundamentalist populations. Indeed, education turned out to be a more significant determinant of anti-Semitism than social class: the poorly educated registered as more anti-Semitic than the well educated, regardless of income or occupational status. Yet among the college educated, the authors learned, the higher the status and income, the greater the prevalence of anti-Semitic attitudes. Negroes, the index showed, responded no differently from whites, except with regard to the "economic" portion of the questionnaire; twice as many Negroes as whites believed that Jews were dishonest and exploitative in business practices. Also, unlike the white respondents, among Negroes younger age and higher education tended to increase the level of anti-Semitism.

Education, or the lack of it, the authors were certain, was *the* independent variable in determining the extent of anti-Semitic bias. Yet the relation between education and anti-Semitism, though strong, turned out to be imperfect: there was still a persistence of anti-Semitism among educated people, white and black. Selznick and Steinberg probed a variety of related factors in search of the culprit—level of educational sophistication, exposure to the mass media, tolerance of cultural diversity, and, of course, authoritarianism and anomie. Still, the correlations, where they appeared, suggested not a causal relationship but rather a syndrome.

In sum, 16 percent of the respondents were revealed to be consistently free of anti-Semitic prejudice, rejecting anti-Jewish stereotypes, opposing social discrimination, and declaring they would vote against an anti-Semitic candidate. At the opposite end of the opinion scale were the 5 to 10 percent who could be characterized as out-and-out anti-Semites. The majority occupied the vast middle ground, not favoring anti-Semitism but lacking the determination to oppose any of its manifestations. Anti-Semitism, Selznick and Steinberg concluded, is widespread in the United States, though not in virulent form. For rectification they looked to educational institutions, which, with all their shortcomings, "are the primary means whereby the individual is integrated into the ideal norms and values that constitute and sustain a democratic and humane society."

For Gary T. Marx, the study of anti-Semitism, even within his more specialized context, was secondary. His primary concern in *Protest and Prejudice* was to examine the climate of opinion in the black community regarding the civil rights movement; Negro attitudes toward Jews were of subsidiary interest. In October 1964 he interviewed over 1,000 Negro adults in various parts of the country, North and South. To probe the depth and extent of civil rights militancy and/or extremism in the black community, Marx fashioned a survey-analysis index which revealed most Negroes to be moderates, overwhelmingly rejecting black nationalism. And, like his illustrious namesake, he too found religion to be the opiate of the people, encouraging quietism rather than protest.

As for anti-Semitism, Marx certified from his data that most blacks were not anti-Semitic—or, at any rate, not more so than whites. Three out of ten nonsouthern Negroes (a higher proportion than among Southerners) registered as anti-Semitic on Marx's index. Most Negroes (75 percent) thought Jews were neither better nor worse than white Christians, while 20 percent said Jews were better and 5 percent said worse. By this calculation Marx concluded that *"Jews were seen in a more favorable light than other whites by a four-to-one ratio"* (italics in the original). Comparing his data with those of the Selznick-Steinberg study, Marx at first found no consistent pattern of differences between blacks and whites in anti-Semitic attitudes, but an "Index of Predisposition to Economically Based Anti-Semitism" showed that Negroes registered high. Marx explained the prevalence of such anti-Semitism as the consequence of the blacks' "actual experiences with Jews in the economic world." "While Negro anti-Semitism is deplorable," he summed up, "it certainly is more *understandable* than white anti-Semitism" (my italics).

In the social sciences, questions of methodology are inextricably linked with questions of substance. Before proceeding further, we might therefore do well to consider the subject of survey analysis, a matter of no small pertinence to our discussion in view of the fact that the technique in question has established itself as dominant in the sociological investigation of American anti-Semitism. Is survey analysis an adequate tool for the study of a phenomenon as complex as anti-Semitism? To what extent has survey analysis itself affected the conceptualization of the problem? Finally, do the studies represent survey analysis at its best? Some answers to these questions, I trust, will emerge from the discussion that follows.

Survey analysis developed out of two diverse but not unrelated fields, market research and the study of propaganda. As new interviewing and statistical techniques were developed to elicit, describe, and measure public opinion on a wide range of matters, *vox populi*, hitherto absent from social or historical records, became a source of scientific information. Paul F. Lazarsfeld, author of the path-breaking work *The People's Choice* (a study of the 1940 presidential election), is generally acknowledged as the founder of survey analysis. His contributions to the discipline included the development of sophisticated mathematical formulas to study the interrelation of assembled data; the invention of the "panel," a body of respondents whom surveyors periodically reinterview; contextual analysis; and, indeed, the whole apparatus of survey analysis—administration, training, data gathering, analysis, publication, even funding. Not content with a technique that depended solely on statistical data and quantification for its findings and insights, Lazarsfeld had always been aware of the need to diversify. In 1933, the year of his arrival in the United States from Germany, he set down, in a paper entitled "Principles of Sociography," four basic methodological rules:

a. For any phenomenon one should have objective observations as well as introspective reports.
b. Case studies should be properly combined with statistical information.
c. Contemporary information should be supplemented by

information on earlier phases of whatever is being
studied.
d. One should combine "natural and experimental data."
By experimental, I meant mainly questionnaires and
solicited reports, while by natural, I meant what is
now called "unobtrusive measures"—data deriving from
daily life without interference from the investigator.*

It would be unfair to demand that the survey analysts of
the *Patterns in American Prejudice* series adhere to the ideal
standards, standards the master himself could not always
observe. Still, I, for one, found the reliance on survey data,
in both *Protest and Prejudice* and *The Tenacity of Prejudice*,
to the near exclusion of other data, intellectually constricting.
To be sure, Gary Marx occasionally drew upon literary,
historical, and journalistic sources, but then, as if to retain
survey-analysis purity in his text, he relegated this material
to footnotes. Selznick and Steinberg used even fewer auxiliary
sources. Their various findings must therefore stand or fall
entirely on the basis of the quantitative empirical data. Yet
how does one measure the extent and intensity of anti-
Semitism? Is there a National Bureau of Standards for the
study of social phenomena which has specified the standard
content, density, or weight of anti-Semitism?

In survey analysis, the standard measuring procedure for
all phenomena is scaling. As we have seen, the scale, or
index, can be constructed from a collection of statements
to which respondents are asked to register degrees of assent
or disagreement ("a lot," "a little," "not at all"). Each item
is designed to elicit a specific attitude or opinion, and their
grouping reflects the conception that certain attitudes and
opinions form a single general outlook. The critical process

* Paul F. Lazarsfeld, "An Episode in the History of Social Research: A
Memoir," in *The Intellectual Migration: Europe and America, 1930–1960*,
ed. Donald Fleming and Bernard Bailyn (Cambridge: Harvard University
Press, 1969), pp. 282–283.

involved in constructing a scale lies in the selection and formulation of items that will provide a valid continuum and thus serve as an accurate and sensitive measuring device. The items selected for the scale naturally reflect the surveyors' hypotheses about the significant variables under study. Obviously, formulation of the items also entails problems, since the wording can influence the response. After the scale items are finally drawn up, techniques for the testing of validity are applied; these are designed to enforce the scale's empirical objectivity.

As should be evident, in good survey analysis everything depends on the ingenuity of the scale. How good, then, is the anti-Semitism scale of the ADL studies? Unfortunately, no one thought to draw up a *uniform* scale that might be applied to all the surveys in the series and that might therefore yield a more scientific understanding of the varieties of anti-Semitism. Instead we are given a patchwork of scales, with each study constructing a different index, using different items, in different quantities, often differently formulated. *Christian Beliefs and Anti-Semitism* used six items for its index; *The Apathetic Majority*, three; *Protest and Prejudice*, nine; *The Tenacity of Prejudice*, eleven (seven of Marx's items were the same as Selznick and Steinberg's). *Wayward Shepherds* changed the ground rules and formulated an index that differed from the one used in *Christian Beliefs and Anti-Semitism*. The anti-Semitism index in *Adolescent Prejudice* consisted of eight items, a few similar to, but none identical with, the eleven-item index in Selznick and Steinberg. Of the various authors, Marx alone employed "positive" items—that is, items favorable toward Jews. ("Positive" items, the experts tell us, are more likely to elicit the accepted "tolerant" responses and are thus less satisfactory in tapping hostile attitudes.)

Given this variety, what is one to make of the different

indices? Are the scales of Glock, Marx, Steinberg and
Selznick, and the others comparable to the Fahrenheit,
Celsius, and Réaumur scales—that is, although they use
different measuring units, do they measure the same
phenomenon? Are the anti-Semitism scales interchangeable
and their findings convertible? Obviously not, for anti-
Semitism has no commonly accepted boiling or freezing
point; no standard weights or intervals have been assigned
to religious anti-Semitism, political anti-Semitism, economic
anti-Semitism, authoritarianism, or ethnocentrism. Altogether,
the disparity among the various scales raises serious doubts
as to their validity. That the Survey Research Center made
no attempt to standardize a scale to measure anti-Semitism
is not very reassuring; nor is the fact that barely any use
was made of the pioneer anti-Semitism scale developed in the
early 1940s by Daniel J. Levinson and R. Nevitt Sanford
for *The Authoritarian Personality*. Among other advantages,
that 52-item scale distinguished between opinions and attitudes, and probed different images of Jews as individuals,
as a group, and as a culture.

A claim of survey analysis is that it can transcend the
surveyor's subjective hypotheses. Yet in the very construction
of the apparatus for the gathering and measuring of empirical
data, subjectivity inevitably plays a role and must, in the
end, color the findings themselves. The fiction of total impartiality in social research has come under attack by, among
others, Gunnar Myrdal, who in the interest of honesty and
greater objectivity has made the suggestion—in which I
concur—that social scientists disclose the personal and
political values underlying their research.* This is a tricky
business, however. Values may at times be so deeply in-

* Gunnar Myrdal, *Objectivity in Social Research* (New York: Pantheon,
1969).

ternalized that the researcher has genuine difficulties in standing aside and acknowledging them. Even the selection of topics shelters subjective viewpoints and values that can infiltrate research, sometimes innocently and subconsciously, occasionally with the intention to influence and manipulate. The reader is at a loss. He does not have even the poker player's option of paying to see the bidder's hand.

The Tenacity of Prejudice is a good example of how the researchers' premises—in this case, with regard to what constitutes the ideal society—have led to a misreading of the data. Selznick and Steinberg, it will be recalled, concluded that education was the independent variable in anti-Semitism, even though anti-Semitism continued to persist among the educated. That irregularity was most pronounced in the following items designed to measure intolerance: attitudes of non-Jews toward intermarriage with Jews, toward the exclusion of Jews from social clubs, and toward the continued observance of Christmas in the public schools. Respondents who otherwise came out very low on the anti-Semitism scale here registered as "intolerant"; in fact, the more educated a respondent, the greater the level of his "intolerance" on these items. As already noted, the authors looked for assorted explanations, but the data nevertheless remained intractable.

The fault, I suggest, lies not in the data but in the attitudes held by Selznick and Steinberg about the nature of American society and of group relations. These attitudes are nowhere set forth explicitly, but they are revealed by a close reading of their approach to the data. We see, for instance, that they consider a Christian intolerant if he is against intermarriage with a Jew. By the goose/gander rule, they must therefore also regard as intolerant Jews who are opposed to intermarriage. In so doing, however, they are forced to ignore considerations that apply with far greater weight to Jews than to American Christians. By making approval of intermarriage a barometer of tolerance, Selznick and Steinberg must logically regard a commitment to group survival as an obstruction to the creation of a prejudice-free, neutral society. Oddly enough, for a study that purports to gauge anti-Semitic feeling, nowhere is an effort made to deal with the question of the legitimacy of group life, religious or ethnic. Selznick and Steinberg seem to believe that anti-Semitism must be combated because it is the ultimate obstacle to Jewish assimilation. Jewish survivalists, on the other hand, start from the premise that anti-Semitism constitutes a peril to Jewish continuity.

If their commitment to the neutral society has caused them to misread their data, the enthrallment of Selznick and Steinberg with education distorts their conclusions. Indeed, the emphasis on education as *the* countervailing force to prejudice exposes the weakness of this method of relying exclusively on attitudes and opinions without referring to ancillary or supplementary considerations, such as the capacity of social and political institutions to absorb and neutralize group conflict. Moreover, nothing that one has learned from contemporary and historical sources supports confidence in the healing properties of education in overcoming prejudice. Especially nowadays, when a college education is no longer a bulwark against the superstitions of astrology, when propaganda of the Third World and the Palestine Liberation Organization can flourish on college campuses as the New Received Truth, and when rationalism on the campuses is not only straight and square but dead, we can scarcely depend on educational institutions to provide defenses against the blandishments of ethnic prejudice.

Gary Marx makes no bones about the values he holds. In the preface to *Protest and Prejudice*, he writes:

With respect to my own values, I have been involved in the civil rights struggle and am concerned with the issues of which this book treats. The effect of my personal concerns on the analysis of the data has, I hope, been minimal. However, someone with a different commitment might have written a different book.

The message is even more explicitly spelled out in the dedication, which reads:

To those oppressed because of their racial, religious, or ethnic identity in the hope that they will become more militant and more tolerant and thus transcend evils so long and cruelly perpetrated by man on man.

It therefore comes as no surprise, given his "commitment," that Marx should have produced a thoroughly tendentious piece of work, which, when all is said and done, stands as an uncritical apology for black militancy. (The *tendenz* is further adumbrated early in the book when the author, in another lapse from social science cool, enthusiastically endorses Malcolm X's highly ideological description of American society as "the American Nightmare.") Such a partisan approach, of course, is not likely to view the black militants as engaging, in thought or deed, in violence and racism. By Marx's criteria, antisocial behavior can be explained simply as justified protest: *tout comprendre, c'est tout pardonner*—an attitude better suited to social workers, perhaps, than to social scientists.

Marx's text is distinguished throughout by a tension, to borrow Guenther Roth's phrase, "between partisanship and scholarship." Which raises a question about his techniques. Were the scales he devised intended to buttress his predictions, or were they merely slipshod efforts? For example, Marx constructed an "Index of Conventional Militancy," meaning "the kind of militancy manifested by the conventional civil rights groups in 1964." It consisted of the following eight items (the "militant" response appears in parentheses):

1. A restaurant owner should not have to serve Negroes if he doesn't want to. (Disagree.)
2. An owner of property should not have to sell to Negroes if he doesn't want to. (Disagree.)
3. Before Negroes are given equal rights, they have to show that they deserve them. (Disagree.)
4. Negroes who want to work hard can get ahead just as easily as anyone else. (Disagree.)
5. In your opinion, is the government in Washington pushing integration too slow, too fast, or about right? (Too slow.)
6. Negroes should spend more time praying and less time demonstrating. (Disagree.)
7. To tell the truth, I would be afraid to take part in civil rights demonstrations. (Disagree.)
8. Would you like to see more demonstrations or less [sic] demonstrations? (More.)

Agreement with the first four items registered as bigotry —but is militancy the converse of bigotry? And the last four items, while more germane than the first to civil rights "militancy," have an antiquated ring about them, even for the dark ages of 1964. That was the year, after all, of the Mississippi Freedom Summer, which was supported by the full spectrum of civil rights groups. Up north, the moderate ("conventional") groups were all under pressure from the militants, and the militants in turn were under pressure from the extremists. Yet Marx's militancy scale—whose items tread rather gingerly, it seems to me—registered most respondents as moderate rather than militant, even in New

York, even in Chicago. Blacks in Atlanta were less militant than their counterparts in Birmingham. Nothing, it seemed, was what it appeared to be. Was the index at fault? Was the sample at fault? Were the interviewers at fault?*

Another example: Marx's "Index of Support for Black Nationalism" consisted of the following four items: (1) refusal to fight for the United States in the event of a war; (2) giving American Negroes their own state; (3) singling out the Black Muslims as a group doing the most to help Negroes; (4) singling out Malcolm X as the leader doing the most to help his people. The data disclosed that less than 1 percent of the respondents agreed with three or more of the statements, leading Marx to conclude, somewhat triumphantly, that "reports of a 'rising tide' of black nationalism . . . were widely misleading." Meanwhile, social researchers at UCLA, studying aspects of the Watts riot, found that 30 percent of their respondents indicated signs of black militancy.† Their measuring devices differed from Marx's, and they themselves indicated the greater effectiveness of their scale over Marx's in tapping the presence of black militancy.

The radical shifts in the civil rights movement have, of course, turned Marx's sociology of the black community in 1964 into ancient history. Was he an innocent victim of unpredictable change? The folk wisdom cautions: forewarned is forearmed. The one constant characteristic of the

* In 1968, George Gallup scrapped a poll his organization had conducted in Harlem for the *New York Times*. Reporters on a follow-up story discovered that two interviewers had falsified some of the data. A researcher engaged in a pilot study in New York City of Negro attitudes toward Jews, commissioned by the American Jewish Committee through Columbia's Bureau of Applied Social Research, discovered that one of her interviewers had falsified a whole set of interviews with young black militants.

† See T. M. Tomlinson, "Ideological Foundations for Negro Action: A Comparative Analysis of Militant and Non-Militant Views of the Los Angeles Riot," and T. M. Tomlinson and Diana L. TenHouten, "Method: Negro Reaction Survey," in *Los Angeles Riot Study*, Institute of Government and Public Affairs, University of California, Los Angeles, June 1, 1967.

civil rights movement since the Supreme Court decision of 1954 has been change. In 1955 the Montgomery bus boycott catapulted Martin Luther King, Jr., into national prominence; in 1960, Negro college students organized the first sit-ins in North Carolina; in 1963 the March on Washington gave the highest national sanction to civil rights protest and demonstration. A year later the urban riots began. Given the fact of change, it remains a mystery why Marx did not avail himself of the protection that survey analysis provides through the techniques of sociological prediction. Prediction for social action is really what sociology is all about, at least to its activists. Comte's *savoir pour prévoir* still remains the sociological watchword.

In 1964, as in 1960 when the sit-ins began, young, college-educated Negroes provided the impetus for the changing patterns of black protest. Yet Marx sampled young and educated blacks only randomly. Only 13 percent of his respondents had some college education; only 22 percent were between eighteen and twenty-nine years old. Had Marx, extrapolating from the trend of young, college-educated militants, drawn a larger sample from this group, his survey might have had more validity. Indeed, the role of strategic elites in influencing social behavior calls into question the usefulness of studies of mass opinion in some contexts. Such studies minimize the roles of opinion molders, political leaders, and social activists, and blur the selective impact of propaganda. In his postscript to the paperback edition of *Protest and Prejudice*, Marx at last confronted this problem. His final paragraph delivered the coup de grace not only to his own study but to the entire enterprise of *Patterns of American Prejudice*:

> *The important questions are clearly not so much how many, but who, how intensively, and in what way?* As the unprecedented domestic violence in the late 1960's and the

changing tone of much black-white dialogue indicates, playing the numbers game with public-opinion data can be conducive to highly unrealistic assessments. . . . "Mass" in polls of black opinion can be an umbrella concept for a highly diverse collectivity which includes the youthful unskilled and unemployed, and ideologically articulate college students, as well as a great many older, more passive people. Everyone's opinion does not count the same, and opinions are changing—if not fast enough for the most radical, certainly much too fast for the most conservative. [Italics in the original.]

Let us return to the subject of black anti-Semitism. In opening his discussion of this subject, Marx immediately takes the sting out of the problem by remarking that "anti-Semitism is a 'normal' aspect of our culture" and a component of "our common culture"—shared, that is, by white and black alike. (Would he, I wonder, characterize racism as "normal" in the same way?) Attitudes, he adds, are "fashioned from experiences," and "for Negroes, anti-Semitic stereotypes appear to be much more related to actual experiences with Jews in the economic world." Hence, while Negro anti-Semitism is to be "deplored," it is also, according to Marx (and as I have already noted), "certainly . . . more understandable than white anti-Semitism." In confusing attitudes with social realities, in assigning to subjective feelings the authority of objectivity, Marx would seem to have fallen into a trap that critics of survey analysis have long warned about. The late Theodor Adorno, who never cared much for survey research anyway, put it this way: "What was axiomatic according to the prevalent rule of social research, namely, to proceed from the subjects' reactions as if they were a primary and final source of sociological knowledge, seemed to me thoroughly superficial and misguided."*

* Theodor W. Adorno, "Scientific Experiences of a European Scholar in America," in *Intellectual Migration*, ed. Fleming and Bailyn, p. 343.

The formation of attitudes is a complex matter to which experience, of course, contributes. But anti-Semitism, like all prejudices, is also a creature of propaganda and of indoctrination in centuries-old hatreds; its unhappy recrudescence in some black literature today is a phenomenon which Marx ignores altogether.

Marx's treatment of black anti-Semitism is generally on the capricious side. He begins by minimizing its existence; then he changes course to say that, yes, there is anti-Semitism in the black community, but that it derives from experience; finally, in yet another shift, he maintains that the anti-Semitism in question is but a reflection of Negro hostility toward all whites. In one of his extra-survey-analysis footnotes, however, Marx himself offers evidence to refute this last contention—a passage from Claude Brown's *Manchild in the Promised Land* which would seem to indicate that blacks do distinguish between Jews and other whites. Negro folklore, says Brown, pictures all white people as mean and stingy. If a man is more mean than he is stingy, he is white —Christian or cracker; if he is more stingy than mean, he's a Jew. The sophistication of this piece of folklore should be sufficiently conclusive to indicate that black anti-Semitism is exactly that and nothing else, harking back as it does to the stereotype of the Jew as swindler and exploiter, as ancient a stereotype as that of the Jew as Christ-killer. The new articulateness of today's American blacks—many of whom form an uprooted peasantry becoming urbanized—simply gives fresh currency in the United States to one of Europe's oldest myths. It is indeed only in terms of the myth that one can understand the psychological process that makes this urban peasantry blame the Jews rather than the other ethnic groups whose occupational roles afflict Negroes far more severely than do Jewish merchants and landlords. The salience of the Jew as Jew, not as merchant or landlord, sets the dynamics of prejudice moving. And it is the myth, more than the experience, which makes it possible for young blacks today to parrot the pseudo-scientific mouthings of anti-Semites in Germany and Austria of 100 years ago.

In 1968, when anti-Jewish fulminations on the part of various black militant groups rose to a particularly strident pitch, there were many, including some Jews, who sought to minimize the significance of what was being said. This was not surprising. Nor was it surprising that these apologists should have adduced *Protest and Prejudice*, with its imposing array of statistics and tables, all at the service of "scientific, objective truth," in support of their contentions that black anti-Semitism was of no significance; that where it existed it was deserved; and that, in any event, Jews weren't being singled out as Jews but as whites. Finally, *Protest and Prejudice* was invoked as evidence for the "fact" that blacks were not even particularly anti-Semitic—at any rate, not more so than whites, and perhaps less so. Of course, the use of the "protective authority" of science, in Max Weber's phrase, to advance partisan commitments is nothing new. Still, it was saddening to see yet another instance of scholarship pressed into the service of ideology, even if Gary Marx's effort lent itself only too readily to the purpose at hand. Perhaps more distressing is the apparent concurrence of other social scientists in the political uses of scholarship.

Survey analysis even at its best, free from intrusive values and obtrusive politics, is, with its single focus on opinion, not properly geared to study the etiology of anti-Semitism. Useful for periodic pulse-taking, it nevertheless serves ultimately to limit our understanding of anti-Semitism, which is a phenomenon marked by a high degree of multiformity and contradictoriness. A pariah people everywhere for most of their history, Jews have been persecuted for believing in Judaism and excoriated for disbelieving; despised when poor and loathed when rich; shamed for their ignorance of the host culture and rebuffed for mastering it; denounced as capitalists and assailed as Communists; derided for their separatism and reviled for their assimilationism. In the course of its long life, anti-Semitism has also assumed pseudorational guises, e.g., the Christian "teachings of contempt," the theories of alleged Jewish economic control and manipulation, the ideologies of alleged Jewish political domination or cultural pollution. The very persistence of anti-Semitism, as Shmuel Ettinger of the Hebrew University has argued, consolidates and intensifies the syndrome. Historical precedents, historical folk memory—these, almost inevitably, have at various times combined with other factors to make the Jews expedient scapegoats and expendable victims (as witness the resurgence of anti-Semitism in Poland, where only 8,000 Jews remain in a population of 34 million).

Studying anti-Semitism as strictly an American phenomenon, without reference to its occurrence elsewhere in time and geography, strikes me as a highly provincial exercise. The specificity of anti-Semitism in America, to be sure, rests in indigenous political traditions and institutions, and it is important to know how these have affected certain forms of anti-Semitism, but the themes, images, and ideas from which anti-Semitism draws its force have throughout history been transnational and transcultural. (Thus, for example, the imported racist theories of Gobineau and Houston Stewart Chamberlain played a part in the passage of restrictive U.S. immigration laws during the 1920s.) Indeed, anti-Semitic mythology often assumes a life of its own, with its own peculiar pattern of migration. The *Protocols of the Elders of Zion*, consigned yesterday to the ash heap of history, has today been resurrected for use by Arab propagandists. And the eighteenth-century European myth of the Illuminati, a somewhat less notorious variant on the theme of the international conspiracy, still persists in our own day, feeding the anti-Semitic prejudices of many a homegrown American bigot, as Lipset and Raab indicate in their historical overview.

Survey analysis, in my opinion, is by its nature unequipped to investigate the historic images and themes of anti-Semitism that still flourish in their American variety, or to trace their passage from one culture to another. How, then, can survey analysis, all by itself and without the support of other disciplines, be expected to perform the more difficult but necessary task of locating a specific variety of anti-Semitism within a meaningful historical continuum? Time, in the two books we have been discussing, was frozen at October 1964, when the interviews were conducted. But what does that date represent? Was October 1964 part of a continuing stable time, a time of long duration and slow motion? Was it part of a deceptive slow-motion time, continuously interrupted by abrupt crises? Or was it cyclical time, regular or irregular? Or retarded time—time-lagging time? Or explosive time?* Society is in constant motion, yet social time is marked by intervals of different duration. Do opinions and attitudes match the patterns of societal time? Are they behind or ahead? Do they reflect a period's decline or beginning, or even a period of flux?

In *Jews in the Mind of America*, Ben Halpern elucidated a persuasive theory of a perennial syndrome called anti-Semitism, "compounded of simultaneous or alternating toleration and hostility." That syndrome exists in the time of Jewish history. But other rhythms of time flow outside and around, as well as through, Jewish history, quickening or

* See Georges Gurvitch, "Social Structure and the Multiplicity of Time," in *Sociological Theory, Values, and Sociocultural Change*, ed. Edward A. Tiryakian (New York: Harper & Row, 1967).

retarding Jewish time. For instance, a new theory of cyclical societal expansion in the United States, propounded by P. M. G. Harris, makes this claim:

> It turns out that not just the bread and butter in our society since 1870 . . . but the essence of American social structure—linking personal opportunity, community growth, institutional development, and societal change—since its very inception has always reflected, and re-created, cyclical fluctuations in rate of expansion of our population.*

Drawing from many academic disciplines, theories, and research methods, in a complex demographic-historical study that locates, identifies, and describes cyclical fluctuations, Harris concludes that there appears to be a 22½ -year cycle of oscillating socioeconomic conditions in America, with concomitant wide-ranging effects on the family, socialization, life cycles, and educational and economic opportunity. The "mood of the nation," Harris declares, "also goes through swings or cycles adhering closely to the familiar interval." Is it not possible that anti-Semitic prejudice, too, is woven into the tapestry of this cycle, and should not social scientists address themselves to investigating this possibility?

It is to be hoped that subsequent volumes in the *Patterns of American Prejudice* series will contribute more to our understanding of anti-Semitism in America than their predecessors. Perhaps if survey researchers were to yield some of their disciplinary autonomy and sovereignty and begin to share the insights of other fields of study, their work might progress beyond the commonplace and self-indulgent. Certainly the study of anti-Semitism is too serious a matter to be left to the exclusive attention of survey analysts.

* P. M. G. Harris, "The Social Origins of American Leaders: The Demographic Foundations," *Perspectives in American History* 3 (1969):311.

14

SMUT AND ANTI-SEMITISM

"WE ARE THE MEMBERS OF THE MASTER RACE!" So an American rock group calling itself The Dictators proclaims in its record album. Another rock group, Blue Öyster Cult (the umlaut seems to be part of the message), sports a quasi-swastika emblem and specializes in songs like "Career of Evil," "Subhuman," "Dominance and Submission." Other rock performers wear swastikas and Iron Crosses as adornments.

Trade in Nazi memorabilia has become a multimillion-dollar business. Among the best-selling souvenirs are portraits and photographs of Hitler, Himmler, and company; Wehrmacht, Luftwaffe, and SS guns, daggers, swords, and knives; uniforms of the Nazi armed forces and the SS, including helmets, jackboots, and belt buckles; SS and Nazi Party insignia and paraphernalia—identification tags, collar tabs, rings, arm patches, badges, medals. "The stuff that sells best," a storekeeper told a reporter, "are concentration-camp objects. Photographs, shots of concentration camps. That's what people want." Women's sexual fantasies, according to a recent trashy book, now include not only the "conventional" masochistic fantasies of rape and beating but also fantasies of torture in concentration camps.

The Golden Boys of the S.S., a film with an all-male cast, boasted in ads that it was "the first daring look at the secret tortures and brutal pleasures" of those golden boys. An earlier film, no doubt to accommodate those who like straight sex with their sadomasochistic kinkiness, *Ilse the She-Wolf of the S.S.* was set in a Nazi concentration camp where medical experiments were conducted and male prisoners were sterilized. A new Italian-produced film, *Lieben-Camp*, titillates with the promise that it will show "violence and horror in a female concentration camp."

This latest compost of sex, sadism, violence, and Nazism is a kind of pornography of the Holocaust—in William S. Pechter's epithet, "death-camp chic."* In the mid-1970s this pornography surfaced from its mean haunts and dark corners into the popular culture through motion pictures with artistic pretensions. Liliana Cavani's film *The Night Porter*, for instance, reduced the Holocaust to sadomasochistic sexual exercises between an SS officer and his lovely virgin victim, first performed in a concentration camp and then reenacted in a postwar reunion. Seducer and seduced, torturer and victim become locked in an embrace of sexual perversity. In this film, as in Lina Wertmüller's *Seven Beauties*, the concentration camp, even the death camp, serves as a kind of prefabricated locale, with its images of sadism built in— whips, beatings, tortures, naked bodies, blood, urine, excrement. The film writer and director are thereby spared the effort of creative imagination. At the same time, the subject

* William S. Pechter, "Obsessions," *Commentary* 61 (May 1976):76.

of Nazi terror, parasitically exploited, confers upon the film a political seriousness which its content does not deserve.

The Nazis, who mastered, refined, and mass-produced methods of torture and murder, continue to fascinate today's generation of sadomasochists and other consumers of the culture of pornography. Every five years or so this nexus of sex, violence, and Nazism manifests itself in a new combination. In the early 1960s, for instance, lower-class youth in big-city high schools formed vandalizing and terrorizing gangs whose status symbols were German and Nazi insignia. In the mid-1960s, motorcycle gangs appropriated those Nazi elements, intermixing them with lawlessness and random violence. The more notorious of the groups were the Pagans of Newark and Washington, D.C., the Misfits of New York, the Aliens of Queens, the Deuces of Cleveland, and most disreputable of all, Hell's Angels and Satan's Slaves of California. The leader of the Cleveland Deuces used to call himself Adolf Hitler; the Misfits used to parade in Jewish areas shouting "Heil Hitler!"

A police raid on a Greenwich Village apartment in 1966 uncovered hundreds of thousands of dollars of stolen goods, burglars' tools, marijuana, pornographic photographs and films, torture devices, and Nazi literature and paraphernalia. The apartment itself was decorated with Hitler's photograph and a huge Nazi flag. One of the arrested men, a German-born naturalized American citizen, belonged to Hell's Angels. These motorcycle gangs disturbingly recalled the motorcycle cult of pre-Hitler Germany, the uprooted and jobless men of the Free Corps, the toughs, drinkers, and brawlers, with a yen for pornography and blood, who became the brawn of Hitler's first army, the brown-shirted Storm Troopers. Hell's Angels have been described as desperate men, without education, jobs, status, above all without a future: "In a world increasingly geared to specialists, technicians, and fantastically complicated machinery, the Hell's Angels are obvious losers, and it bugs them."*

That same year, 1966, a most bizarre crime came to trial in Chester, England. A 27-year-old store clerk, Ian Brady, and his 23-year-old girl friend, Esther Myra Hindley, a stenographer, had been arraigned on charges of having murdered, in a two-year period, a 17-year-old boy, a 12-year-old boy, and a 10-year-old girl, and of having buried their bodies on the desolate moors. The case became known as the Moors Murders and attracted national attention. The English novelist and critic Pamela Hansford Johnson was asked by the *Sunday Telegraph* to write her impressions of the trial.†

Brady and Hindley committed the murders for no other purpose than their own pleasure. They were acting out the fantasies about which they had read in works by the Marquis de Sade and other sadomasochistic writers. The victimized children had been tortured and sexually abused, photographed in pornographic poses, their screams and pleas for mercy tape-recorded. Finally they were murdered and buried.

The house near the moors where Brady and Hindley satisfied their cravings for blood, erotica, and murder had a library of some fifty books, which Miss Johnson categorized as (1) sadomasochistic (e.g., *The History of Corporal Punishment, Orgies of Torture and Brutality, Sex Crimes and Sex Criminals, The Life and Ideas of the Marquis de Sade*); (2) titillatory (e.g., *Sexual Anomalies and Perversions, Cradle of Erotica, Kiss of the Whip*); and (3) books

---

* Hunter S. Thompson, *Hell's Angels: A Strange and Terrible Saga* (New York: Random House, 1967).

† Pamela Hansford Johnson, *On Iniquity: Some Reflections Arising out of the Moors Murder Trial* (New York: Scribner's, 1967).

on Nazism and Fascism, including a copy of *Mein Kampf* and two self-teaching German manuals.

Miss Johnson described the attraction that Nazism had for both Brady and Hindley. Brady, even as a schoolboy, was said to have been obsessed with Nazism, often playing records of Hitler's speeches. That obsession continued to grip him, for on his first date with Myra Hindley he took her to a film of the Nuremberg rallies. As for Hindley, she kept in her room a picture of Irma Grese, the highest-ranking SS woman in Auschwitz, hanged in 1945 as a war criminal. Grese, according to an Auschwitz survivor, was "the most depraved, cruel, imaginative sexual pervert" that she had ever encountered.

The relationship between the Brady collection of sado-masochistic literature and the murders which Brady and Hindley committed led Miss Johnson to discuss our "Affect-less Society." This was a term she used to describe a society in which boredom sparks the search for gratification in sex and violence, in which sadomasochistic adventures lead not only to the atrophy of moral sensibility but also to the very triumph of evil accomplished. Miss Johnson cited a passage from de Sade's *Juliette* which was read at the Moors trial, a passage upon which Brady used to brood:

> Destruction is Nature's method of progress, and she prompts the murderer to destruction, so that his action shall be the same as plague or famine. . . . In a word, murder is a horror, but a horror often necessary, never criminal, and essential to tolerate in a republic.

It was not inconceivable, Miss Johnson argued, that this passage might have provided Brady and Hindley with precisely the rationale and self-justification they needed to commit their tortures and murders.

Miss Johnson's book, published in 1967, was uncannily

prophetic. In 1969, in Los Angeles, members of Charles Manson's "family" killed seven people in a blood-steeped orgy of savagery and sadism. One victim was stabbed a dozen times, another forty times, a third more than fifty times. Charles Manson, a common criminal and a freaked-out drug addict, was also a cult leader manipulating sex to attract and keep his followers. Believing himself to be both Satan and Jesus, he advocated murder as part of a crazy scheme to set off a national massacre, after which he would become the country's ruler. Besides the sex, drugs, sadism, violence, and murder, there was also ideology. Though he was barely literate, Manson claimed to have read Nietzsche. He believed, he said, in a "master race." He admired Hitler, often speaking of him as a model, instructing his followers that "Hitler had the best answer to everything," that Hitler was a "tuned-in guy who leveled the karma of the Jews." In one interview, Manson showed an explicit anti-Jewish streak, and during one of his trials he often wore a Storm Trooper's black uniform.*

Lurid sex and violence have traditionally accompanied Nazism. George Steiner, commenting on the relations between pornography and Nazism in the course of reviewing *The Olympia Reader*, a literary-pornographic cornucopia, argued:

> That those who turn to Sade, to books on torture or to the interminable floggings and humiliations detailed in a number of Olympia Press publications *also* dream of Hitler and the beauteous SS, of pogroms and the sexual torment of children is an obvious yet profoundly disturbing truth. . . . It makes it doubly important that we reexamine the political,

* All details from Vincent Bugliosi, *Helter Skelter: The True Story of the Manson Murders* (New York: Norton, 1974), especially pp. 296–317, 633–638.

psychological, social aspects of "total freedom" of publication at this particular time and place. "Total freedom" of publication includes Streicher on the need to castrate all Jews; or any flysheet instructing us of the racial inferiority and sexual aggressiveness of Negroes or West Indians.*

In a prophetic essay written in 1952, shortly before his death, Lewis Corey traced the influence of de Sade and his philosophy of perversion among nineteenth- and twentieth-century writers, artists, and intellectuals who "were overwhelmingly *anti-humanist, anti-liberal, and anti-democratic*" (italics in original), and among self-styled revolutionary elites who thought themselves superior to the "vulgar herd" and whose sexual violence and despotism became intermingled with political violence and despotism.† The Italian decadents, Corey pointed out, turned to Mussolini; the artistic and literary cults turned to Hitler. "The Nazi elites," Corey wrote, "were adepts in the practices of sadism, from homosexuality to lust-murder. Their concentration camps became a kind of 'public brothel' where sadistic practices flourished, including hypochorematophily [sic], necrophilia, and anthropophagy."

We have heard a good deal in the last decade about the liberating properties of pornography. Purveyors and consumers alike, it is said, learn to free themselves of false modesty and inhibiting morality; expression is open, spontaneous, fresh, innocent, etc., etc. But we hear little of the debilitating effects of pornography and its political implications. So long as pornography is a private pursuit, it is a

* George Steiner, in *The Times Literary Supplement*, May 26, 1966; see also Steiner's "Pornography and the Consequences," *Encounter* (March 1966):46–47.
† Lewis Corey, "Marquis de Sade—the Cult of Despotism," *Antioch Review* (Spring 1966):17–31.

matter of individual and private morality, of interest and concern primarily to the prurient and/or the puritanical. But when pornography goes public, it produces "a truly pagan *Kulturpolitik*," to use the words of a bureaucrat in Goebbels's Propaganda Ministry. The deluge of sadomasochistic, sexually titillating, and violence-glorifying books, magazines, and movies, many of which draw upon the Nazi experience, cannot be without effect. Pornography is not cathartic because it is not art, whatever pretentious claims may be made in its behalf. Pornographic works are merely bad art, repetitive, banal, and cruel, and they can succeed only in dulling and deadening any sense of human worth, joy, or pain; in rendering brutality, sexual deviation, and scatology commonplace and habitual; in making its consumers affectless.

Pornography affects not only morality; it also affects morale. It releases infantile desires and fantasies, disconnecting the dreamer from reality, and is thus admirably suited to undermining a community's morale. When the Germans invaded Poland in 1939, Miss Johnson noted, they flooded the bookstores with pornography. In 1940, Reich Minister of Propaganda Josef Goebbels conceived a plan to turn the French against the English, proposing at a meeting of his department chiefs to fake a "pornographic diary" of an English prisoner of war, with a detailed and salacious account of his bedroom adventures in Paris with the wives, sisters, and sweethearts of French soldiers who were at the front. This pornographic document, in pamphlet form, was to be dropped by the Luftwaffe on concentrations of French troops.* Whether the "diary" was ever used, I cannot say. Curt Riess, in his biography of Goebbels, refers to porno-

---

* Sefton Delmer (British Psychological Warfare), "The Secret Minutes of Dr. Goebbels," *The Times Literary Supplement*, November 9, 1967.

graphic photographs and letters circulated among French soldiers immobilized on the Maginot Line. The Germans were not alone in these efforts to demoralize the French; the French Communists assisted them, since the Soviet Union was then Germany's ally.

Pornography and Nazism have mutually reinforced each other over the decades. The antihumanists and sadists were those who helped to create and develop Fascism and Nazism. Those movements, in turn, bred new generations of antihumanists and sadists, providing ever-increasing audiences for the consumption of pornography, plain and political. Today a sizable population views the Third Reich's terrors and murders only through a prism of pornography. Their loss of moral affect becomes a loss of political affect. Morally dulled, they become more vulnerable to the appeal of antihumanist movements and eventually more receptive to the obscenity of anti-Semitism.

15

IN HITLER'S SERVICE:
Albert Speer

THE ABLEST AND "LEAST CORRUPTED" member of Hitler's
court—thus did H. R. Trevor-Roper characterize Albert
Speer, Hitler's architect and wartime minister of armaments.
Sentenced at Nuremberg to twenty years' imprisonment for
his use of concentration camp labor and his deportation of
foreign workers, released from prison in 1966, Speer is now
one of the last survivors of Hitler's court. His memoirs,
Inside the Third Reich (New York: Macmillan, 1970),
drafted surreptitiously during the years he was imprisoned
in Spandau, present a view of that court—its routine com-
monplaces and its diabolical intrigues—that no other work
has yet offered. His prison notes, *Spandau: The Secret Diaries*
(New York: Macmillan, 1976), supplement the memoirs
with more recollections of the days of power, now viewed
from the perspective of Nuremberg, and with sardonic
accounts of his fellow prisoners, those eminences of the
German dictatorship who, like him, escaped hanging by the
Allied Military Tribunal.

By family background and upbringing, Speer would not have seemed a likely candidate for Hitler's retinue. He was born in Wilhelmine Germany (Mannheim, 1905) into wealth and high social status. His father and grandfather were architects. Politics at home were liberal, his father was an eager subscriber to the *Frankfurter Zeitung*. Speer attended the best private schools, read poetry, enjoyed music, climbed German mountains, and paddled German rivers. In 1927 he received his architect's license from the Institute of Technology in Berlin and the following spring, at twenty-three, he became the Institute's youngest teaching assistant.

The Berlin Institute was meanwhile becoming a center of Nazi propaganda and activity. In 1930, Speer's students persuaded him to attend a student meeting where he would hear Adolf Hitler speak. The experience turned out to be decisive. A few weeks later, Speer applied to the Nazi Party for membership, and in January 1931 he was accepted. His activity as a Nazi began with an unpaid assignment to decorate district party headquarters in Berlin; then he did Goebbels's ministry and home. In July 1933 came another critical juncture in Speer's life, the assignment to design the architectural background for the first party rally in Nuremberg. Hitler himself approved Speer's sketches at a brief impersonal encounter, during which it appears he took a liking to the young architect; soon thereafter, Hitler recommended that Speer assist Paul Ludwig Troost in redoing the chancellor's residence in Berlin. The rest followed swiftly. Invited into the inner circle, Speer was seated at Hitler's side at dinner; at twenty-eight, he had been propelled into the very center of power in Germany. Remembering that period, Speer writes: "For the commission to do a great building, I would have sold my soul like Faust. Now I had found my Mephistopheles."

Speer spent much of the next eight years in Hitler's

company—he became his personal architect after Troost's death in 1933—satisfying Hitler's megalomania by designing buildings and monuments of monstrous proportions for the Thousand Year Reich. Once the war began, Speer naturally became involved in the problems of the entire German construction industry and developed a working relationship with Fritz Todt, minister of armaments and munitions. In February 1942, after Todt's death in a mysterious plane crash and a month before Speer's thirty-seventh birthday, Hitler appointed him as Todt's successor. In September 1943 his authority was expanded; he became minister of armaments and war production, one of Nazi Germany's most powerful men.

What kind of man was Speer? The portrait that emerges from his memoirs and diaries reveals ambition and haughtiness, with talents that matched the avarice of his ambition and the indulgence of his narcissism. Even as an inexperienced young man, unfamiliar with the exercise of power and dazzled by his own swift elevation, Speer contrived to keep apart from the other members of Hitler's court. His origins, his class, his education combined to make him contemptuous of the stupid, the bunglers, the blunderers. Besides, Hitler had chosen him personally. Speer now says that he was not interested in politics. He was an architect, an artist. He was admitted into Hitler's entourage not as a Nazi, not as a politician seeking power, but on his own merit, so to speak. For years he stood aside from the court intrigues, detached and superior. Only after he became a minister did he take part—for the good of Germany, he asserts—in the Byzantine machinations of the court.

Speer's self-esteem, his need to stand apart from, and above, the other Nazi leaders, manifested itself at the Nuremberg trial. Whereas the other defendants chose to shift blame for the acts of Nazi Germany to the now dead and vanished, Speer, dissociating himself from Hitler's entourage, publicly assumed a share of responsibility (although like the others he pleaded "not guilty"). His assumption of responsibility reflected not only the creditable pride inherent in an attitude of noblesse oblige but also, I believe, Speer's lifelong ambition to appear more honorable than his colleagues, to appear, indeed, *the* most honorable of the Nazi leaders. Even in Spandau, Speer continued to separate himself from his colleagues, to see himself as the only one among the remnants of Hitler's court who could and did admit that the Nazi universe was not only irrecoverable but also irredeemable.

Speer emerges from his memoirs above all as Hitler's man, eagerly submissive to that indescribable yet irresistible magnetism, until the very end elated by Hitler's praise and distressed by his reproaches. If Hitler had had the capacity for friendship, Speer said at Nuremberg, he would have been his friend. The only place in his memoirs where Speer reveals his emotions is in the account of his reaction to news of Hitler's death—news that he had been expecting. Unpacking his suitcase, he found Hitler's framed portrait: "When I stood the photograph up, a fit of weeping overcame me." In the twenty years in Spandau, haunted by Hitler, Speer sought an explanation, a justification for the thrall in which his Führer held him. In the third year of his imprisonment, sensing that he no longer felt loyalty to Hitler, Speer asked rhetorically, "Is that betrayal?" In the eighteenth year he came to blame Hitler for his condition. "Hitler accorded me," Speer wrote on January 30, 1964, marking the thirty-first anniversary of the Nazi accession to power, "my triumphs, acquaintanceship with power and fame—but he also destroyed everything for me." Thus Speer lifted from his own shoulders the burden of responsibility for Nazi crimes which he had so gallantly assumed at Nuremberg and thrust it back upon his once beloved, now betrayed, Führer.

Not before February 1945 did Speer begin to realize that in defeat Hitler was prepared to let Germany be destroyed, historic buildings and all.* Only then did he begin to extricate himself from Hitler's mesmeric power. In the last cataclysmic days of the war he rushed about Germany, countermanding Hitler's scorched-earth policy, trying to salvage what could be salvaged of Germany's industry and transportation as a basis for postwar survival. On April 16, 1945, he wrote an appeal to the German people—never delivered, because of his still lingering loyalty to Hitler—to put a halt to Hitler's destructive policies. The appeal concluded:

> The military blows which Germany has received during the last few months have been shattering. Our fate is no longer in our own hands. Only a more merciful Providence can change our prospects for the future. We ourselves, however, can help save ourselves not only by going about our work industriously, facing the enemy with dignity and self-confidence, but also by becoming more modest in our hearts, by practicing self-criticism, and by believing unshakably in the future of our nation, which will remain forever and always.

That was Speer's personal credo. The course he wanted Germany to choose was one he chose for himself. His memoirs are a vehicle for self-criticism, practiced in the mode of emotional austerity. "My moral failure," he concludes the memoirs, "is not a matter of this item or that; it resides in

---

* Speer himself was not without a streak of nihilism. Berlin set aflame by Allied air raids entranced him. "No doubt about it, this apocalypse provided a magnificent spectacle."

my active association with the whole course of events."
No confessional repentance. No plea for forgiveness. No
"fit of weeping."

What of the Jews and their annihilation by the German
state in which Speer wielded such great power? Speer in
his memoirs says that he did not know. But not quite. In
an exercise of Ciceronian preterition, Speer says he will no
longer say that he did not know even though "it is true that
I did not know what was really beginning on November 9,
1938 [*Kristallnacht*], and what ended in Auschwitz and
Maidanek." He himself was no anti-Semite nor did he ever
become one, Speer writes, but "Hitler's hatred for the Jews
seemed to me so much a matter of course that I gave it no
serious thought." Yet hardly any of Hitler's anti-Semitic
remarks remained in his memory: "In those hundreds of
tea-times . . . Hitler scarcely ever said anything about the
Jews, about his domestic opponents, let alone about the
necessity of setting up concentration camps." As a matter of
fact, Hitler's published table-talk and Goebbels's diary
indicate that he said a lot about the Jews, and on days when
Speer was present. Perhaps Speer did not listen, shutting
out of his awareness first those spoken words, later those
overt acts of the *Kristallnacht* that he himself characterized
as "the vulgar business of carrying out a policy proclaimed
in the anti-Semitic slogans printed on streamers over the
entrances to towns." He was too fastidious for such "vulgar
business."

But in the seventh year at Spandau, still entangled in
Hitler's toils, Speer recalled that on a walk alone with Hitler
late in 1942 in Berchtesgaden, Hitler began to rant about
the Jews. He blamed the Jews for World War I, for the
armistice, for the stab in the back. "The Jews," Hitler raved,
"made me go into politics." Never before, Speer remarked

in his diary, had he realized how absolutely essential the figure of the Jews was for Hitler.

But Speer disclaimed and continued to disclaim knowledge of Hitler's ideas, plans, and program to destroy the Jews. At Nuremberg, Justice Jackson cross-examined Speer about his use of slave labor and his knowledge of anti-Jewish policies. "I knew that the National Socialist Party was anti-Semitic, and I knew that the Jews were being evacuated from Germany," Speer replied, denying further knowledge or complicity. When asked what he did know, Speer testified that when he took office in February 1942, the party was demanding the removal of Jews still working in armaments factories. Because he desperately needed labor, Speer convinced Party Secretary Bormann to issue a circular permitting Jews to continue at this work and extending protection to their employers from political denunciation. That situation lasted until September or October 1942, Speer said, when Hitler "insisted emphatically" that the Jews be removed, and gave orders to that effect. Still, Speer managed to keep the Jews on in factories until March 1943, when they "finally did have to get out." This admission was elicited by a document presented by the prosecution, in the form of a letter written by Fritz Sauckel, plenipotentiary for the allocation of labor, Speer's colleague under Hitler and his co-defendant at Nuremberg.* The letter read:

At the end of February, the Reichsführer SS [Himmler], in agreement with myself and the Reich Minister for Armaments and Munitions, for reasons of state security, has removed from the places of work all Jews who were still working freely and not in camps, and either transferred them to a labor corps or collected them for removal.

* Implicated in the misuse of Jewish concentration camp inmates, Sauckel was hanged in Nuremberg prison, October 16, 1946.

A year later, just two weeks after the German intervention in Hungary, Speer asked for 100,000 Hungarian Jews as forced laborers. Hungary was then the only country where Jews still survived in substantial numbers. (He must surely have known then that the European Jews had suffered some terrible fate.) In a letter to Hitler arguing his case, Speer complained that Sauckel was unwilling to use the Hungarian Jews. Although conceding that the presence of Jews was disturbing also to him personally, Speer emphasized that this was an emergency, and that since the Jews were in concentration camps, using them would not offend the sensibility of the German people.*

In his memoirs Speer recalled that his old friend Kárl Hanke, then *Gauleiter* of Lower Silesia, warned him in the summer of 1944 never, under any circumstances, to accept an invitation to a concentration camp in Upper Silesia. "He had seen something there which he was not permitted to describe and moreover could not describe." Speer, now believing that his friend was referring to Auschwitz, criticizes himself for not having tried to find out what was happening there.

Auschwitz served two competitive but also mutually reinforcing purposes, mass murder and slave labor. The slave labor installation was the I. G. Farben Buna works, designated as Auschwitz III (Auschwitz I was the base camp; Auschwitz II was the main killing center). Of the 35,000 slave laborers who were brought there, at least 25,000 died; a worker's life expectancy ranged from one to four months. Extant documents show that Speer knew a lot about Auschwitz III. It was thus impossible for him not to have known about Auschwitz II.

---

* From a Speer file, Bundesarchiv of Koblenz, summarized in Eugene Davidson, *The Trial of the Germans* (New York: Macmillan, 1966), p. 497.

Both mass murder and slave labor were in the jurisdiction of the SS, under Himmler. Mass murder was an enterprise of the SS security department, headed by Reinhard Heydrich and, after his assassination, by Ernst Kaltenbrunner.* Slave labor was the business of the SS economic and administrative department, headed by Oswald Pohl.† In the normal course of his work, Speer had frequent contacts with Pohl and one of his staff, Hans Kammler, head of the construction division.‡ Kammler had distinguished himself by fanatical ambition in all his undertakings: he had built the installations at Auschwitz—the gas chambers, the synthetic rubber plant (Buna works), the sewage system. Speer remarks that in both career and methodology Kammler was his mirror image, and that he "rather liked his objective coolness." But Speer omits to say anything about his conference with Pohl and Kammler on September 15, 1942, or about developments thereafter.§

The SS, always ambitious to extend its enterprises, had put two items on the agenda for this conference: enlarging the camp at Auschwitz III in view of the "eastern migration" (this was at the peak of the mass deportations from Poland), and "taking over complete armament tasks of major proportions by the concentration camps." As to the first item, Speer approved the purchase of building materials to construct

* One of Speer's co-defendants, hanged in Nuremberg prison, October 16, 1946.
† Condemned to death in the trial of the Concentration-Camp Central Administration at Nuremberg, November 3, 1947; executed June 8, 1951.
‡ Speer describes Heydrich and Kammler as if they were twin Rover Boys: "Both Reinhard Heydrich and Hans Kammler were blond, blue-eyed, long-headed, always neatly dressed, and well bred." Speer says that he never read *Mein Kampf*, but he must have learned from Hans F. K. Gunther's *Rassenkunde* that the cephalic index of the Nordic race was around 75—that is, long-headed.
§ For sources and analysis, I am indebted to Raul Hilberg, *The Destruction of the European Jews* (Chicago: Quadrangle, 1967).

300 barracks for 132,000 inmates. As to the second, which was more complicated, Speer at first thought the SS security department should take some 50,000 Jews out of the free economy and send them into concentration camps. But nothing came of the whole plan because Speer later decided, after an inspection tour of the Mauthausen concentration camp, that the SS construction plans were too extravagant. On April 5, 1943, Speer wrote to Himmler that since he could not supply the necessary building materials, the SS should henceforth apply the principle of *Primitivbauweise* (primitive construction)—meaning that concentration camp inmates should work with their bare hands and cheap materials. In a later letter, Speer complained to Himmler about the inefficiency of slave labor: the inmates were dropping dead too fast, particularly in Auschwitz.

From the Nuremberg Trial until today, Speer has insisted that he knew nothing of the murder of the Jews. The evidence which I have cited from Speer's records, found among the captured German documents, disprove his innocence. Now Heinrich Himmler himself has provided irrefutable corroboration of Speer's complicitous knowledge.* Speer and Himmler both addressed a meeting of *Reichsleiter* and *Gauleiter* of the Nazi Party, convened in Posen on October 6, 1943. In his memoirs Speer described how he lectured the assembled officials on the priorities of armaments production, but he did not mention Himmler's presence or Himmler's speech at that meeting. But Himmler, in his speech, addressed some remarks directly to Speer, probably turning to him, seated on the platform among the dignitaries.

---

* See the important article by Erich Goldhagen, "Albert Speer, Himmler, and the Secrecy of the Final Solution," *Midstream* 17 (October 1971):43–50. Goldhagen here translated a substantial extract from a hitherto unpublished speech by Himmler.

What did Himmler speak of on that occasion? As in his most notorious speech, delivered two days earlier to top SS officials, Himmler here expatiated on the destruction of the Jews:

> I ask you really only to hear and never to talk about what I tell you in this circle. The question arose: What should be done with the women and children? I decided here too to adopt a clear solution. I did not deem myself justified in exterminating the men, that is to say, to kill them or to let them be killed, while allowing their children to grow up to avenge themselves on our sons and grandchildren. The hard decision had to be taken: *This people must disappear from the face of the earth.*

A few minutes later, Himmler described the difficulties he had had in "clearing" the Jewish ghettos, because the German heads of the defense enterprises using ghetto slave labor had complained that the annihilation of the Jews was interfering with the war economy. "Of course," Himmler continued, turning to Speer, "all this has nothing to do with Comrade Speer, you cannot do anything about it. It is those alleged defense enterprises that Comrade Speer and I jointly will clean out during the coming weeks and months."

Wittingly or unwittingly, Speer erased Himmler's talk from his mind, consigning it to the same oblivion which he reserved for all other uncomfortable memories, especially those touching on the Jews. How else could he present himself as a man of honor? In an interview in 1971, asked what he would have done then, in those days, had he known about the murder of the Jews, Speer replied that that was a question whose "answer does not help me to sleep at night." But his diary does not mention sleepless nights for this reason. Indeed, though Speer recounts some of his bad dreams at Spandau, none was ever about Auschwitz.

In 1944 the London *Observer* characterized Speer as the "very epitome of the 'managerial revolution,' " symbolizing the "pure technician . . . with no other original aim than to make his way in the world and no other means than his technical and managerial ability." It is the image in which Speer has chosen to cast himself—the technician, without politics, without loyalties, morally neutral, devoted only to his machines and his technical tasks. But this is an incomplete and self-serving portrait. In the case of Speer, it is cited to insulate him from the emotional shock of Nuremberg and to obscure the roots of his attraction to the Nazi movement and his passionate attachment to Hitler.

In his final statement at Nuremberg, Speer turned modern technology into an accomplice of the Hitler regime. Hitler's dictatorship, he said, was the first to have "made complete use of all technical means in a perfect manner for the domination of its nation." The radio and the loudspeaker, he charged, deprived 80 million people of independent thought—the most exaggerated claim yet made for the mass media. And he warned, "Today the danger of being terrorized by technocracy threatens every country in the world." Thus was technology made to share responsibility with German leadership for crimes against humanity.

To be sure, technical advances and scientific discoveries have increased the potentialities for human destruction in general. But in thinking about how the Jews were killed, one marvels less at the sophisticated technical facilities (there were none) available to the murderers than at human determination: Heydrich's mobile killing battalions murdered about 1 million Jews with rifles and machine guns alone. Nor can it be claimed that the installations at Auschwitz, Bełżec, or Majdanek represented a significant technological innovation, scientifically speaking. Not the craft of the machine but the cunning of the mind was responsible for

Nazi Germany's rationalized and bureaucratic system of murder.

Speer endured the procession of endless days in Spandau in self-discipline and self-pity. He has, he believes, done his penance; he feels that his case should be closed. Of this he has convinced a vast reading public which has credulously swallowed his account, taken in by his boundless vanity, trusting his distortions and misrepresentations.* As we have seen with regard to the Jews, the Speer that emerges from the memoirs and the diaries is not the historic Speer, because Speer the memoirist has concealed and suppressed the truth. The historic Speer—the man who truly existed in the past, not the self-serving present recreation—was a man who exploited millions of enslaved human beings without humane or ethical considerations. *That* Speer was convicted of crimes against humanity and sentenced to twenty years in prison. He has served his sentence, but he can never erase his past.

---

* The only other critical evaluation of Speer's memoirs that I know of is by Geoffrey Barraclough, "Hitler's Master Builder," *The New York Review of Books*, January 7, 1971.

16

AN OBEDIENT KILLER:
Franz Stangl,
Commandant of Treblinka

IN 1942, SS *Hauptsturmführer* Franz Stangl became commandant of Treblinka, an annihilation camp in German-occupied Poland where an estimated 800,000 Jews were murdered. Before that, he had been commandant at Sobibór, also an annihilation camp in Poland. There a quarter of a million Jews were murdered. Stangl qualified for those posts because of his experience as police superintendent at one of the euphemistically titled "euthanasia" stations, where the National Socialist German government murdered defective and mentally ill "Aryan" Germans, regarding them as "racially valueless material" and consequently as "unworthy life."

After the war, Stangl was arrested by U.S. Army intelligence officers who identified him merely as an SS officer. When his connection with the "euthanasia" program was uncovered, he was transferred in 1947 from the internment camp to a prison in Linz, but he escaped on May 30, 1948, making his way to Rome. There high-ranking Catholic clergy provided him with identity papers which they had obtained from the Red Cross. Stangl then went to Syria, where his family soon joined him. They prospered in Damascus, but moved to Brazil in 1951, eventually settling in a São Paulo suburb, enjoying a normal middle-class life. In February 1967, having been traced and located through the tireless efforts of Simon Wiesenthal, Stangl was arrested by Brazilian police at the request of the Austrian government. In June 1967 he was extradited to Germany to stand trial there as a war criminal.

The trial began May 1970 in Düsseldorf. Stangl was charged with responsibility for the murder of 400,000 Jews at Treblinka during the time he was commandant. Denying guilt for any wrongdoing, Stangl persisted in protesting his innocence. "The Lord God knows me," he said in his closing statement in December 1970, "and my conscience does not condemn me." The court ruled otherwise. Stangl was found guilty as charged and was sentenced to life imprisonment. He appealed the sentence. On June 28, 1971, awaiting the outcome of his appeal in a Düsseldorf prison, he died of a heart attack, having already had a coronary in 1966.

During April and June 1971, when he was in prison, Stangl was interviewed for about seventy hours by Gitta Sereny, a journalist living in London. The book which she composed is the product of those interviews, augmented by conversations with Stangl's wife and a host of other people who knew him, worked with him, or were survivors of Treblinka.* A mélange of personal journalism and pop history, the trifling mixed with the significant, the book talks too much yet in the end tells too little.

---

* Gitta Sereny, *Into That Darkness: From Mercy Killing to Mass Murder* (New York: McGraw-Hill, 1974).

To be sure, the commandant of Treblinka is a subject worthy of a book whose objective, as Sereny herself put it, would be "to penetrate the personality of a man who had been intimately involved with the most total evil our age has produced." Yet that objective was not attained because Sereny has given us little more than the naked raw material of Stangl's conversation—lies interwoven with truth—without the corrective depth of historical perspective, without the unsentimental focus of psychiatric analysis. Her method is affable discussion; her approach, as she indicates, the "open mind," whatever that may mean in an encounter with a man responsible and culpable for the murder of more than half a million men, women, and children. (The personal affability developed into a personal relationship. Sereny says that Stangl came to regard her as his friend, whereas she, definitely not seeing herself as his friend, nonetheless once even brought him a special soup that he liked.)

Sereny seems to have had fantasies of bringing Stangl to confront his deeds and confess his guilt. This was apparently a sort of rescue fantasy: she envisioned herself as saving his immortal soul and redeeming him for all eternity, like a character in a Dostoyevsky novel.

Intent on her Dostoyevskian ploy, Sereny tells us that on two occasions Stangl expressed guilt. "I must acknowledge my guilt," he said when he was describing his first involvement with the Nazi police apparatus in his native Austria, immediately after *Anschluss* early in 1938. "I should have killed myself in 1938." Later, at the end of the last interview and the day before he died, Stangl said: "My guilt is that I am still here. . . . I should have died. That was my guilt." In both instances the expression of guilt hangs limply in the air, without reference, without specificity, without context. Yet Sereny closes her book with a melodramatic flourish: "I think he died because he had finally, however briefly, faced himself and told the truth; it was a monumental effort to reach that fleeting moment when he became the man he should have been." Thus, in a triumph of sentimentality over reality, Sereny conferred a posthumous humanity upon a man who had dehumanized himself.

Stangl's statements were, however, no expression of guilt, but merely attempts to please, to be liked. He knew that Sereny wanted him to admit guilt, even though that precisely was what he had been denying all his life. Would this man, who for twenty-five years had eluded the police, who had lived an ordinary life despite his career as a mass murderer, who had remained unrepentant and unconfessing throughout his trial—would this man jeopardize his court appeal, prejudice his legal case, risk his last opportunity for freedom? But by saying "I'm guilty, I wish I were dead," without specifying what he was guilty of or remorseful for, he ventured nothing. That statement, he doubtless shrewdly calculated, would please the nice lady. Besides, it was appropriate to the whining self-pity and the tears he occasionally shed—for himself only, never for his victims.

Admission of guilt means acceptance of culpability and responsibility for one's acts, self-reproach for having committed a sin or a crime. Once in the course of these interviews Stangl addressed himself directly to the question of responsibility. Sereny recorded his statement without comment or explication: "I am responsible only to myself and my God. Only I know what I did of my own free will. And for that I can answer to my God. What I did without, or against my free will, for that I need not answer." Stangl had said the same thing in his closing statement at his trial. The meaning was unmistakable. He held himself innocent of wrongdoing and would take no responsibility for acts which he committed in obedience to orders. As for autonomous acts, that was no one's business but his own, between him and his God, as he put it. The statement reveals a man without moral or religious standards by which to distinguish right from wrong, for whom obedience to authority is the highest morality, even when that authority commands him to commit mass murder. Stangl's words conjure up an image of an automaton, programmed for obedience, ready to kill at the flick of the switch. The Germans have a word for this: *Kadavergehorsam*, corpselike obedience.

Stangl was *Kadavergehorsam*, a passive man who did what his superiors asked of him, always eager to please those in authority. He was always taking jobs he said he did not want, always working under people whom he did not like or whom he even feared, always submissive, never refusing, never backing out, never dissenting, never objecting. Even in Düsseldorf prison he tried to please. The prison staff, Sereny noted, "*liked* him," stressing what she thought was an incongruity.

Stangl's wife and daughters liked him too. Like Rudolf Höss, the commandant of Auschwitz, and like many other SS killers, Stangl was a good family man. Stangl's wife, whom Sereny interviewed and sentimentalized, must have suited him well. When she first learned from one of Stangl's assistants about the kind of work her husband did at Sobibór, "her thoughts were in a whirl." She confronted Stangl in hysteria and that night, she told Sereny, "I couldn't bear him to touch me." Still, several days later, she admitted, she "let him again." Höss's wife seems to have had more human feeling. Höss told a psychiatrist that after his wife found out what he was doing, "we rarely had desire for intercourse."

An obedient man, a kind man, Stangl was also an efficient man. He had been transferred from Sobibór to Treblinka to bring order out of the indescribable chaos that had overtaken the incumbent commandant, unable to cope with the mass arrivals of some 200,000 Jews from the Warsaw ghetto within a month. Everywhere in Treblinka bodies lay decomposing and putrefying in the open. Germans walked knee-deep in Jewish clothing, goods, and money. Everywhere the nauseating smell of death saturated the air. But Stangl was a veritable Hercules in the Himmlerian stables, and it did not take him long to tidy up Treblinka. He brought system and order into the killing process. A year later, when it was all over, the Jews murdered, their possessions distributed according to detailed specifications to various German state and party institutions, Stangl was one of those SS functionaries whose services Himmler acknowledged by bestowing upon him the *Kriegsverdienstkreuz*, the War Cross of Merit.

Stangl was a quick study and a good learner in the school of murder, combining the functions of the "desk murderer" —arranging the schedules and handling administrative matters associated with that large killing enterprise—and chief executioner, supervising the actual annihilation process and its sequences. Not only had he been inoculated with National Socialist ideology to sustain and justify his acts, but he had also been armed with the psychological and linguistic mechanisms to deflect guilt and reinforce denial. "A transport," Stangl told Sereny, "was normally dealt with in two or three hours." That sentence is a paradigm of Nazi-Deutsch vocabulary and syntax. The noun "transport," vague and abstract, conceals the terrible reality: 5,000 exhausted and terrified Jewish men, women, and children arrive at Treblinka's railroad ramps, having traveled for long hours, often days, sometimes even weeks, penned in like cattle, without water, without sanitary facilities. Stangl in his white riding clothes, his SS men, and their Ukrainian helpers greet the Jews upon their arrival, whipping them toward their destination in the gas chambers. "To deal with" is a vague

and nonspecific verb which in Nazi-Deutsch became an
esoteric or euphemistic word for murdering, nearly always
used in the passive construction. Thus, no agent was responsible for the murdering—the murders appeared to be an act
of nature. Stangl's description of his morning's work stands
in stark juxtaposition to the rest of his remarks, as he described to Sereny his daily routine at Treblinka:

> A transport was normally dealt with in two or three hours.
> At 12 I had lunch—yes, we usually had meat, potatoes,
> some fresh vegetables such as cauliflowers—we grew them
> ourselves quite soon—and after lunch I had about half an
> hour's rest.

Still, though Stangl remained without guilt and without
remorse for his deeds, without pity for his victims, he had
not entirely succeeded in repressing the horror attendant
upon the enterprise in which he had been engaged. In
response to Sereny's questions he admitted that he had
never thought of those hundreds of thousands of people he
had murdered as human beings. He then recalled an experience in Brazil. He had been riding on a train that had stopped
next to a slaughterhouse. The cattle in the pens stared up
into the train. "I thought then," Stangl said, " 'look at this;
this reminds me of Poland; that's just how the people looked,
trustingly, just before they went into the tins.' . . . I couldn't
eat tinned meat after that." Though he denied his responsibility and guilt, he could not quite suppress his physical
revulsion and horror for the killings. Yet he mastered that
horror by displacing the memory of human beings with the
image of penned animals awaiting slaughter.

In the twenty-five years since he had murdered hundreds
of thousands of Jews, Stangl seemingly retained his prewar
notions about them; SS indoctrination had been so thorough

that his mind remained impenetrable to any conception of the Jews grounded in historical reality. What was the reason, Sereny asked him, for the annihilation of the Jews? Twice he gave exactly the same reflexive reply: "They wanted the Jews' money." Astonished by Sereny's disbelief, Stangl reassured her: "But of course. Have you any idea of the fantastic sums that were involved? That's how the steel in Sweden was bought." The bare statement, totally devoid of moral sensibility, suggests the peak of the iceberg, hinting at the seven-eighths substratum of anti-Semitism still in Stangl's mind.

In National Socialist ideology the Jews were regarded as racial enemies who, as a biological menace to the existence of the "Aryan" Greater Reich, had to be destroyed. Believing that Jewish possessions had anyway been unfairly wrested from the "Aryans" by cunning and deceit, the National Socialists thus justified themselves as the legatees of Jewish property. Stangl's explanation about the reason for killing the Jews indicates that he still clung to his old ideas about Jews, but would say only what he thought would be acceptable. He was shrewd enough to realize that Sereny, whom he wished to please, would be displeased if he disclosed the ideological infrastructure, as it were, of his anti-Semitic notions. Therefore he adhered to what he regarded as objective evidence: after all, the financial and material yield of the despoiled property of nearly all European Jews—not only of the 6 million who were murdered—had been quite substantial.

Just as National Socialist anti-Semitism remained unrepudiated in Stangl's mind, so his murderousness remained intact and encapsulated in his heart until the very end. Dr. Henry V. Dicks, in his book *Licensed Mass Murder*, a sociopsychological study of eight SS killers, elaborating on

findings by Dr. A. Hyatt Williams about convicted killers
in a British prison, set forth the hypothesis that his SS killer
subjects harbored a "murderous enclave in the personality,"
defined as a predisposition to murder-lust caused by early
childhood experiences but usually repressed and strongly
controlled in later life. National Socialism and especially the
SS released these restraints and succeeded in launching such
men on killer careers. After the war, these killers reverted
to their overcontrolled "normal" lives; yet that enclave of
murderousness continued to exist within the psyche. Stangl
may have been that kind of man. When he talked about his
work at the "euthanasia" station and at Treblinka, Sereny
noted, his face coarsened, his voice became harsh. In the
last interview, Stangl underwent those same physical changes
when he was commenting on the stupidity of people he had
worked with at the Volkswagen plant in Brazil:

> There were idiots amongst them—morons. I often opened
> my mouth too wide and let them have it. "My God," I'd
> say to them, "euthanasia passed *you* by, didn't it," and I'd
> tell my wife when I got home, "those morons got over-
> looked by the euthanasia."

In that statement Stangl revealed himself for what he was
—a killer at heart. Despite Sereny's unwarranted sentimental
interpretation of Stangl's words, he had in fact never given
evidence of a tortured conscience or of the expiative suffering
of guilt. In his book about Dostoyevsky, Berdyaev says that
"the torments of a man's conscience are more frightening
than the severities of a whole code of law, and he looks at
his legal punishment as a relief from his moral torture."
Measured against that authentic Dostoyevskian standard of
the redemptive power of confessing guilt, Stangl remained
at his death what he had been in life—a brutal and un-
regenerate murderer.

17

BLEACHING THE BLACK LIE: The Case of Theresienstadt

"IN GERMANY," Friedrich Reck-Malleczewen noted in his diary in February 1942, "the lies have a blond character." German nationalism colored, indeed double-dyed, all life, painting the dirty deeds of National Socialism in blond hues. Heinrich Himmler, himself no mean liar, informed his SS officers in 1943 that truthfulness had become a rare virtue in Germany. Lying prevailed in Germany no doubt because Adolf Hitler, High Master of the Big Lie, had demonstrated time and again that lying in the service of the National Socialist state and the German *Volk* was not only ideologically desirable but also politically rewarding. Besides, in Hitler's Germany, lying was regarded not as a policy to be exercised exclusively by elite rulers in behalf of the state, as prescribed in Plato's *Republic*, but as a necessary technique to be used at all levels of state and party hierarchies in implementing National Socialist policy.

But not all German lies were blond. When the Ninth

Commandment was violated to conceal the transgression of the Fifth, German lies were black as hell, black as murder. The blackest of German lies were concocted to carry out the "Final Solution of the Jewish Question."

The "Final Solution of the Jewish Question" was the German code name for the planned, systematic murder of the European Jews. Under cover of this code name, the Germans annihilated 6 million Jewish men, women, and children and destroyed the thousand-year-old civilization of East European Jewry. Assigned top priority by Hitler, the Final Solution was carried out with determination and the requisite efficiency, even at considerable cost to the conduct of the war against Russia and the Western Allies.* To facilitate this vast undertaking of mass murder, the Germans spun intricate webs of lies, most designed to disarm and deceive their victims, "aggressive lies" (Ira S. Wile's classification), to advance German goals and thwart resistance to them. The Germans also erected facades of lies to deceive the bystanders, the world's putative watchful eyes and wakeful consciences—the Red Cross, the churches and their clergy, resistance movements, Allied political leaders. These were "defensive lies," fabricated to avoid detection of, and consequently punishment for, crimes far more heinous than lying. All over Europe the Germans told the Jews that they were being sent away elsewhere for labor service. "Resettlement for work in the East" became the master cover lie, concealing mass murder carried out through mass shootings by specially trained units in the open air on territory seized from Russia, or through mass gassings in the specially constructed death camps on Polish territory.

In Kiev in September 1941, for instance, German occupa-

---

* See my book *The War Against the Jews 1933–1945* (New York: Holt, Rinehart and Winston, 1975), especially pp. 140–147.

tion authorities posted notices ordering the Jews to assemble for "resettlement" and marched them off to the outskirts of Kiev at the desolate ravine of Babi Yar. There the SS murder squads, designated as *Einsatzgruppen* (special-duty groups), shot more than 33,000 Jews in two days. In Lublin, the SS officers in charge of the "evacuation" of the Jews, which began in March 1942, told the officials of the Jewish Council, half of whom were to be "evacuated," that they would resume their administrative functions in their new residence.* But they, along with some 30,000 other Jews from Lublin, were sent straight to the death camp at Bełżec and into the gas chambers. In the Warsaw ghetto, the official German orders to the Jewish Council on July 22, 1942, stated that "all Jewish persons, regardless of age and sex," would "be resettled in the East," and that "each Jew to be resettled" would be allowed to take fifteen kilograms of luggage with him and provisions for three days. However, the freight trains from Warsaw transported them to Treblinka, where they needed no provisions.

Often the Germans elaborated on the official lies to adapt to particular situations. In small towns and villages, for instance, many Jews, having learned that "resettlement" meant death, fled to adjacent forests or found other nearby hiding places when they learned that the Germans were organizing roundups of Jews. The Germans then improvised new lies and ruses. Allowing an interval of several days to elapse, they dispersed their forces and planted reports that the coast was clear, that the Jews in hiding could return home safely. Seduced by the lie, the Jews returned and were trapped. In some places, the idea of "resettlement" was embellished by German sadism. Loading unwitting Jews on

---

* The texts of these and other documents are in my book A *Holocaust Reader* (New York: Behrman House, 1976).

trains destined for death camps, the SS told them that they were being transported to Palestine.

At Treblinka, a death camp where 800,000 Jews were murdered, Commandant Franz Stangl had a sham railway station built, with a clock, ticket windows, timetables, and signs indicating train connections to Warsaw and Bialystok, all contrived to create in the minds of the arriving Jews the false notion that Treblinka was a place from which departure was just as feasible as arrival.

The lies continued into the inmost chamber of murder. Following the style set in the euphemistically titled "euthanasia" stations, where thousands of mentally ill and incurably sick Germans were murdered, the gas chambers in the death camps were identified as "shower baths." The Jews were told that they and their clothes had to be disinfected before they could be assigned to their new places of work. Crowding the Jews into the gas chambers, the Germans continued to lie even then, instructing them to breathe deeply and thus cleanse their lungs.

While planning the final details involved in executing the Final Solution, Reinhard Heydrich, head of the most dreaded police institution of all Europe, the *Reichssicherheitshauptamt* (Reich security main office, RSHA), which had been entrusted with the task of coordinating all aspects of the Final Solution, evolved another stratagem in the web of lies. (He called it a "tactical measure.") He would establish a camp for Jews that, while fulfilling routine functions in connection with the Final Solution, would also be (or would appear to be) a model institution whose existence could refute charges that the Germans mistreated or even killed Jews. Such a model camp would be the blond lie to disguise the black lie, an ambitious and intricate falsehood designed to "document" the "truth" of a still greater falsehood. As a locus for this model camp, Heydrich chose the town of

Theresienstadt in Bohemia, about thirty miles north of Prague.

Built in 1780 by Joseph II to commemorate his mother, Empress Maria Theresa, Theresienstadt was a walled fortress town at the confluence of two rivers, with some 200 two-story buildings and 14 huge stone barracks. Abandoned as a garrison by the 1880s, Theresienstadt languished as a civilian town with a stagnant economy. Its population was some 7,000 when the Germans early in 1939 annexed the Czech provinces of Bohemia and Moravia (Slovakia became a separate puppet state), designating them as a German protectorate.

On September 24, 1941, Hitler appointed Heydrich as Protector of Bohemia and Moravia, in the expectation that this ruthless man, whom he later eulogized as "the man with the iron heart," would terrorize the Czechs and subdue popular unrest, which was then widespread in the region. Heydrich's new assignment was not intended to—and definitely did not—divert him from his responsibilities with regard to the Final Solution, nor did it diminish his consuming interest in it; his appointment as Protector merely enlarged his area of operations, putting at his disposal the resources of Bohemia and Moravia.

On October 10, 1941, less than two weeks after assuming his new office, Heydrich was already familiar with Theresienstadt and had decided that it would serve admirably as an assembly place at which to concentrate the Czech Jews before deporting them to death in accordance with plans and schedules still to be worked out.* Across the river

* For this narrative about Theresienstadt I have relied primarily on the two authoritative books by H. G. Adler: *Theresienstadt 1941–1945: Das Antlitz einer Zwangsgemeinschaft* (Tübingen: J. C. B. Mohr, 1955), and *Die verheimlichte Wahrheit: Theresienstädter Dokumente* (Tübingen: J. C. B. Mohr, 1958).

from Theresienstadt stood a small fortress, *die kleine Festung,* which was designated as Gestapo headquarters for Theresienstadt operations and which would also house a prison, convenient to the camp yet discreetly out of sight. In a few weeks, Jewish forced-labor brigades, recruited from Prague and Brno for heavy construction work at Theresienstadt, began to transform the fortress town and its barracks into a detention camp. The Czech Jews began to arrive at the end of 1941, and the local civilian population was evacuated shortly thereafter. (In keeping with the habitual sequence of events in National Socialist Germany, the official decree establishing Theresienstadt as a "Jewish settlement" and ordering the evacuation of the local Czechs was issued after the fact, on February 16, 1942.)

Already, in October 1941, Heydrich had darkly adumbrated his cunning plan to make Theresienstadt more than a transit camp for the Czech Jews on their way to annihilation. He elaborated more concretely on his idea of setting it up as a "privileged camp" at the Wannsee Conference on January 20, 1942.*

The Wannsee Conference—its name taken from the meeting site, the pleasant suburban Berlin lake—was an interministerial conference called by Heydrich to coordinate administrative matters relating to the Final Solution as they impinged on the various jurisdictions of the German state and Nazi Party bureaucracies. There, in an expansive presentation outlining the development of the Final Solution, Heydrich also described his plan to assign to an old-age ghetto those Jews from the Greater Reich (Germany, Austria, and the Protectorate) who were over sixty-five. Theresien-

---

* The minutes of the Wannsee Conference appear in full in my *Holocaust Reader.*

stadt, he said, was under consideration for this purpose. Also, Jews with World War I decorations (Iron Cross, First Class) and with serious wartime disabilities would be assigned to old-age ghettos. "With this efficient solution," Heydrich summed up triumphantly, "the many interventions"—presumably by Germans in high office who still had connections with Jews or part-Jews—"will be eliminated at one stroke."

The idea of exemptions for Jewish veterans from the German dictatorship's anti-Jewish measures had originated with Marshal Paul von Hindenburg back in April 1933, when he had appealed to Hitler against the summary dismissals from the civil service of war-wounded judges, lawyers, and civil servants in the judiciary: "If they were worthy to fight and bleed for Germany, then they should also be considered worthy to continue serving the Fatherland in their professions." Hitler promised, somewhat gracelessly, to take Hindenburg's "noble motives" into consideration in the legislation then being drafted to legitimate the removal of the Jews from the civil service. Subsequent anti-Jewish legislation did indeed exempt various categories of Jewish World War I veterans and permitted them to retain their jobs, but by 1938 even those exemptions were revoked. Still, personal interventions continued to be made from time to time for prominent persons, and Heydrich, aware of the possibility that a general might apply on behalf of a much-decorated "non-Aryan" war hero or that a top government bureaucrat might intervene for a part-Jewish partner in a mixed marriage, envisaged Theresienstadt as a wholesale solution to such requests for exemption. In Theresienstadt these individuals would be separated from the "Aryan" population and interned, yet would remain on tap if need be, in response to inquiry or investigation.

While elaborating this aspect of Theresienstadt's simulating function, an even craftier idea occurred to Heydrich and

Himmler: the operation of Theresienstadt as an old-age ghetto would in itself supply the cover for the more monstrous lie of the Final Solution, "resettlement for work in the East." The existence of a model old-age ghetto, consisting of elderly Jews exempted from labor service in the East because that would be too severe a hardship for them to sustain, would give credence to German claims that the Jews had indeed been deported to labor and not to death.

During the early months of 1942, Heydrich perfected his design for the "propaganda camp," as Theresienstadt was thenceforth to be called by insiders in the SS. Most Czech Jews who first populated the camp, except for selected ones over sixty-five, were dispatched on their ultimate journey eastward—to ghettos and death camps—in the spring to make room for the "privileged" Jews. When Heydrich was assassinated in May 1942 by members of the Czech underground, the whole scheme to operate Theresienstadt as a cover for the Final Solution had already been worked out. Administrative responsibility for Theresienstadt was thereafter lodged with the RSHA office IV B 4, "Jewish Affairs and Evacuation Affairs," headed by Adolf Eichmann, who had worked under Heydrich. Theresienstadt's three successive commandants were all recruited from Eichmann's staff.

In June 1942 thousands of elderly Jews and war-wounded and war-decorated Jewish veterans began to arrive at Theresienstadt, to become unwitting actors in the sinister charade. They were duped even before they were sent away, the RSHA having evolved a minor-scale deception that would bring the German dictatorship material gain as well as propaganda benefit. German and Austrian Jews who still had some personal property and private means were induced to sign "home-purchase contracts," under which they assigned their remaining assets in exchange for a "lifelong guarantee of residential accommodations and board," including also medical care. But when the Jews came to Theresienstadt, with their possessions, clothing, and books, they were assigned not to the modest private quarters they had been hoaxed into buying, but to tiered bunks in cheerless barracks. Remonstrating, they exhibited their contracts their title to decent accommodations and board, but it did not take them long to realize they had been defrauded and deceived.

Actually, Theresienstadt was operated like the ghettos in Eastern Europe. Its Jewish population was forcibly enclosed within a circumscribed area from which unauthorized departure was punishable by death. The old Hapsburg barracks and the dilapidated two-story buildings, including the unused storefronts, were turned into communal quarters where at times as many as 50,000 Jews were crowded in misery and distress. Bunks were constructed in four and five decks, so tightly packed that no one could sit upright at the edge of a bunk. Often people did not have even enough room to stretch out.

Hunger, cold, and disease stalked the ghetto, ravaging the aged men and women already afflicted by the emotional shock of displacement and rejection. The ghetto hearse, an ornate four-posted wagon, a macabre relic of the past, now drawn not by horses but by Jews, transported the dead to the cemetery and delivered bread to the public kitchens, sometimes simultaneously.*

The SS ruled the ghetto with terror. Ghetto Jews were punished for writing unauthorized letters, for covering up escapes, for drawing and painting scenes of the authentic misery of Theresienstadt. The RSHA wielded the only power

* The artists of Theresienstadt left a poignant record of this and other aspects of Theresienstadt. See Gerald Green, *The Artists of Terezin* (New York: Hawthorn Books, 1969) and *The Book of Alfred Kantor* (New York: McGraw Hill, 1971).

in the ghetto, but to reinforce Theresienstadt's fraudulent facade, they assigned the management of the ghetto's internal administration to a Jewish council whose three top officers represented the uprooted Jewish communities of Berlin, Vienna, and Prague; thus the imposture of "Jewish autonomy" was established. But, in fact, the only truly autonomous activity of the Jewish captives in Theresienstadt was the expression of their stubborn will to live and to survive the Third Reich.

In February 1943, Ernst Kaltenbrunner, Heydrich's successor, believing there were too many Jews in Theresienstadt —the count then stood at 46,000, nearly half over sixty years old—and using as justification the possible spread of a typhus epidemic, proposed to Himmler that 5,000 of those over sixty be removed and sent to Auschwitz. Aware of Theresienstadt's role as a "propaganda camp," Kaltenbrunner assured Himmler that, as had been done with previous deportations from Theresienstadt to Auschwitz, the Jews to be taken would be exclusively those "who have no special connections or contacts to draw on and who hold no high war decorations of any kind." But Himmler, who precisely at that time was ordering the total destruction of the Warsaw ghetto, sent a message through his personal secretary rejecting Kaltenbrunner's proposal:

> The Reichsführer SS does not desire the deportation of Jews from Theresienstadt because thereby the intention that the Jews in the old-age ghetto of Theresienstadt live and die in peace would be obstructed.

The facade of Theresienstadt as a propaganda camp was, then, to be preserved, even though for the time being it was not exhibited. The stage and cast were being held in readiness for the occasion when the show would be put on. The first tryout came in June 1943, when Theresienstadt was opened to two representatives of the German Red Cross. Their guide was one Eberhard von Thadden, Eichmann's opposite number in the Foreign Office, who dutifully followed Eichmann's instructions as to what to show. From the RSHA's standpoint, that visit was not successful. The German Red Cross representatives were reportedly "very upset and unfavorably impressed by their visit," having found the ghetto "frightfully overcrowded," the Jews "seriously undernourished," and medical care entirely insufficient.* After that visit, occasional parcels from the International Red Cross, mostly drugs and medical supplies, were permitted to be shipped to Theresienstadt. Perhaps the German Red Cross made its point, but more likely the RSHA eased up so that the arrival and receipt of such parcels, however infrequent, would give credence to the claims of the propaganda camp.

To ease the overcrowded conditions, Eichmann did in September 1943 what Kaltenbrunner had unsuccessfully proposed to Himmler the previous February. He shipped more than 5,000 Jews from Theresienstadt to Auschwitz, but the deportation this time had a new twist, intended to preserve the fiction of Theresienstadt. Instead of deporting just old people or those unfit to work, Eichmann selected families and allowed them to take their possessions. They were kept in isolation on the vast grounds of Auschwitz for six months, during which period they were forced to send postcards to friends and relatives in Theresienstadt praising their new accommodations. Thus the RSHA expected to dispel suspicion and disquieting rumors about where those 5,000 Jews had been sent. (Only thirty-seven of them survived.)

During the next few months, von Thadden several times

---

* Roswell D. McClelland to John W. Pehle, executive director of the War Refugee Board, confidential letter, October 26, 1944. A copy of this letter is in my possession. See also Adler, *Die verheimlichte Wahrheit*, pp. 304–307.

conducted visiting dignitaries around Theresienstadt, but no special efforts appear to have been made to enhance the camp's conditions, presumably because those guests were well disposed toward the German dictatorship and cared little about the Jews.

Theresienstadt, meanwhile, was fulfilling its function as a propaganda camp in bolstering the German effort to deport the Jews from Denmark. In no European country had the Germans encountered as much resistance as in Denmark in September 1943, when the planned deportation measures aroused the opposition of Danish leadership and the entire Danish population. To reassure top Danish officials that no harm would befall their Jewish nationals, Werner Best, German plenipotentiary in Denmark, told them on the eve of the attempted roundup that the aged and unemployable would be sent to Theresienstadt, "where the Jews enjoyed self-government and lived in decent conditions."* But few Danes believed him. A few days before the roundup scheduled for the night of October 1, the Danes managed to warn, conceal, and then transport most of the 7,000 Danish Jews to safety in Sweden. Somewhat fewer than 500 Danish Jews fell into German hands. They were all sent to Theresienstadt rather than Auschwitz, as had been the case with the Norwegian Jews, no doubt because the RSHA now realized with what persistence the Danes would pursue the fate of their nationals. Indeed, shortly after the roundup, Danish authorities began to demand from Best and other German authorities the release and return of the deported Jews. Danish welfare authorities immediately applied for permission to send letters and parcels to Theresienstadt. (The

---

* Raul Hilberg, *The Destruction of the European Jews* (Chicago: Quadrangle, 1967), p. 362.

Germans never approved the shipment of parcels, but the Danes nevertheless sent about 700 parcels monthly, containing food, medicine, and vitamin pills, some of which were let through.) The Danish Red Cross petitioned to visit Theresienstadt to see the Jews and their conditions.

Pressured by the Danes on all sides, Best appealed to Eichmann, who was in Copenhagen on November 2, opportunistically urging Eichmann to accede to the Danish demands. Two days later, Eichmann, back in Berlin, having cleared with headquarters, wired Best that the RSHA agreed in principle that the Danish Red Cross could visit Theresienstadt, but not before the spring of 1944. The Danes insisted on an earlier date but were rebuffed by Eichmann himself on December 14, 1943, and again in February 1944, when he said that a visit before May "would be undesirable." On May 16, Himmler himself gave permission for the visit. Finally, on June 13, 1944, eight months after the deportation of the Danish Jews, the RSHA informed the Red Cross that the date for the visit to Theresienstadt had been fixed for June 23, 1944.[*]

The long postponement of the Danish request is surely to be attributed to the RSHA's determination to proceed with caution, avoiding the blunders of overconfidence which had marred the visit of the German Red Cross in June 1943. The RSHA realized that the forthcoming Danish Red Cross visit, if properly prepared, organized, and managed, could provide an ideal opportunity to demonstrate to the world at large Germany's solicitude for elderly Jews and to dispel reports about slave labor and death camps. This supersanguine expectation stimulated the SS to a grandiose scheme. They would transform Theresienstadt's exterior into a dazzling

---

[*] Leni Yahil, *The Rescue of Danish Jewry* (Philadelphia: Jewish Publication Society, 1969), pp. 291–305.

fantasy, while the misery would persist unchanged behind the false front.

At the end of 1943 the bitter comedy of Theresienstadt's potemkinization* began under the guise of a major "beautification" program. A new camp commandant, SS *Obersturmführer* Karl Rahm, was brought in to set the pace. Neither money nor effort was spared. Even nature was enlisted: Eichmann was said to have postponed the Danish visit to the spring because the trees in bloom would enhance the landscape.

Under Rahm's brisk supervision, the streets began to be repaired, smoothed, and cleaned. Some abandoned buildings in poor condition were torn down. Others were repaired, cleaned, and painted on the outside. Block by block, the beautification program proceeded. The stores which had been converted into living quarters were now transformed into elegant shops, painted, refurbished, with charming outdoor signs reading "grocery," "bakery," "pharmacy," "lingerie," "perfumery." (These false fronts appear frequently in the work of the Theresienstadt artists as grotesqueries.) The SS even brought in appropriate merchandise as stock to authenticate the fraud.

The town square, which had been closed off, was now opened and its grounds cultivated. A splendid lawn was laid with little bypaths for strollers. A total of 1,200 rose bushes were planted. A music pavilion, complete with bandstand and park benches, was erected. A café with sidewalk tables added to the illusion of a delightful spa. A children's playground was constructed, with up-to-date installations, furniture, and adornments. The hospital, various children's quarters, public kitchens, as well as other institutions to be

* Modern critical history destroys our childhood myths. The scholars now say that Grigori Aleksandrovich Potemkin was an efficient and responsible administrator who most likely did not loot the treasury of Catherine II and did not erect sham villages to deceive her.

inspected, were all renovated and refurnished; necessary equipment was brought in. Every place was cleaned and scrubbed.

With accelerating frequency, inspection teams and supervisory committees checked on the progress of the beautification program. Each review generated new orders for further improvements. By May most of the exterior transformation had been accomplished. A Theresienstadt prisoner remarked that "even the great Potemkin would have been green with envy at the sight of so much ingenuity."

The next stage was to provide the sort of living accommodations for the so-called "prominent" Jews and many of the Danish Jews that would attest to the lie of Theresienstadt. To make space and at the same time to fortify Theresienstadt's reputation as an old-age ghetto, the RSHA in May 1944 deported about 7,500 Jews to Auschwitz, most of them young and able-bodied. The space that became available was used to set up new residential quarters, all on the ground floor of the small buildings. Since the RSHA did not plan to take its visitors upstairs, Jews vacated from the lower floor were crammed into the communal quarters upstairs, where the only beautification was the placement of flower-pots on the outside windowsills.

The living quarters of the prominent Jews were cleaned, painted, and refurnished. Paintings which had been robbed from the abandoned homes of Czech Jews sent to Auschwitz were hung on the walls. The places which had been prepared for some of the Danish Jews were not assigned, however, before June 20. The next day they were allowed to inspect their new quarters, and only on June 22, just one day before the Red Cross visit, were they permitted to move in with their few belongings. A Danish couple with a five-year-old son rejoiced in the ultimate luxury, the privacy of a room of their own. The amenities delighted them:

. . . a real lamp shade, curtains for the windows, and a flowerpot; besides the three beds, a wardrobe, a real table, and a proper chair (what a thrill!), and a night table. There was no more space for any more furniture. A trim name-plate on the door and a blue quilt on the bed.

About seventy Danish Jews, for whom such accommodations were not available or not considered worth providing, were invited to attend a nonexistent concert in a barracks and were kept there in isolation for the duration of the Red Cross visit.

In the last days of preparation, the SS authorities, using terror as their educational tool, began to coach the Jews on how to behave while the foreign visitors were on the grounds of Theresienstadt. The Jews were instructed and rehearsed as to how they were to dress, where they were to be stationed, and what they were to say. Children too were coached and bribed with food about what to say and how to behave. The adults were warned against trying to pass unauthorized information about Theresienstadt and its real conditions. The Danish Jews especially were reminded that their continued exemption from being deported was contingent on their obedience to SS orders. Those whose families had been sent to slave-labor camps and about whom some inquiry might be raised were interned under Gestapo surveillance in barracks out-of-bounds for the guided tour. Ailing, emaciated, ragged, and crippled Jews were warned to remain in their upper-floor barracks and keep off the streets. Just before the visitors were due, the Jewish workers who delivered the bread were provided with white gloves to wear while they were on exhibit. At the last minute the pavements were washed with soap and polished as if they were parquet floors.

As the deadline for the Red Cross visit neared, tension in the Theresienstadt ghetto increased. The Jewish Council was particularly apprehensive, since the Germans had threatened to hold them responsible for any untoward conduct. But with that traditional Jewish optimism which history has so frequently belied, many Jews hoped that some good, some change for the better, might ensue from the visit.

At last came June 23, 1944, a pleasant summer day. The visiting commission arrived, consisting of two Danes and a Swiss medical man, Dr. M. Rossel, representing the International Committee of the Red Cross (ICRC). The Danes, who had never met Dr. Rossel before, were Dr. Frants Hvass, head of the Political Section of the Danish Foreign Ministry, and Dr. E. Juel-Henningsen, vice-chairman of the health administration in the Danish Ministry of Interior, the latter representing the Danish Red Cross.

The welcoming committee consisted of a half dozen SS officers, but only Rahm wore his SS uniform; the rest— including the head of the security police and security service in the Protectorate, and even the top SS officials from Berlin —were dressed in the false colors of mufti. Von Thadden and a delegate of the German Red Cross were also present. When the Danes and the Swiss entered the gates of the Theresienstadt ghetto, they were received by Dr. Paul Eppstein, the "eldest" of the Jewish "self-government." In the ghetto's town hall, the delegation's first stop, Eppstein delivered a short lecture on how the ghetto was organized and administered, in accordance with the briefing he had been given by the RSHA. Like all the Jews of Theresienstadt, Eppstein had been instructed by terror, the German threats of reprisals having ensured his compliance. In fact, the day the visitors arrived, Eppstein still had a black-and-blue mark under his eye, the lingering evidence of a blow Rahm had given him a few days before.

The visitors were then conducted on the tour which had been so long and so diligently in preparation. They stayed in Theresienstadt for about eight hours and were shown everything that had been constructed, cleaned, painted, and adorned especially for the occasion. The visitors talked to ghetto Jews whom they encountered on their tour—those encounters too were planned—or whom the Danes particularly inquired about, but except for one fleeting moment no conversation was conducted out of the earshot of the SS. Once Dr. Rossel had the opportunity for a private word with Dr. Eppstein, asking him what he thought would be the ultimate fate of the ghetto population. Dr. Eppstein said that he knew no answer to this question and added that he personally "saw no way out."* That was Eppstein's desperate attempt at esoteric communication, but it fell on deaf ears. Dr. Rossel proved to be the ideal dupe, more gullible and credulous than any old, frightened Berlin Jew hoaxed into buying an apartment at Theresienstadt. The Danish officials, for their part, persisted in their inquiries about their nationals in the ghetto, but showed little interest in the others.

For the Reich Jews in Theresienstadt, that day was one of anguished disappointment. Their expectation that the Red Cross Commission might see behind the facade and penetrate the truth of Theresienstadt was crushed. Leo Baeck himself commented:

> They appeared to be completely taken in by the false front put up for their benefit. . . . Perhaps they knew the real conditions—but it looked as if they did not want to know the truth. The effect on our morale was devastating. We felt forgotten and forsaken.†

On July 19, 1944, Dr. Hvass and Dr. Juel-Henningsen reported at the Danish legation in Stockholm on their visit

---

* McClelland to Pehle, October 26, 1944.
† Leo Baeck, "A People Stands Before Its God," in *We Survived*, ed. Erich H. Boehm (Santa Barbara, Calif.: Clio, 1966), p. 294.

to Theresienstadt to a small group of interested Jews, two of whom represented the Committee to Aid Persons Deported from Denmark. Their summary of Hvass's remarks intimates that the Danes had opted for prudence rather than fault-finding, as a more judicious means of serving the interests of the incarcerated Danish Jews. Though Hvass appeared for the record to be moderately satisfied with conditions as he saw them, at least with regard to Danish nationals, the report reflects a state of credence suspended, judgment suspended, censure suspended. Dr. Hvass pointed out that at Theresien-stadt conversations had been "discreetly" observed.[*] The Danes had apparently decided that by appearing to have been hoodwinked, by making the Germans think they had been taken in by the grand pretense, they could continue, perhaps even intensify, their aid to the Danish prisoners. Indeed, their vigilance in the end saved the Danish Jews from the fate which was the common lot of the German, Austrian, Czech, and Dutch Jews in Theresienstadt—deportation to the gas chambers of Auschwitz. Those other Jews were truly forgotten and forsaken.

As for Dr. Rossel, the Swiss ICRC representative, his acceptance of everything he had seen (his own eyes!) and everything he had been told (his own ears!) was total and complacent. The report which he prepared for his superiors in the Red Cross was exactly what the Germans had hoped for—a totally uncritical, even approving affirmation of their propaganda.[†] Rossel's report does not sufficiently illuminate

---

[*] "Conditions in Theresienstadt, According to Danish Report," October 13, 1944, prepared by Otto Leyvsohn and Kai Simonsen, on a meeting at the Danish legation in Stockholm on July 19, 1944. An English translation is in my possession.

[†] "The Theresienstadt Ghetto," report of visit of June 23, 1944, by Dr. M. Rossel, delegate of the International Committee of the Red Cross. An English translation from the French original is in my possession. The McClelland letter, cited on p. 264, contains a penetrating commentary on Rossel's report.

his personality or motives. Was he merely deficient in intelligence or common sense? That would be a sad reflection on his genetic heritage. Was he simply a pompous, vain man swayed by flattery and the VIP treatment which the Germans gave him? A sad reflection on his character. Or was he nurturing certain political sympathies for the Third Reich? A most sad and unfortunate reflection on the institution which employed him. The report itself can serve various classroom exercises, not least as a model for the unreliability of eyewitness reports in establishing historical truth.

"Immediately on entering the ghetto," Rossel wrote, "we were convinced that its population did not suffer from undernourishment." He was even persuaded by German assurances that the Jews in Theresienstadt ate not merely just as well but even better than non-Jews elsewhere in the Protectorate. In fact, he remarked, "certain articles even reach the ghetto, which are almost impossible to find in Prague." The Jews of Theresienstadt were well dressed too, he noted:

> The smarter women were all wearing silk stockings, hats, foulards and carried modern handbags. The young men seemed also well turned out, some of them even were flashily dressed.

Furthermore, Dr. Rossel commented, "certainly there are few populations whose health is as carefully looked after as in Theresienstadt."

In his summation, Rossel was all naiveté:

> We must say that we were astonished to find out that the ghetto was a community leading an almost normal existence, as we were prepared for the worst. We told the SS officers who escorted us that what astonished us most was that it

should have been so difficult for us to obtain permission to visit Theresienstadt.

That "almost normal existence" was what Rossel had characterized variously as a "collectivist" or "communistic" society, as if in some way insinuating something about Jewish political preferences. The aftertaste of those remarks is definitely unpleasant.

Most perilously poised between obtuse neutrality and Nazi sympathy was Rossel's concluding paragraph. In its entirety it read:

> Our report will change nobody's opinion. Each one remains free to condemn the Reich's attitude towards the solution of the Jewish problem. If, however, this report should contribute in some small measure to dispelling the mystery surrounding the Theresienstadt ghetto, we shall be satisfied.

In Rossel's mind, impartiality was the fair approach toward the "Reich's attitude towards the solution of the Jewish problem." While he granted everyone the freedom to condemn the Reich in this regard, his report clearly indicated that he himself did not do so and that he considered Theresienstadt a wholly appropriate and unobjectionable "solution" to the Jewish question.

Rossel believed the false German assurances that Theresienstadt was an *Endlager*, a camp of final destination, from which no one was deported elsewhere. But in the months following the Red Cross visit, some 25,000 of the Theresienstadt Jews were sent to the gas ovens in Auschwitz. Only 10,000 remained by the end of 1944. Nevertheless, the comedy continued to run for selected audiences. On April 6, 1945, while the battle of Germany was raging, with Russian and American forces converging from east and west, two Swiss Red Cross delegates visited Theresienstadt, seeing only what the Germans wanted them to see. "The total picture of the town," they reported with acumen equal to Rossel's, "makes a very favorable impression."

Two weeks later, when Berlin was already surrounded, Himmler was ready to betray his lifelong Führer and save his skin through phony negotiations on behalf of Jews who were already nearly all murdered. Theresienstadt was one of his bargaining points:

> Theresienstadt is not a camp in the ordinary sense of the word, but a town inhabited by Jews and governed by them, in which every manner of work is to be done. This type of camp was designed by me and my friend Heydrich, and so we intended all camps to be.*

Thus the man who had complained that truthfulness had become a rare virtue in Germany was at the very end exploiting the lie of Theresienstadt as his passport to legitimacy. But it was then too late for fraud and deception. The charnel smell of Europe under Hitler's Germany gave away the whole dark truth.

* Quoted in Gerald Reitlinger, *The Final Solution*, 2nd ed., rev. (South Brunswick, N.J.: T. Yoseloff, 1968), p. 179.

18

BLAMING THE JEWS:
The Charge of Perfidy

WITH EACH PASSING YEAR the murder by Hitler's Germany of 6 million Jews, for no other reason than that they were Jews, becomes increasingly harder to comprehend. The gigantic proportions of the annihilation dwarf the puniness of the rescue. Why did no one in the world stop the slaughter?

From time to time, extremists of both right and left—Jewish and non-Jewish—offer answers to this imponderable question. Though they argue from diametrically opposed premises, they come to the same conclusions: the Jewish leaders then were to blame, and the Jewish leaders today are to blame. That simple answer ignores the historic evidence and disregards the historic complexities, but it had a certain vogue during the 1960s, when the word "establishment," capitalized, became a term of opprobrium.

A few years before Hannah Arendt leveled her sweeping and unfounded charges against the *Judenrat* as an instrument of Jewish collaboration with the murderers of Jews, Ben Hecht, an American novelist and playwright, charged all Jewish leaders—there and here, then and now—with perfidy. Hecht, who often in his adult life had played the role of enfant terrible, had long been identified with the Revisionist movement, a right-wing dissident group that had broken from the Zionist Organization. His book *Perfidy*, published in 1961, delivered a brutal message. "Everyone," Hecht charged, "Great Britain, the United States, and the leaders of world Jewry—traitors all! Murderers." He concentrated especially on the case of the Hungarian Jews. Long out of print, the book nevertheless continues to enjoy an underground reputation, and though most recruits to the Jewish Defense League have never heard of Hannah Arendt, many are acquainted with Ben Hecht's *Perfidy*. It is consequently worth examining the book whose message still resonates in some Jewish quarters.

Perfidy is a scenariolike version of the famous Kastner case, with heroes, heroines, villains, and flashbacks. In 1954 in Jerusalem one Malkiel Greenwald was brought to trial for libel. He had, in an issue of the mimeographed political gossip sheet he published, accused Rudolf Kastner, while a member of the rescue committee of the Jewish Agency in Budapest, of collaborating with the Nazis and thus being implicated in the murder of Hungarian Jews. Kastner, a respected member of Mapai, had been employed by the Israeli government and the Jewish Agency in various posts. Previous innuendos by the seventy-two-year-old Greenwald about other worthies had gone unnoticed, but unexpectedly, the government decided to come to Kastner's defense and sued Greenwald for defamation. Though Greenwald was the defendant, Kastner was the one really on trial. The case became a vehicle for the rightist Herut, the Revisionist

Israeli political party, to vilify the Jewish Agency and Mapai. The Revisionists had then reached bottom in Israel's political life, with barely more popular support than the Communists or the Arab parties. Thus, the Greenwald-Kastner case, which should have examined certain aspects of the Holocaust in the light of the profoundest problems of morality, became the ground for a political duel between the ins and the outs. Greenwald, a member of the Mizrachi, was deeply sympathetic to the Irgun. His son had died fighting with the Irgun; his daughter had been in the Irgun underground. Greenwald's talented young defense counsel, Samuel Tamir, at twenty-three had been acting Irgun commander of Jerusalem. Kastner stood for the Establishment—the Jewish Agency and Mapai. His counsel was Hayyim Cohen, Israel's attorney general.

Greenwald had accused Kastner of failing to warn the Hungarian Jews of the planned deportations to Auschwitz, of rescuing only his relatives and friends, and of sharing in the ransom the Nazis had collected from the Jews. The charges were not new. Back in 1946 the Zionist movement, Mapai, and the Haganah had held secret hearings on Kastner's transactions with Adolf Eichmann, Kurt Becher, and Dieter Wisliceny. Apparently, none of Kastner's detractors—as numerous as his defenders—had been able to make a conclusive case against him.

Joel Brand, who had worked with Kastner in the Jewish Agency's rescue committee in Budapest, was a witness at the Greenwald-Kastner case. Brand, a quiet, unassuming man, had been catapulted into world prominence in May 1944, when Eichmann sent him abroad on a mission to offer the Allies Jews in exchange for trucks.

Early in the trial, Tamir succeeded in establishing beyond a shadow of doubt, despite Kastner's original denials, that Kastner had voluntarily given an affidavit to the International

Military Tribunal at Nuremberg on August 4, 1947, on behalf of SS Colonel Kurt Becher, and that the Allies had released Becher on the strength of Kastner's statement. This immediately provoked wonder as to why the Israeli government was supporting Kastner so loyally. From then on, nothing went well for Kastner.

The trial dragged on for nearly nine months, and then Judge Halevi took another nine months to write a 300-page judgment that almost completely upheld Greenwald's charges. In negotiating with the Nazis, Kastner "had sold his soul to the devil," Halevi ruled. Only one charge was not proved, that Kastner had shared in the loot paid to Becher to rescue the Hungarian Jews. Sidestepping the Herut-Mapai argument, Halevi addressed himself to the question of individual morality in negotiating for Jewish lives with the Nazis. But he could scarcely have been unaware of the political effects of his decision. The next day the attorney general announced that the government would appeal the case to the Israeli Supreme Court. Thereupon, Herut and the Communists each brought motions of nonconfidence before the Knesset for the government's handling of the case. When the General Zionists abstained, the government failed to obtain enough votes for confidence, and Prime Minister Sharett submitted his resignation.

On March 4, 1957, while the Supreme Court was deliberating his case, Kastner was shot in the street by assassins and died some days later. Another nine months elapsed before the five judges of the Supreme Court issued their decision on the government's appeal: all upheld Halevi's finding on Kastner's guilt for testifying at Nuremberg on behalf of Becher, but only two upheld the lower court's verdict that Kastner had been guilty of collaboration with the Nazis and had acted in bad faith with regard to the Hungarian Jews. Had Kastner not been murdered, the case would have come to court again, and presumably the moral issues would have been confronted. For it was Kastner's moral wartime behavior that was, in reality, sub judice. No one can know whether Kastner would ultimately have been vindicated or condemned.

A court of law is perhaps not the place for deciding the kinds of questions involved in Kastner's behavior. The law is the embodiment of a code of morality in normal society. To what extent can that code apply to human behavior in extreme situations? We have ample evidence of how variously morality expressed itself in the will to survive in such institutions as the ghetto, the concentration camp, the places of hiding. Between the extremes of self-sacrifice so that another might survive and the sacrifice of another so that the self might survive, there was a range of action that the law could not easily foresee and a subtle complexity of motives that the law could not readily distinguish as right or wrong. Yet this ought not to preclude the attempt to investigate the events, nor curb the ambition to make moral and historical judgments. Hecht was right in wanting to render judgment on Kastner, morally and politically. Lord Acton and Isaiah Berlin, who have both written of the historian's need to apply moral standards, could be cited in his defense. But Hecht was neither a good historian nor a fair judge. It is important to consider what limits on action and freedom of choice the Nazis set for the Jews, and how this affected the moral decisions of men like Kastner.

The Nazis had demanded the creation in each ghetto of a *Judenrat* through which they were to manipulate the fate of the Jewish community. At the outset, there were among decent and honorable Jews two points of view. There were those Jews who opposed participating in the *Judenrat* because it could only be an instrument of Nazi policy, and there were those who believed that responsible Jewish participation might alleviate the situation. We know now which side was right. The lesson was bitterly learned by Adam Czerniaków, the first chairman of the *Judenrat* in Warsaw, who committed suicide when he realized he could not halt the mass deportations to Treblinka. But there were others with abnormal self-confidence and a near messianic belief in their own abilities to save the Jews. Jacob Gens, whom the Nazis appointed chief of the Vilna ghetto, was such a one.° On the lowest level were the Jews who joined the ghetto or concentration camp police, perhaps only to gain immunity (did they know how brief?) from deportation, and whose self-justification was that they would be kinder to the Jews than Polish, Ukrainian, or German overseers.

Kastner was one who believed that "nothing was unholy in a holy struggle," as one observer has noted. Until German troops occupied Hungary in March 1944, the situation of Hungarian Jews was wretched but not desperate. Limited rescue activities were possible. An underground Jewish committee in Budapest worked with church agencies, the International Red Cross, and the neutral foreign embassies. The Swedish government gave Raoul Wallenberg, a Swedish businessman, diplomatic status in Budapest, where he conducted a rescue program conceived and supported by the U.S. War Refugee Board and the American Joint Distribution Committee (JDC). Bribery and graft had been used with some success on the Hungarians and Slovakians. When Eichmann arrived with the German troops, Kastner was among those who favored negotiating with him to try to rescue the Jews. His considerable talents for negotiation, to

° For more on the *Judenrat*, see Lucy S. Dawidowicz, *The War Against the Jews 1933–1945* (New York: Holt, Rinehart and Winston, 1975).

which even his detractors testified, were, to be sure, inflated by an enormous vanity and self-assurance.

Kastner was a more complex human being than the caricature of a traitor that Hecht made of him. Hecht was neither a historian nor a chronicler, but as a novelist and playwright, Hecht might have been expected to show more understanding and compassion for the plight of men put in intolerable situations. Kastner, it is true, in accepting Eichmann's conditions and bargaining for some Jews on those terms, betrayed the trust of his position. Can we therefore condemn him as a traitor, perfidiously leading Jews to their death, in exchange for the comforts and luxuries of his position as chief negotiator with the Nazis? Or can we see him as a self-deluded egotist, obsessed with the sense of his historic mission to save some Jews? I agree that Kastner must in the end stand condemned. But since Hecht did not prove his particular case against Kastner, I cannot accept his particular judgment. No one, I am afraid, will ever learn any more what Kastner did for good or evil, to what extent he was acting for the Jewish Agency, and how deeply the power of his position corrupted him. Hecht condemned Kastner for trying to bargain with the Nazis for Jewish lives. But he described Joel Brand's mission to the Allies on behalf of Eichmann as a "savior mission." In justifying Brand's negotiations on Eichmann's offer of "a million Jewish lives for a few thousand trucks," Hecht was only trying to discredit Jewish and Allied leaders for not having consummated the deal.

Would it really have been possible for the Allies to accept the Eichmann proposal? Eichmann had promised that the 10,000 trucks would be used only on the Eastern front. Did Hecht expect Britain and the United States to trade Jewish lives for Russian lives? Besides, we now know that Eichmann never kept his promise to Brand to hold off the deportations, but instead kept sending Hungarian Jews to the gas chambers at Auschwitz without respite. The Brand mission was meant also to feel out the Western Allies about a separate peace. In his innocence, Brand had no idea of what the whole drama was about, and how small a part he was playing in a great spectacle. Hecht appears not to have known that the Western Allies informed the Russians of Eichmann's proposal and that, though they all rejected the offer, efforts were made by the Jewish Agency and the Allies to maintain contact in case something might develop on the rescue of the Jews. Nor was Hecht aware that the Germans had sent out new feelers for negotiations through Kastner and Eichmann's assistant, Becher, proposing discussions with the Joint Distribution Committee, to pick up where Brand had left off. It is also well known that with the approval and knowledge of the State Department and War Refugee Board, the JDC arranged to have its Swiss representative, Saly Meyer, negotiate with Becher; that the British and Russian governments were kept informed; and that promises of Allied postwar aid to the Germans were made in an effort to halt the mass murder.

Hecht tells none of this. Obsessed with the notion of perfidy and sellout, he sees only that Britain refused to buy the Jews from Eichmann's agent because Britain wanted most of all to halt Jewish immigration into Palestine, and that Weizmann, Sharett, and Ben Gurion acquiesced. We are back to the old quarrel between the Haganah, the Jewish army in Palestine, and the Irgun, the dissident underground army, and back to the time when Weizmann opted for partition, with a small state having a Jewish majority, whereas the Revisionists wanted all of Palestine. This was the real reason that Hecht hated Weizmann and accused him of unimaginable, but quite imaginary, callousness toward the European Jews.

Surely Weizmann was as much concerned for the European Jews as Ben Hecht. Even Menachem Begin, today's head of the Israeli Revisionist movement and the man who led the Irgun when its chief contribution to the war effort was killing British soldiers in Palestine, was more charitable toward Weizmann. Begin quoted Randolph Churchill as saying that his father used to avoid Weizmann during the war. "Whenever I see him," Winston Churchill was supposed to have said, "I can't sleep at night." It was Weizmann who proposed to the British that they bomb the gas chambers of Auschwitz, a fact which Hecht suppresses. Auschwitz was not bombed, but not because Weizmann didn't try or care.*

The fact remains that the Jews were not rescued. Nothing was done or, to be precise, nothing substantial enough to stand up against the stark statistics of 6 million murdered.

Perhaps the Jews were not rescued because no one, not even Ben Hecht, realized until it was too late how final was to be the solution to the Jewish problem. Even the Jews in Warsaw who lined up at the railway station for bread and jam rations to take on their "resettlement" trip did not know or did not believe the reports of eyewitnesses about Treblinka. So, a fortiori, the Jews in London or New York. The Joint Emergency Committee for Jewish Affairs, consisting of all major Jewish organizations in America, was formed in March 1943. Its first important business was to submit a memorandum to the Anglo-American Refugee Conference, which opened in Bermuda on April 19. That was the day the 50,000 surviving Jews of the Warsaw ghetto, one-tenth of the original population, rose up against the Germans. It

* The British were not alone to blame. There is reason to believe that the Russians rejected the idea of allowing their fields to be used by British bombers to take off against Auschwitz, and also vetoed a plan to blow up the rails leading to the death camps.

was too late then for most of the European Jews. Four months later, Peter Bergson set up the Emergency Conference to Save the Jewish People of Europe, another in a series of Irgun fronts to raise money for arms to fight the British. Its one accomplishment, so far as I know, was that its proposal to establish a U.S. commission to rescue European Jews brought about the creation of the War Refugee Board. Synchronizing intergovernmental and private agency programs for relief and rescue, the Board worked together with JDC, the Orthodox *Vaad Hatzalah*, the *Bricha* (the Jewish Agency's underground rescue teams), HIAS, and others. Nevertheless, it was too late. The war was an effective barrier against negotiations, bargaining, large-scale rescue, and substantial relief. The only way, it seemed then, to halt the murder of the Jews was to defeat the Germans as rapidly as possible.

Something might have been done sooner, before Pearl Harbor and even before September 1, 1939, to rescue Jews wishing to escape Europe, had the United States been more receptive. But economic depression, anti-Semitism, and isolationism prevailed. Whispering campaigns spread the rumor that refugees in the United States were taking the jobs away, and the Jewish defense agencies were busy publishing statistics to show it wasn't true. Patriotic organizations and congressmen rallied round to prevent passage of a bill to admit 20,000 refugee children from Germany. Ships, unable to land their human cargo, wandered over the seas until they found a watery grave. Why were we Jews not more energetic? Some were fearful, for themselves and for the good name of American Jews. Others construed the rescue of Europe's Jews in terms of Palestine, and Palestine in terms of a Zionist political solution. Now we agree that there should have been marches on Washington. A hunger strike of thousands of Jews around the White House and the Capitol might have had a response. In the daily papers the Irgun's wasteful full-page ads—which Hecht wrote—did shock people out of their torpor, even if only to contribute to the Irgun.

Timidity, miscalculation, and misjudgment are merely venial sins as compared to "perfidy." Hecht, however, was intent on exploiting the bitter tragedy of the Holocaust for partisan political advantage. The Kastner case had been conducted in that spirit, and even Joel Brand finally realized it. Withdrawing earlier accusations of treachery against Sharett and Weizmann which Tamir had wrung from him, Brand cried out that Tamir wanted "to help one party by exploiting the spilt blood of the Jews."

This is precisely what Ben Hecht did, too.

19

RESISTANCE: A
Doomed Struggle

RESISTANCE, the dictionary informs us, can be defined as an underground organization of private individuals of a conquered and occupied country who conduct acts of sabotage and carry on guerrilla warfare with the goal of overthrowing and expelling the enemy. Such resistance is classically exemplified by Tito's National Liberation Movement under German occupation and by the Soviet partisan movement during World War II, both significant auxiliary military organizations. Resistance movements elsewhere, especially in Western Europe, operated on a more modest and less aggressive military scale, but nearly everywhere their objectives were determined by overall Allied strategy, and each mission of a resistance group was designed to advance the Allied military effort and to incapacitate or weaken the Germans.

Given this definition of resistance, how can one speak of

resistance among the East European Jews, imprisoned in tightly sealed enclosures which the occupying Germans designated as ghettos but which were actually urban forced-labor concentration camps? How can one speak of resistance in the slave-labor barracks of Auschwitz, a place whose mere name evokes terror and horror? Neither ghetto nor slave-labor camp fitted into Allied military calculations, for the incarcerated prisoners, being totally without mobility, could not blow up trains or railroad tracks, could not destroy German goods and supplies. They had no access to military information; they could not observe troop movements. Under ceaseless surveillance, they could not receive clandestine airborne shipments. They could not even communicate directly with the outside world.

Nevertheless, though they were imprisoned, isolated, and under the constant whip of German terror, the ghetto Jews and the Auschwitz slave laborers managed to organize resistance movements. Perhaps most remarkable were the resistance groups which Jews conspired to set up in the death camps themselves: in Treblinka, Sobibór, and even in the annihilation center at Auschwitz. To be sure, these resistance groups did not conform to the dictionary definition of resistance, nor to the conventional notions of underground resistance that Hollywood films have glamorized. Generated in ghettos and in the slave-labor and death camps, these resistance movements were anomalous, and consequently most people know little, if anything, about them. Yet even those who know something have been insensitive to the conditions of extreme persecution under which these resistance movements were created and under which they operated.

The history of Jewish resistance in Eastern Europe evolved in two distinct phases. The first phase, from the time the

Jews came under German occupation until early 1942, when they inferred that the Germans intended to destroy them, is comparable to the history of the West European resistance movement throughout the entire occupation. The second and final phase of Jewish resistance, after mid-1942, was the period of planning, organizing, and carrying out armed resistance to the Germans, a phase which most European resistance movements did not enter at all until Allied forces actually stood at their gates.

Unlike today's fatuous questioners who ask, "Why didn't they resist?," the Jews in the ghettos, as well as underground leaders throughout Europe, understood how unavailing would be their armed resistance against the Germans and how wasteful, without commensurate benefit, of human life. All Europe lay prostrate under German military might and SS terror. The Polish, French, and even the Soviet armed forces had collapsed utterly under the onslaught of superior German military power. The occupied peoples of Europe, total captives of their German rulers, were in deep shock.

Slowly, cautiously, underground resistance movements began to emerge from the remnants of war-shattered political and social organizations. Their functions were everywhere alike: protecting and rescuing movement leaders from German terror, planning escape routes, establishing chains of contacts, rebuilding their organizations on a conspiratorial basis, and above all communicating with their members and a wider periphery through the issuance of underground— that is, forbidden—newspapers, flyers, and posters. Everywhere the first tasks of resistance movements were to maintain their organizations, raise the morale of their members, inform the public at large of their political goals, provide guidance and leadership. In the ghettos of Eastern Europe the underground organizations of the prewar leftist Jewish parties performed precisely the same tasks, though they had far fewer resources of manpower, supplies, and outside contacts than their French, Italian, Dutch, or Polish counterparts.

The Germans quickly taught the resistance movements the cost of overt resistance. A case in point was the Communist-organized general strike in Amsterdam, Hilversum, and Zaandam in February 1941, which the Germans suppressed with overpowering brutality and terror. The severity of German reprisals soon committed the resistance movements in Western Europe to a prudential policy, for the costs outweighed the benefits. (Other calculations prevailed in Eastern Europe, where the Soviet partisan command and the Communist-led partisans in Yugoslavia and Greece decided that no cost in human life was too dear in fighting the Germans.)

The Jewish underground organizations in the ghettos for the most part shared the prudent outlook of the Western resistance. The Jews had learned from the first days of the German occupation that any violent act against the Germans would succeed only in unleashing upon the whole ghetto the full fury of German terror. The idea of collective armed resistance—assuming that the Jews could even assemble the merest arsenal with which to attack the Germans and would have the opportunity to engage them and the terrain on which to fight—was obviously not just romantic and quixotic but actually suicidal. The Jewish underground, therefore, continued a policy of disciplined self-restraint, trying to bring comfort to the people and to provide leadership for the community within the impossibly narrow and immorally cruel limits set by the Germans.

But when in 1942 the underground ghetto leaders concluded that death was their only option anyway, they decided to choose death through resistance. Such resistance was conceived in nearly all the East European ghettos, planned in many, and actually accomplished in several, the Warsaw ghetto being the most renowned. The purpose of that resistance was to thwart the Germans in deporting the Jews to their deaths; its function was symbolic and affective rather than substantive and instrumental. It was a resistance of despair. Perhaps the trapped and isolated Jews, like the suicide wanting to be saved from his own hand, hoped that their desperate resistance would at last bring succor from the outside world.

At the same time that Jewish armed resistance was taking shape, the Soviet and Polish partisan movements were also being formed. (The Red Army command needed about a year after the German invasion to take control of the ex-soldiers' guerrilla groups and another year to stabilize and centralize the partisan organization.) In some ghettos, especially in Lithuania and Eastern Poland—that is, in territory where the partisans were being organized—a real option became available to a relatively small number of ghetto Jews, those who had physical stamina and at least a small supply of weapons. In nearly all these ghettos the Jewish underground debated whether to engage in armed resistance in the ghettos in order to halt their liquidation or to escape to the woods and join the partisans.

The decision depended on various factors: the depth of solidarity with the ghetto, even unto death; a sense of noblesse oblige not to abandon those who had no other champion; the viability of the partisan option and one's personal commitment to the Soviet Union; and, finally, the attitude of the official communal leadership (*Judenrat*), especially in terms of providing funds and supplies. In some ghettos—Kovno, Bialystok, and Vilna, for example—the decision to send armed groups of young people into the forests to join the partisans represented communal policy (*Judenrat* and/or underground), determined in a few instances by the hope that the ghetto itself might escape destruction or by the desire to give the young people an opportunity to fight the Germans. Certainly, except perhaps for fanatically dedicated Communists, all the Jews who joined the partisans hoped to revenge themselves upon the Germans and also, wherever possible, to rescue Jews from final destruction.

Reuben Ainsztein, in his book *Jewish Resistance in Nazi-Occupied Eastern Europe* (New York: Barnes & Noble, 1974), calculates that some 20,000–25,000 Jews fought in the Soviet partisan movement and that another 5,000 joined the leftist Polish partisans, in both cases constituting a disproportionately high percentage of all partisans. (Jews, it has been estimated, also made up an extremely high percentage of the French underground.) Apparently, few Jews were in partisan units of the Polish Home Army, the underground organization directed by the Polish government-in-exile, doubtless because of the pandemic anti-Semitism among Polish army men and officers.

Though most Jews were motivated to join the partisans to pursue "Jewish" objectives, their Jewish energy was very soon directed into general military and political channels. The policy of the Soviet partisan command was to break up the solid Jewish units which had emerged from the ghettos and to disperse the Jews among other units. Jews were seldom permitted to hold positions of authority in these units. Their proposals to carry out "Jewish" missions (revenge against known Germans who had murdered Jews or liquidated ghettos; rescue of endangered Jews) were nearly always vetoed and, if executed, were severely punished on the ground that such missions contravened the purposes and goals of the partisan movement.

Furthermore, the Soviet partisan government was riddled with anti-Semitism. In the partisan movement, Soviet as well as Polish, the Jews were exposed to anti-Semitism as raw as the elements. Jews were abused and exploited by the partisans and even murdered—sometimes for their weapons and sometimes because they had no weapons.

Thus, for reasons beyond the resources of the Jewish partisans to alter or modify, the partisan movement did not in any substantial way affect the fate of the Jews under German occupation. Like Jewish soldiers in the Allied armed forces, Jewish fighters in the partisan units in Eastern Europe were part of a large and complex military organization whose political objectives were as important as their military targets. (For Communist-directed partisan movements, political goals may have been even more important, as postwar politics demonstrated.) The Jews in the partisan movement, under firm discipline and hierarchical authority, were assigned tasks that were synchronized with Soviet strategy and goals. That strategy and those goals embraced neither the defense of the Jews nor their rescue. Except for a few isolated cases, at best dubiously documented, no partisan movement undertook missions to help Jews or punish their murderers.

Of course, all efforts to incapacitate and eventually defeat the Germans served a "Jewish" purpose, for only the utter downfall of the Germans could save the Jews. But we know now that the German dictatorship did not want only victory and conquest of Europe. The murder of the Jews was just as vital to them. The Allies, however, fought with both their conventional and auxiliary military forces to prevent Germany's conquest of Europe, but never tried to halt the murder of the Jews. As a matter of fact, civilian Danes, Bulgars, Italians, French, and even a tiny minority of civilian Poles did more to save Jews than did the partisan movement.

The hopelessness of Jewish resistance to the Germans becomes even more sharply impressed in the mind when we compare the situation of the Jews with that of the Poles who were enslaved in the German industrial enterprises at Auschwitz. However wretched their circumstances, the Poles, who formed various conspiratorial organizations in the camp, could still turn for aid—through underground channels—to their government, then in exile in London. The Jews, in contrast, had no government, no political voice to speak for them, no authority to issue arms and supplies to them. Yet even the Poles, under the yoke of German terror, could not make resistance a viable operation. At one time, the head of a Polish underground group of slave laborers in Auschwitz, himself a former Polish army officer, hoped to set off an uprising in the camp. He believed that he could, through Polish Home Army headquarters, get arms and supplies dropped from English planes flown by Polish pilots. Thus equipped, his men would attack the SS forces and liberate the imprisoned slave laborers. Several times he proposed this plan, through couriers, to Home Army headquarters in Warsaw and then in person, after his escape from Auschwitz in April 1943. Serious consideration was apparently given to the idea, for on August 24, 1943, Władysław Banaczyk, minister for home affairs of the Polish government-in-exile, radioed the Polish underground in Warsaw that the English staff had expressed its readiness to bomb Auschwitz, especially the factories producing synthetic rubber and gasoline, and that the Polish government would link this with a mass liberation of the prisoners.

But the scheme never materialized. Józef Garlinski, in his book *Fighting Auschwitz: The Resistance Movement in the Concentration Camp* (London: Julian Friedmann, 1975), explained that the costs were too high without expectation of success. He realized, as too few of our contemporaries do, that the resistance forces "were too few and too poorly armed, that the underground organization inside the camp was almost helpless and the SS garrison too numerous and well equipped."

That statement best sums up the situation of resistance movements in extreme situations—the Jews in the ghettos, the prisoners in the slave-labor installations, even the burial commandos in the death camps. Given those conditions of overpowering German might and terror, the wonder is not that there was so little resistance, but that, in the end, there was so much.

20

BELSEN REMEMBERED

"IT IS BETTER to go to the house of mourning than to the house of feasting," Koheleth advised, but for all his worldliness he did not anticipate that one could go to both simultaneously. The occasion was back in November 1965, when the World Federation of Bergen-Belsen Associations sponsored a dinner at the Waldorf-Astoria to mark the twentieth anniversary of Belsen's liberation.

I had worked among the survivors of the Holocaust in the Jewish displaced persons' camp at Belsen in 1947, but for many years now had lost touch with my friends among them. The invitation to dinner (black tie optional, but appropriate) had summoned up dormant memories about who survived and who did not. I decided to go, but mocking my own sentiment, I mocked the incongruity of the occasion. I would go not to feast but to participate in the commemoration and observe the feasting.

Nearly a thousand guests thronged the grand ballroom; a full-sized symphony orchestra was assembled on the stage; dozens of Jewish notables were installed on a two-tiered dais. Amid the glitter of gowns and the gabble of gossip, beneath a huge trilingual banner exhorting "Remember," the speeches began. The survivors themselves spoke in flat and insipid phrases, unable to revive memory. I wanted the relief of silence from the flow of banality, yet chided myself that a fastidiousness for style was Jamesian rather than Jewish. (But later that evening Elie Wiesel, accepting the Belsen Association's first Remembrance Award, for *The Town Beyond the Wall*, spoke of the need for "an accumulation of silence." Job's comforters, Wiesel reminded us, sat with him seven days and seven nights, and none spoke a word.)

When Josef Rosensaft, former chairman of the Central Committee of the Liberated Jews in the British Zone of Germany, rose to speak, the tedium was replaced by tension. His own unconsumed passion to tell and retell his tale ignited his words. Suddenly, I did not mind his rhetoric, nor even the occasional theatrical effects. At his bidding we rose to remember the dead. As each of us stood in the silence of his memories, the lights dimmed. The ghostly and evocative strains of the *Ani Ma'amin*, played by the orchestra's muted strings, sounded as if wafted from the other side of this life, perhaps from the mass graves at Belsen.

The DP camp of Belsen, in the bleak landscape of the sandy Lueneburg heath, was housed in the concrete barracks of a former German Army Panzer Training School, about a mile from the site of the Bergen-Belsen concentration camp. Summer there is brief and cool. In spring and fall the chill and damp penetrate your bones. In winter, I am told, ice formed in the corridors of the barracks.

The flatness of the landscape was relieved here and there by sparsely wooded areas. But I could take no pleasure in them, suspecting every young forest of camouflaging a graveyard. Before 1943, when Belsen became an internment camp for Jews holding foreign citizenship papers who were to be exchanged for German civilians abroad, the Germans had operated it as a Russian prisoner-of-war camp. Whether any Russians left that camp alive, I do not know, but some 50,000 were buried there in terraced mounds, separated by trellises made of birch branches. Birch saplings and young fir trees lined the graveled paths. One path in the Russian cemetery led to a moss-covered wooden platform on which stood a tall thin cross of birch. A bare wooden sign identified the surrounding mounds of mass graves and wooden crosses as the *Cimitero Italiano.* (How these Italians came to be buried there, I never knew.)

Belsen was altogether a place of graveyards and tombstones. The Jewish graves stood on the site of the concentration camp, under the bare sky, without the protection or concealment of trees. Some mass graves contained a few hundred bodies, others as many as 5,000. In a corner of the field, a handful of monuments marked individual graves—a miniature cemetery set against the anonymous vastness of the mass graves. Wherever you stood on this necropolis, you thought you must be treading on corpses. (On the first anniversary of their liberation, the Belsen survivors dedicated a modest monument to the memory of 30,000 Jews murdered in Belsen, the inscription paraphrasing Job: "Earth conceal not the blood shed on thee!")

In 1944, Belsen was turned from an exchange camp into a camp for the sick (in Nazi-Deutsch double-speak, a "recovery" camp), and in the last months of the war Bergen-Belsen became a dumping ground for thousands of slave-labor survivors from Auschwitz and other camps that the Germans had begun to dismantle and destroy before the Allied armies came upon them. Besides prisoners, Belsen inherited from Auschwitz *Hauptsturmführer* Josef Kramer, who became top officer, and a complement of other Auschwitz officials.

On April 15, 1945, when the 11th Armored Division of

the British Second Army entered Bergen-Belsen, they came upon 40,000 sick, starving, and dying prisoners (25,000 women), mostly Polish and Hungarian Jews, and 10,000 corpses stacked in high heaps. To be sure, in the hierarchy of horror, Belsen had ranked low. Auschwitz, Bełżec, Chełmno, Majdanek, Sobibór, Treblinka—these were the great killing centers, where the Germans innovated and perfected the technology of mass murder. But the British had their first direct encounter with death camps at Belsen, and their shock made Belsen a byword for terror. The *Times* correspondent began his story: "It is my duty to describe something beyond the imagination of mankind."

Typhoid, typhus, tuberculosis, dysentery spread. In the first four weeks after liberation, another 13,000 died. The British senior medical officer set up an emergency hospital in the officers' hostel of the Panzer training school, from which the Wehrmacht had fled. The less critically ill were evacuated to the training school's concrete barracks. Under British supervision, the German and Hungarian SS began to collect the corpses. When the remains were buried in mass pits, the camp huts and the SS installations were razed. At the entrance to the desolate waste, the British erected two signboards, in German and English:

This is the site of

THE INFAMOUS BELSEN CONCENTRATION CAMP
Liberated by the British on April 15, 1945.
10,000 unburied dead were found here,
Another 13,000 have since died.
All of them victims of the
German New Order in Europe
And an example of Nazi Kultur.

(Those signs no longer stand, but in 1947 they were included in the standard necrological tour on which we took visiting dignitaries.)

As soon as they could, Western Jews returned to their countries; non-Jews were moved to another camp. The East European Jews, declining repatriation, remained—awaiting visas, passports, certificates, exit permits from infernal Europe. The British, meanwhile, wanted the Panzer barracks for their soldiers and prepared to evacuate the Jews to a camp at Lingen, near the Dutch border. But they had reckoned without Josef Rosensaft.

Rosensaft had arrived in Belsen just a week before the British, in a contingent of 4,000 slave laborers from Dora. Born in Będzin, Poland, in 1911, he was raised in a traditional Jewish family. Before the war he led an ordinary life, buying and selling scrap metal. Deported in June 1943, he jumped from the transport and escaped, only to be caught two months later and sent to Auschwitz. Assigned to a labor camp nearby, he escaped once more in May 1944, while working on the outside. He returned to Będzin and hid for a time with a non-Jewish family, but the Auschwitz number tattooed on his arm soon gave him away. After months of torture (the Germans suspected he had accomplices) and solitary confinement in Auschwitz, he was sent to Dora as a slave laborer.

A small, wiry man, infinitely resourceful and unpredictably daring, Rosensaft, having survived the Third Reich, could scarcely be intimidated by the British. He found the quarters at Lingen without water, without light, unfit for human habitation. Defying British military orders, he sent the first transport of Jewish evacuees back to the Belsen barracks and prevented the second from setting out. That was how the Jewish DP camp at Belsen began.

The next battle with the British was over names. The British, sharing the Panzer barracks with the Jewish survivors, identified the camp by the name of the nearest town, Hohne; Britons at home, the army explained, became agitated on learning that their soldiers were stationed at Belsen. But determined to keep the remembrance of Belsen alive (a name, he used to say, to make you tremble), Rosensaft persisted and, persisting, prevailed.

Under Rosensaft's direction, Belsen became a self-governing community of about 10,000 Jews who were waiting for exit papers. The first thing to be set up was the tracing service, to seek out the survivors' families all over Europe and relatives all over the world. The American Jewish Joint Distribution Committee began to send in supplies to supplement British army rations. People began to get married and babies to be born. Rabbis, *mohalim, shohatim* plied their trades; Jewish police kept order and Jewish judges held court. Children went to Talmud Torahs and secular schools; adults attended vocational classes. A hand-printed newspaper began to appear; a drama studio was formed; a library was set up. From Aguda to Revisionists, Jewish parties competed for representation on the camp's Central Committee.

Belsen became, as Rosensaft put it, a shtetl. Perhaps it was—the last shtetl in Europe, whose inhabitants, teeter-tottering between despair and exhilaration, were suspended between past and future. Their memories pursued them, waking or dreaming. Once I met a friend in the camp, his hands freshly bandaged: literally leaping out of a nightmare, he had gone through the window. (Even many years later, Rosensaft told me, many survivors preferred street-level apartments because of such recurrent dreams.) Public events were occasions for processions to the cemetery, and the Deuteronomic text "Remember what Amalek did unto thee" became a commonplace. Belsen also had its manic side— mass meetings and vociferous demonstrations, almost always on behalf of a Jewish state, and there was dancing in Belsen's Freedom Square on that Saturday night, November 29, 1947, when the UN voted to partition Palestine.

Not all Belseners went to the new Jewish state; many, even fervent Zionists, chose the United States or Canada. In 1950, Belsen closed down, its residents scattered throughout the new English-speaking Diaspora. But Belsen ties still continued to bind them. In the United States, in Canada, and in Israel, Belsen associations became new-style *landsmanshaftn*, and at their anniversary meetings Belseners display their prosperity and boast of their children's accomplishments.

Rosensaft prospered most of all, and he used his wealth to exercise his paternalistic concern for the dispersed Belsen community. His obsession to keep the memory of Belsen alive endured the rest of his life until his sudden death in 1975. He became our Ancient Mariner, who passed "like night, from land to land," with "strange power of speech" to tell his tale to whosoever would listen.

Having the means to indulge his obsession, he organized annual pilgrimages to the Belsen site and arranged ceremonies of remembrance in New York, London, Montreal, and Israel. He saw to the erection of a Belsen tablet on Jerusalem's Mount Zion, and he watched over the mass graves at Belsen. He established scholarship and loan funds for Belsen survivors, Belsen memorial libraries in Tel Aviv and New York, and an annual Remembrance Award for a work of literature, art, music, or research on the Nazi terror. He subsidized the publication of commemorative books, including a lavishly produced, outsized, 471-page trilingual volume, *Holocaust and Rebirth: Bergen-Belsen 1945–1965*.

He sponsored the commemorative dinners, inviting as his guests non-Belsen writers, journalists, scholars, communal leaders, philanthropists, and rabbis. Through them he tried to involve the whole Jewish community in the memory of Belsen and, against all odds and despite the incongruity of the setting, he somehow succeeded. The Belsen commemoration I attended was not just a private Belsen affair. Briefly, fleetingly, it became a communal service of remembrance, a fragile moment in which we all remembered together.

An ancient Jewish legend has it that when God spoke at Sinai, revealing the Torah, all Israel was present, the living and the dead and those not yet born, so that every Jew in the course of history has had his personal share of the revelation. The late Yiddish poet Jacob Glatstein updated this legend in his poem *Nisht di meysim loybn got* ("The dead praise not the Lord," an allusion to Psalm 115), when he ascribed to all Israel a share also in the Holocaust:

> We received the Torah at Sinai
> and in Lublin we gave it back.
> The dead praise not the Lord,
> The Torah was given for living.
> And so together as all of us stood together
>   at the Giving of the Torah
> So verily, we all died in Lublin.

And, indeed, nowhere in the world, I think, is there a Jew alive today who, if he ponders at all the fact that he is a Jew alive today, has not had his own apocalyptic encounter with the Holocaust. But we keep our share in the catastrophe private and intimate; we do not acknowledge it collectively.

Having no religious or communal authority to decide such matters, those who commemorate the Holocaust are, like those biblical men of war taking booty, every man for himself. Even Rosensaft, who explained his preoccupation with his institutions of remembrance as the surrogates of traditional mourning—*Kaddish* and *yortsayt*—did not keep a fixed date for Belsen commemorative events. For some, April 19, the start of the Warsaw ghetto uprising, has become the date to remember. The Israeli Knesset decreed the 27th of Nisan as Martyrs' and Heroes' Remembrance Day to commemorate "the disaster which the Nazis and their collaborators brought upon the Jewish people and . . . the acts of heroism and revolt performed in those days"; though more Jews observe that date nowadays than used to, it is still not entered on most Jewish calenders and has not entered the consciousness of most American Jews. We have no prayer for the occasion, not even a liturgical poem. In the old days the liturgy accommodated itself to national disasters, assimilating into the service laments and supplicatory poems. But no one writes liturgical poetry nowadays, and the trend is toward cutting services, not adding to them.

Consequently, I am everlastingly grateful to Josef Rosensaft for having given me a public occasion to remember. I came thinking to mock; I left wanting to remember and wanting nothing else but that we all remember.

GLOSSARY OF HEBREW AND YIDDISH TERMS

alef: the first letter of the Hebrew and Yiddish alphabets.

aliyah: "ascent"; the being called up for the reading of a portion of the Torah during the synagogue service.

Ani Ma'amin: "I believe"; credo based on the Thirteen Articles of Faith formulated by Maimonides and included in the morning service (the twelfth article, expressing belief in the coming of the Messiah, was set to music and became a hymn sung by pious Jews in the concentration and death camps).

aspirantur: research training program.

baal-tefillah: a leader of the synagogue service.

baal-teshuvah: a penitent, one who returns to the observance of Judaism.

bar mitzvah: "son of the commandment"; a boy who at the age of thirteen formally takes on the obligation to observe the commandments of Judaism.

bet din: a rabbinical court.

bet midrash: a house of prayer and religious study.

bimah: a raised platform in the synagogue from which the Torah is read.

borerim: arbitrators.

davvenen: to pray.

dayan: a judge in a rabbinic court.

ezrat nashim: the women's section in the synagogue.

Galut: "exile"; the Jewish condition of homelessness following the destruction of the Second Temple.

goldene medine: the golden land, used to describe the United States.

haftarah: the reading from the Prophets following the reading of the portion of the Torah during the synagogue service.

Haggadah: the liturgy for the seder service.

hakkafah: "circuit"; circling the *bimah* with the Torah scrolls during the festival of Simhat Torah.

Halakhah: Jewish religious law.

hametz: leavened bread, food not permitted for Passover.

Haskalah: enlightenment, secular culture.

Hatan Bereshit: "bridegroom of Genesis"; the person called up to read the first portion of the Torah during Simhat Torah.

Hatan Torah: "bridegroom of the law"; the person called up to read the last portion of the Torah during Simhat Torah.

heder: an elementary religious school.

hevrat bikur holim: a society to visit the sick.

kaddish: "consecration"; the doxology recited, with congregational responses, at the close of prayers in the synagogue; also mourner's *kaddish,* recited by mourners and on *yortsayt.*

Kallat Torah: "bride of the law"; a Reconstructionist formulation.

kasher: to prepare food or utensils according to Jewish dietary laws.

kashrut: Jewish dietary laws governing foods permitted for consumption and their preparation.

kavanah: devotional intent.

kehillah: Jewish community organization.

ketubah: a marriage contract.

kiddush: the blessing recited over a cup of wine to consecrate the Sabbath.

landsmanshaft: a self-help society of people who emigrated from the same town or region.

mahmir: a strict interpreter of Jewish law.

mame-loshn: mother tongue; applied particularly to Yiddish.

maskil: an adherent of *Haskalah*, a man of secular learning.

mehitzah: a screen separating the women's section from the main part of the synagogue.

mekil: a lenient interpreter of Jewish law.

minyan: the quorum of ten adult male Jews required for congregational prayer.

mitzvah: a religious commandment, a good deed.

mohel: a circumciser.

Pirke Avot: Wisdom of the Fathers, a treatise of the Talmud.

rebbe: a Hasidic rabbi.

rimonim: finial Torah ornaments, usually silver, placed upon the protruding staves of the rolled Torah scroll.

seder: the home service of the first night of the Passover festival (repeated the next day by those who keep the second day of the holiday), during which the participants read the Haggadah and eat a ceremonial meal.

Shema: the initial word ("Hear") of the confession of Jewish faith, which proclaims God's unity; recited in the daily prayers.

Shemoneh Esreh: "eighteen"; a major section of the daily, Sabbath, and holiday prayer service, basically consisting of nineteen (originally eighteen) benedictions.

shohet: a ritual slaughterer.

shtetl: a small town in Eastern Europe with a substantial Jewish population.

shul: a synagogue.

siddur: a prayerbook.

sofer: a scribe, a copyist of Scriptures.

tachles: practical purpose, career goal, end in sight.

tallit: a prayer shawl.

talmid khokhem: a learned Jew.

targum: Aramaic translation of the Scriptures.

tefillin: phylacteries.

tehinna: a supplicatory prayer, recited quietly, often composed in Yiddish for the use of women.

trefa: unkosher, forbidden according to dietary laws.

treyfene medine: unkosher, impure country.

vov: the sixth letter of the Hebrew and Yiddish alphabets.

yeshiva: an institution for the pursuit of Talmudic studies and for rabbinic training.

yidishkayt: Judaism, Jewishness.

yodei sefer: persons who are literate, knowing Jewish religious texts.

yortsayt: the anniversary of a death.

yud: the tenth letter of the Hebrew and Yiddish alphabets.

zedakah: charity.

INDEX

Index